"*The Snapping of the American Mind* brilliantly switches on a very bright light in the reader's mind, illuminating all the lies, deceptions, and illusions with which the Left has successfully captured millions of Americans' hearts and minds. An absolute must-read in the Age of Obama."

—JAMIE GLAZOV, EDITOR OF *FRONTPAGEMAG.COM* AND HOST OF *THE GLAZOV GANG*

"David Kupelian's latest book, *The Snapping of the American Mind,* is worth the investment of your time to read. As every form of evil, unethical, ridiculous, bizarre behavior is normalized by the mainstream gatekeepers of America, we ask ourselves, 'Are we losing our minds as a society?' Kupelian answers that question with a resoundingly well-researched conclusion. Read it!"

—MICHELE BACHMANN, FORMER CONGRESSWOMAN AND
REPUBLICAN PRESIDENTIAL CANDIDATE

"David Kupelian is a fearless writer, unafraid to take on the nasty, intolerant secular left that continues to remake America in its own image. *The Snapping of the American Mind* is the newest installment in David's fearlessness. He does not shy from political judgment, cultural judgment, or even theological judgment—a rare but refreshing frankness in this new age of non-diverse 'diversity.' From his opening exposé of 'Bizarro America' to his chronicles of the new 'Disinformation Age,' the 'Real Zombie Apocalypse,' what he suitably calls 'Gender Madness,' and, alas, his warnings of 'False Messiahs,' David Kupelian has once again given us a must-read in these times of political turbulence and cultural insanity."

—PAUL KENGOR, AUTHOR OF *TAKEDOWN* AND PROFESSOR OF
POLITICAL SCIENCE AT GROVE CITY COLLEGE

"*The Snapping of the American Mind* clearly reveals how the secular Left has brought about the 'fundamental transformation' that Barack Obama promised before becoming president. But as David Kupelian documents, this transformation, which includes de-Christianizing our culture, indoctrinating our children, and forcing acceptance of all sorts of bizarre sexual and social behavior, is taking a terrible toll on the American people's mental, emotional and spiritual wellbeing. Fortunately, Kupelian also points the way to national and personal renewal."

—PHYLLIS SCHLAFLY, AUTHOR, LAWYER, AND FOUNDER OF EAGLE FORUM

"Everyone who loves freedom should read *The Snapping of the American Mind*. With extraordinary insight from diverse perspectives author David Kupelian reveals the Far Left's America-hating assault on the foundations of societal sanity. This book is a stunning exposé of all that is evil and delusional in the Liberal-Progressive plan to destroy the American miracle. A moral tour de force!"

—LYLE ROSSITER, M.D., FORENSIC AND GENERAL PSYCHIATRIST AND
AUTHOR OF *THE LIBERAL MIND*

"Maybe once in a generation are we so graced with a communicator like David Kupelian. His matchless ability to unpack the complicated issues of our day with absolute crystal clarity is nothing short of genius, a gift from God which he has shared once more. In *The Snapping of the American Mind*, David explores the root cause of our age of lawlessness and moral anarchy, yet somehow leaves us filled with hope for American revival and renewal. It's just the book Americans need at such a time as this."

—MATT BARBER, COLUMNIST AND ASSOCIATE DEAN AT
LIBERTY UNIVERSITY SCHOOL OF LAW

THE
SNAPPING
OF THE
AMERICAN
MIND

HEALING A NATION BROKEN BY A LAWLESS
GOVERNMENT AND GODLESS CULTURE

DAVID KUPELIAN

WND Books

TO MY GOD, MY FAMILY, AND MY BELOVED BUT TROUBLED COUNTRY

ᴣᴇ

THE SNAPPING OF THE AMERICAN MIND

Published by WND Books, Washington, D.C. WND Books is a registered trademark of WorldNetDaily.com, Inc. ("WND")

Book designed by Mark Karis

WND Books are available at special discounts for bulk purchases. WND Books also publishes books in electronic formats. For more information call (541) 474-1776 or visit www.wndbooks.com.

Hardcover ISBN: 978-1-942475-08-8
eBook ISBN: 978-1-942475-09-5

Library of Congress Cataloging-in-Publication Data available.

Printed in the United States of America
15 16 17 18 19 20 MP 9 8 7 6 5 4 3 2 1

CONTENTS

INTRODUCTION

America, like all nations, has endured its share of mega-crises. We've had military conflicts that claimed the lives of hundreds of thousands; economic disasters, like the Great Depression, that left millions destitute; disease pandemics, including the Spanish flu, which killed 675,000 Americans; catastrophic earthquakes and other natural disasters; and, of course, the 9/11 terror attacks. We've also endured serious social upheaval, including a devastating Civil War!

Yet we Americans, a resilient and optimistic lot, have always persevered and ultimately prevailed—a truism borne out by every generation's near-sacred mission to leave their exceptionally blessed nation a better place for their children and grandchildren.

Today, however, many fear those days are over, and that naught but trouble lies ahead.

It's not just the daunting array of current geopolitical threats—wars, terrorism, de facto invasion by millions of illegal immigrants, unpayable national debt and economic disintegration, *1984*-style surveillance, and a palpable and ever-increasing loss of freedom—all causing high anxiety over an uncertain future. It's also a growing conviction that government itself, whose primary reason for existence is to protect its citizens, has instead become Americans' greatest nemesis.[1]

To be sure, the American political scene has always been tumultuous, rife with raucous criticism of government and the president. A few decades ago, Richard Nixon became so mired in scandals, "enemies lists," and "dirty tricks" that he had to resign.[2] And Jimmy Carter openly acknowledged the nation's "malaise" and "crisis of confidence" in response to his appeasing and spectacularly inept leadership.[3]

In the 1990s, a scandal-plagued Bill Clinton, though not convicted, was impeached for perjury and obstruction of justice. Yet with Barack Obama, America has been thrust into an entirely new and almost surreal realm. For no other occupant of the White House, however controversial or unpopular, has ever inspired such a widespread conviction among the populace that a sitting American president and wartime commander in chief actually *hates* the very nation he was elected to lead and is sympathetic toward her enemies.

Indeed, Americans seem shell-shocked by a president superficially depicted as incompetent, oddly disconnected, and blinded by ideology, but who upon closer examination can be seen invariably pursuing some deep and unspoken anti-American, anti-*commonsense* impulse in addressing every crisis confronting the republic. Moreover, as we shall soon see, many of those crises have been *purposely created* by Obama and his administration to advance a largely concealed agenda.

This daily roller coaster of scandals and crises, as well as the multiple threats facing the nation during (and often because of) Obama's presidency, would be daunting enough. But add to them a pervasive and wantonly perverse culture that celebrates mindless narcissism and wild sexuality while openly mocking God, morality, and the overarching transcendent sacredness of life that preserved our national soul in previous eras. The result is that Americans today are being affected by political and moral chaos in unprecedented and transformative ways.

Indeed, America is undergoing the progressives' long-promised "fundamental transformation,"[4] and it's not a pretty sight. That much everyone knows.

But what few seem to realize about this "transformation" is that the sheer stress of living in today's upside-down America is literally driving tens of millions to the point of illness, depression, despair, addiction, and self-destruction in a multiplicity of guises.

Consider the following trends:

- Suicide has surpassed car crashes as the leading cause of injury death for Americans.[5] Even more disturbing, *Stars and Stripes* reports that more active-duty U.S. soldiers have been dying by suicide than in combat.[6]

- Shocking new research from the federal Centers for Disease Control and Prevention shows that one in five of all high-school-aged children in the United States has been diagnosed with ADHD,[7] while a large study of New York City residents shows, sadly, that one in five *preteens*—children aged six to 12—have been medically diagnosed with either ADHD, anxiety, bipolar disorder, or depression.[8]

- Equally alarming, one in 10 girls reportedly engages in "self-harm" in the form of "cutting" their bodies with a knife or razor,[9] while New York's state Department of Health reports that "self-inflicted injuries, such as cutting, burning, and pinching, are the second leading cause of hospitalizations due to injury for children ages 15 to 19 years."[10]

- Fully one-third of the nation's employees suffer chronic debilitating stress,[11] and more than half of all "millennials" (18- to 33-year-olds) experience a level of stress that keeps them awake at night,[12] including large numbers diagnosed with depression or anxiety disorder.

- New research also concludes that stress renders people susceptible to serious physical illness,[13] and a growing number of studies now confirm that chronic stress plays a major role in the progression of cancer,[14] the nation's second-biggest killer. Of course, the biggest killer of all, heart disease, causing one in four deaths[15] in the U.S., is also known to have a huge stress component.[16]

- Incredibly, eleven percent of *all Americans aged twelve and older* are currently taking antidepressants—those powerfully mood-altering psychiatric drugs with the FDA's "suicidality" warning label and alarming correlation with mass shootings.[17] Women in their 40s and 50s are especially prone to being diagnosed as depressed, with 23 percent of them—almost one in four—now taking antidepressants.[18]

- Add to that the tens of millions of users of all other types of psychiatric drugs, including, for example, the 6.4 million American children between 4 and 17 diagnosed with ADHD and prescribed Ritalin[19] or similar psycho-stimulants. Throw in the 28 percent of American adults with a drinking problem[20]—that's more than 60 million—plus the 24 million using illegal drugs like marijuana, cocaine, heroin, hallucinogens, and inhalants,[21] and pretty soon a picture emerges of a nation of drug-takers, with well over a hundred million of us dependent on one toxic substance or another, legal or illegal, just to get through life.

- And Americans aren't addicted just to drugs and alcohol, but, it seems, to *everything*: Enormous numbers of men, women, and children are addicted to online pornography (85 percent of young men and nearly 50 percent of young women reportedly watch porn at least once a month).[22] That may be why an astonishing 110 million Americans currently have a sexually transmitted disease.[23] Food addiction is also rampant, with one in three American adults clinically obese, and more than one in six of the nation's youth.[24]

By the way, things are no better across the pond—and may even be worse. One major study concluded that almost *40 percent* of Europeans are plagued by mental illness.[25]

What on earth is going on? Why isn't medical science—and for that matter, all of our incredible scientific and technological innovations in every area of life—*reducing* our stress and lightening our load? Why doesn't the almost-magical availability of the world's accumulated knowledge, thanks to the Internet, make us more enlightened and happy? Why is it that, instead, more and more of us are so stressed-out that we're on a collision course with illness, misery, tragedy, and death?

Most important, what can we do to reverse course? Is that even possible?

"HE *WANTS* PEOPLE TO SNAP"

"Life is difficult," wrote psychiatrist M. Scott Peck at the outset of his international best seller, *The Road Less Traveled*. Stress, difficulties, disappointments, accidents, disease, misfortune, cruelty, betrayal—they're unavoidable in this life.

Yet, during eras when society and families are stable, unified, and fundamentally decent and moral—as, say, America during the 1950s and early '60s—the stress level for each person is minimized, or at least not vastly compounded by a perverse society. Conversely, when, as is the case today, we have widespread family breakdown, a depraved culture that scorns traditional moral values, a chaotic economy, and a power-mad government dominated by demagogues and seeming sociopaths, the normal stresses of life are vastly multiplied.

Worse, subjecting Americans to unbearable stress, conflict, and crisis by Team Obama is not only intentional—it is strategic. Remember, these people are *revolutionaries* (engaged in "bringing about a major or fundamental change," as Merriam-Webster puts it[26]). They are utterly committed to replacing one societal structure—America's constitutional, limited-government, free-enterprise system—with another—a socialist, wealth-redistributionist system run by an all-powerful government.

Such radical change *cannot* be accomplished while Americans are calm, happy, content, and grateful for their blessings. Citizens *must* be unhappy and stressed-out. Indeed, widespread popular discontent has always been the required fuel for the leftist transformational engine.

Just reading a few pages into Saul Alinsky's leftist playbook, *Rules for Radicals,* one encounters repeated confirmation that the very heart of radical "change" is keeping the populace angry, encouraging their grievances, stoking their resentments, and making sure they are continually *upset*. That is the primary psychological dynamic of "community organizing"—and since 2009 America has been led by a community organizer in chief and longtime master practitioner and instructor in Alinsky's Far-Left agitation methods.

Top radio talker Rush Limbaugh picked up on this normally unspoken aspect of Obama's modus operandi when he told his radio audience, "I think he *wants* people to snap. I think Obama is challenging everybody's sanity. . . .The more chaos there is, the more requirement there is for him to step in and control the chaos."[27]

Commenting on Obama's sudden obsession with employing every means possible to deny law-abiding Americans their constitutionally guaranteed right to keep and bear arms, Limbaugh exclaimed, "Obama is literally pushing people to snap, attacking the very sanity of the country. . . . I mean, all of this is so in our face. Everything that people hold dear is under assault, deliberately making people upset! This is not what presidents do."[28]

It's not what presidents do—unless they happen to be leftist revolutionaries, in which case "deliberately making people upset" is *precisely* what they do to accomplish their intended "fundamental transformation."

Fox News analyst Chris Stirewalt alluded to the same phenomenon when he commented on *The Kelly File*, "I might even submit that this is part of an [Obama] administration strategy which says the crazier, the angrier, the madder they can make Republicans . . . the better."[29]

And best-selling author-columnist David Limbaugh put it this way: "One may reasonably wonder whether the militant left in this country is solely dedicated to manufacturing issues to keep the nation in a constant state of uproar, angst and disharmony."[30]

This book will present the case that not only are such allegations true, but keeping Americans in a constant state of uproar, angst, and disharmony constitutes an absolutely essential component of the Far Left's transformation of America.

This process has been ongoing and long precedes Barack Obama. Indeed, Americans could not have chosen as their leader someone as transcendently unworthy of the presidency as Obama without first having allowed their minds and hearts to be captured. Through constant indoctrination, intimidation, and emotional manipulation (as well as being continually rewarded once they have "converted"), a sizable part of the American electorate, to one degree or another, has been programmed over the course of decades by a subversive school system, an equally perverse "news" establishment, and a shameful and degrading culture.

Of course, at the very nucleus of the myriad assaults on traditional America is the rejection—at least by society's elites—of God and the repudiation of the Judeo-Christian values that have long undergirded our civilization. This in turn has led to pervasive societal disintegration and a Pandora's box of endless and unimaginable problems.

What we're about to discover together in this book is that not only are we undergoing a "fundamental transformation of America," but another transformation even more profound, that of Americans *themselves*. And that, it turns out, was the real object all along.

But not to worry. We will also explore creative and sometimes outside-the-box strategies for righting the American ship of state, as well as living well in a dangerous and utterly unpredictable age. And we'll survey the very best, most proven and effective ways to rise above the stress and chaos that seem increasingly to dominate what once was a unified and supremely influential superpower—and even more important, a good, decent, and happy country.

1

BIZARRO AMERICA

As part of my well-rounded childhood, I read *Superman* comic books.

That's right. Also *Superboy, Batman and Robin, Aquaman, The Flash, Green Arrow, Green Lantern*, and others—but my favorite was *Superman*. And one of the most memorable characters in those adventures was a guy named Bizarro.

Created when Superman was exposed to a "duplicate ray," Bizarro was essentially a defective clone of the "man of steel." Ugly, surly, and speaking broken English like Tonto in *The Lone Ranger* (*"Me hate Superman! Him bad!"*), Bizarro's defining characteristic was his total rebellion against everything normal, everything sensible, everything Superman stood for. Indeed, he took pride in being the exact *opposite* of Superman in every way.

Thus, Bizarro eventually relocated to Bizarro World, a cube-shaped planet called Htrae ("Earth" backwards). Life on Htrae followed "Bizarro logic"—meaning it was wrong to act in a right or normal way—and a legal system based on the "Bizarro Code," which decreed it "a crime to do anything well or to make anything perfect or beautiful."[1] For example, I remember reading, as a nine- or ten-year-old Superman fanatic, how on Bizarro World, when the street-sweeping truck came down the road, instead of sweeping up dirt and debris, the Bizarro street-sweeper would actually *throw dust and dirt onto the streets* to make them dirtier! In every area of life, Bizarro folk did the opposite of whatever was logical.

Got the picture?

Now, let's look at today's USA, which increasingly resembles a "Bizarro" version of traditional America—not just different, not just "transformed," but morphed in so many ways into the opposite of what it was in previous generations.

First, for those who weren't around during the 1950s, let me just say that the America of my youth, despite its many shortcomings, was basically confident, prosperous, and overflowing with life, hope, and unlimited opportunity. People were patriotic and our culture was strong and essentially moral. America was the undisputed leader of the world—not just militarily and economically, but in terms of freedom and generosity. (To my liberal friends: Do me a favor and don't tell me, *"But the '50s had racial segregation."* Yes, and today we dismember, poison, vacuum, crush the skulls of, chemically burn, or decapitate three thousand beautiful human babies every single day. So just drop it.)

Compared with the shining and vibrant nation it once was, today's America has become a different country: deeply and angrily divided, unable to deal with crises foreign or domestic, the world's greatest debtor nation with 50 million people on food stamps, rampant divorce and family breakdown, unprecedented sexual anarchy with 110 million with STDs, almost 60 million abusing alcohol, and over 70 million taking mood-altering drugs. On so many levels, America is becoming ever more "bizarro"—diametrically opposed to logic and common sense.

To really understand what's happening, we need to transcend the usual left-right paradigm and dive deep into the heart of the matter.

Although America's bizarro transformation has been in progress for decades, it burst into full bloom in the age of Obama.

Let's take a quick trip back in time to the 2008 presidential election. While much of the public was electrified by the soaring rhetoric of a little-known freshman Illinois senator named Barack Obama, just out of view was his astonishingly disturbing background, replete with communists (Frank Marshall Davis), terrorists (William Ayers), criminals (Tony Rezko), and rabid, anti-American racists (Jeremiah Wright)—not to mention his Islamic education as a boy in Indonesia and his hard-core Marxist orientation in college. But somehow, mesmerized by the prospect of heralding the nation's first black president, the establishment media couldn't be bothered to investigate Obama's qualifications to lead the free world. Just the opposite: he was the object of near-unanimous worship by the major media.

Now, for comparison, bring to mind the same media's treatment of Sarah Palin, the junior half of the GOP ticket opposing Obama in '08.

Essentially a very normal American with strongly held Judeo-Christian values, Sarah Palin had grown up bold and outspoken enough to challenge local political corruption, get herself elected mayor, and later become a popular governor of Alaska.

But once she was tapped by Sen. John McCain to become the Republican vice presidential candidate, an extraordinary phenomenon started to unfold: While studiously ignoring Obama's obviously subversive background, the media instead sent hordes of journalists to Wasilla, Alaska, dumpster-diving for dirt on Palin—investigating who paid for the tanning bed she had installed in the governor's mansion (she did), and whether she is actually the mother of her youngest son, Trig (she is).

The story took on even more bizarre proportions once Election Day arrived and the Republicans lost. One would think the attacks would have ended, especially after Palin resigned the governorship in mid-2009 (in the face of nonstop harassment) and no longer wielded any official power.

Instead, the hatred grew. Consider the following 2011 Twitter comments made about Palin:

"Join us in praying to God that Sarah Palin contracts cancer and dies."

"My hatred for Sarah Palin continues to grow. I think this woman should be assassinated."

"I hope Sarah Palin dies a slow and painful death."

"I hope she dies gnashing her teeth."

"Sarah Palin is the single most dangerous threat to the future of the human race. Thick venomous cretin she is. Someone bloody shoot her."[2]

Mind you, these are only five out of *dozens* of similar Twitter messages, all equally horrendous, calling for an agonizing death for the former governor and VP candidate. They came after a deranged young man named Jared Loughner tried to assassinate Arizona congresswoman Gabrielle Giffords in downtown Tucson—and many people, for some incomprehensible reason, blamed Sarah Palin.

This is not political. Politics cannot account for such dark, otherworldly expressions as "I hope she dies gnashing her teeth" and death threats against the Palins' *children*.

For years, the left and the major media continued the vilification, with both the *Washington Post* and *New York Times* in 2011 begging readers to join in a new witch hunt to find something—*anything*—incriminating or embarrassing in twenty-four thousand newly released Palin e-mails.[3] Again they found nothing.

What explains such bizarrely extreme hatred—reprised in late 2013 when MSNBC host Martin Bashir angrily ranted, on the air, that justice would be well served if someone would defecate in Sarah Palin's mouth?[4]

Shortly after the '08 election, I took a passing stab at this question in my book *How Evil Works*:

Haven't you ever wondered why, when someone on the public stage radiates noble character, common sense and natural grace—like Ronald Reagan did, or more recently Sarah Palin—he or she is regarded by the "big media" with an inexplicable revulsion? Hatred is almost too soft a word. It's because Reagan and Palin manifest the very qualities of character that the jaded media elite lost long ago, and since being thus reminded of their lost innocence is painful and unwelcome, they feel compelled to attack the "reminder."[5]

Later, "Robin of Berkeley"—literary pseudonym for a licensed therapist in Berkeley, California—wrote a perceptive column reaching the same conclusion: "Leftists loathe Palin because she has retained something that was stripped from them years ago: a wholesomeness, a purity of heart. People on the left despise Palin because she shines a bright light on their shame and unworthiness, which they try desperately to deny."[6]

This phenomenon obviously extends far beyond Sarah Palin. Indeed, what we are looking at here is actually the defining phenomenon of modern American life. It capsulizes the underlying reason today's secular-left news media, government, school system, and popular culture mysteriously tend to side with the subversive and perverse, and to demonize traditional Judeo-Christian values—even, as "Robin of Berkeley" put it, to be offended by "wholesomeness" and "purity of heart."

Consider the case of thirteen-year-old Taryn Hathaway of Salinas, California, who, according to news reports, was told by a teacher at her middle school that her drawing of the American flag with the words "God Bless America" inscribed on it was "offensive."[7] How, one wonders, is this possible or even conceivable? What is there about a child's lovely drawing of an American flag, with that reverent three-word phrase added, that could be considered even remotely offensive? What exactly is disturbing about a little girl's innocent expression of love for God and country?

Or how do we explain the high-profile Lisa Miller custody case? After childhood abuse led her into a dysfunctional life of addictions and homosexuality, eventually Lisa found the Christian faith, freedom from her former bondage, and real hope. She left behind the lesbian lifestyle in which she had lived as "spouse" to another woman in a same-sex civil union. And she dedicated her life to raising her little daughter, Isabella, conceived through artificial insemination and born during her brief homosexual cohabitation. Only one problem: The judge demanded that Lisa allow her former lesbian partner to have unsupervised visits with little Isabella, which, according to multiple experts and eyewitness testimony, were so traumatizing to the child that Lisa discontinued allowing the visitations. In response, another judge ruled that Lisa Miller must *give up her daughter entirely*—her own, legal and biological daughter—to her former lesbian lover, who had no biological connection to the child.[8] As a result of such legal perversity, Lisa "kidnapped" her own daughter and left the country, rendering her a fugitive and sending a pastor who helped her to prison.

What would possess a judge to rip a daughter away from her own loving, biological, Christian mother and give the child totally over to a former lesbian partner?

As a working journalist, I can testify that such examples as these are daily occurrences in today's bizarro America. Let's look at a big one.

A NEW KIND OF EXTREMIST

In the early months of Barack Obama's first term, the Department of Homeland Security produced a report[9] warning about the threat of homegrown, radicalized, militant, and potentially violent extremists. And who exactly were these scary people? If you were pro-life, your car had an NRA bumper sticker, you were concerned about illegal immigration or government debt, or especially if you were a returning military veteran—just home after having defended America with your very life—you were potentially a dangerous "extremist" and threat to the country, according to the Obama administration.[10]

Here's how retired Marine Lt. Col. Oliver North responded, in a column headlined "I am an extremist":

> According to the US government, I am an extremist.
>
> I am a Christian and meet regularly with other Christians to study God's word. My faith convinces me the prophecies in the Holy Bible are true. I believe in the sanctity of human life, oppose abortion and want to preserve marriage as the union of a man and a woman.
>
> I am a veteran with skills and knowledge derived from military training and combat. I own several firearms, frequently shoot them, buy ammunition and consider efforts to infringe on my Second Amendment rights to be wrong and unconstitutional.

I fervently support the sovereignty of the United States, am deeply concerned about our economy, increasingly higher taxes, illegal immigration, soaring unemployment and actions by our government that will bury my children beneath a mountain of debt.

Apparently, all this makes me a "right-wing extremist." At least that's what it says in the April 7, 2009 "assessment" issued by the Office of Intelligence and Analysis at the Department of Homeland Security.[11]

Fast-forward a couple of years. After one of several debt-ceiling melodramas in Washington, DC, during which the Tea Party demonstrated the most sanity of any of the main players, the *New York Times'* Maureen Dowd—in a column headlined "Washington Chain Saw Massacre"—characterized Tea Partiers as "cannibals," "zombies" and "vampires." She wrote:

> They were like cannibals, eating their own party and leaders alive. They were like vampires, draining the country's reputation, credit rating and compassion. They were like zombies, relentlessly and mindlessly coming back again and again to assault their unnerved victims, Boehner and President Obama. They were like the metallic beasts in "Alien" flashing mouths of teeth inside other mouths of teeth, bursting out of Boehner's stomach every time he came to a bouquet of microphones.[12]

Let's be crystal clear as to who is being talked about. "Tea Party members" is just a contemporary label for people who in previous generations would have been described as *normal patriotic Americans.*

Normal people—regular, fair-minded, live-and-let-live, law-abiding citizens with traditional values: work hard, save your money, play by the rules, help other people, don't spend more than you have. These are the people being labeled "cannibals," "vampires," and "terrorists."

On cable news, pundit after pundit could be heard parroting the day's talking points, likening Tea Party folk to terrorists.

- MSNBC's Steven Rattner: "It's a form of economic terrorism. These Tea Party guys are like strapped with dynamite, standing in the middle of Times Square at rush hour, and saying, 'You do it my way or we'll blow you up.'"[13]

- Bloomberg's Margaret Carlson: "They strapped explosives to the Capitol."[14]

- MSNBC's Chris Matthews: "The GOP has become the Wahhabis of American government, willing to risk bringing down the whole country in the service of their anti-tax ideology."[15]

Ironically, as former CBS newsman Bernie Goldberg observed during an *O'Reilly Factor* broadcast, "These are people who don't call *real* terrorists 'terrorists.'"[16]

Of course, before Tea Partiers were maligned as "terrorists," "zombies," "cannibals," and "vampires," they were "racists." And before that—even before the name "Tea Party" came into vogue—the same normal American people were maligned as "right-wing extremists" by the likes of the Obama Department of Homeland Security.

Is the picture becoming clearer?

There is a growing and highly influential segment of our society that regards normal, "Ozzie and Harriet," traditional-minded Americans as evil.

THE PICTURE OF "NORMAL"

The early years of the Obama presidency witnessed many Tea Party events colorfully evoking classic Americana, with patriots dressing up as George Washington or Thomas Paine, moms with their kids holding homemade "God bless America" signs, people praying together, a grandmother thoughtfully picking up litter after a rally so the city's maintenance crew wouldn't have too much to do, and so on. The Americans attending these events frequently reminded me of characters out of a patriotic Norman Rockwell painting.

You remember Norman Rockwell: he was awarded the Presidential

Medal of Freedom for painting "vivid and affectionate portraits of our country"[17]—like the man standing up at a town hall meeting to exercise his freedom of speech or the family saying grace before a meal or the crowd pledging allegiance to the flag.

Norman Rockwell painted the country most Americans have long loved and revered.

But did you know there are influential people who *hate* Norman Rockwell paintings? One of the more vocal is Blake Gopnik, the *Washington Post*'s chief art critic for a decade, and now a contributor to *Newsweek* and the *Daily Beast*. Gopnik has written about how much he is "offended" by and even "hated [Rockwell's] art": "I can't stand the view of America that he presents, which I feel insults a huge number of us non-mainstream folks."[18]

"Non-mainstream"? What exactly does that signify? Or maybe a better question is, if Gopnik hates Norman Rockwell's vision of America, what vision does he love?

Here's a possible clue. Gopnik came to the defense of a taxpayer-funded exhibit at Washington's National Portrait Gallery by homosexual artist David Wojnarowicz of a film featuring a crucifix with ants crawling on Jesus' body.[19]

The Wojnarowicz exhibit also featured male sex organs, naked brothers kissing, men in chains, and other offensive stuff the *Washington Post*'s chief art critic defended. But he hated Norman Rockwell's work because of the image of America his art portrays—which many "mainstream" Americans would probably describe as love, affection, and respect for their country. The ants-crawling-on-Jesus video is so incredibly creepy that it makes "mainstream" people want to run screaming from the room. But apparently to some, art that is sacrilegious and nausea-inducing is somehow laudable.

What we're looking at is nothing less than a spiritual polarization of Americans—a divided population fighting on behalf of warring values.

Author Dinesh D'Souza describes the phenomenon this way:

Contrary to what we frequently read and hear, the great American divide is not a clash between conservatives who advocate liberty versus progressives who oppose liberty. Rather, the two sides each affirm a certain type of liberty.

One side, for example, cherishes economic liberty while the other champions liberty in the sexual and social domain. Nor is it a clash between patriots and anti-patriots. Both sides love America, but they love a different type of America. One side loves the America of Columbus and the Fourth of July, of innovation and work and the "animal spirit" of capitalism, of the Boy Scouts and parochial schools, of traditional families and flag-saluting veterans. The other side loves the America of tolerance and social entitlements, of income and wealth redistribution, of slave-revolts and the civil rights movement, of Indian rights and women's rights, of sexual liberation and abortion, of gay rights and gay marriage.[20]

How did we get to this point?

On one level, it's simple to understand: All of us are shaped by other people—first parents and family, later friends, school, college, and work, as well as culture, which today is wildly immoral and corrupting. When we go to school, our common sense and innocence are under attack. The government education system (which we prefer to call "public school") is, just like most of our colleges, dominated by the political and cultural left. For example, a central feature of modern university life, something leveraged across every area—from curriculum to campus culture—is the mainstreaming and *forced acceptance and celebration* of sexual perversion and debauchery, glorified as though it were enlightened and liberating. And all for only sixty thousand dollars a year!

Unfortunately, once we've had our innocence and integrity ripped off and have mysteriously oozed into a darker, more conflicted version of our former self, now when somebody comes along who simply radiates the wholesome qualities we left behind, we feel uncomfortable in his or her presence. In fact, we feel positively threatened, as though there's something malevolent about that person. At the same time, we are attracted to, and feel comfortable around, people who (like us) have been seduced to the "dark side."

Barack Obama is no exception. He has a serious case of this syndrome, sympathizing and identifying with subversive characters while being mysteriously repelled by genuine virtue. Seen at public events with leftists radicals, LGBT groups, or proabortion outfits like Planned Parenthood, Obama's smile is broad and animated; he obviously feels comfortable and *at home* there. Yet he displays a palpable aversion to all that is emblematic of the success of Western Judeo-Christian civilization.

Thus, no sooner was Obama sworn in as president than he immediately got rid of the long-cherished White House bust of Winston Churchill, his aides finally admitting the act after initially denouncing the claim as "100 percent false."[21] Far worse, from the start of his presidency, Obama manifested a mystifying coldness and incomprehension in the presence of Israel's Benjamin Netanyahu. That attitude shockingly escalated during Obama's second term into an all-out effort to defeat the Jewish state's prime minister, complete with Obama's campaign team setting up shop in Tel Aviv to try to turn the election against the sitting leader of a trusted American ally.[22]

FOLLOWING THE BIZARRO CODE

Although an increasingly toxic culture has negatively impacted Americans for decades, this society's degeneration has undeniably accelerated during Barack Obama's presidency.

Incredibly, Obama has made an annual habit of releasing onto America's streets tens of thousands of *criminal* illegal aliens—people who entered this nation illegally, then were convicted in US courts of serious crimes, like murder, rape, and assault—but who, rather than being deported or incarcerated, have been released back into America's communities! The specific crime breakdown for the thirty thousand such criminal illegals released in 2014 wasn't publicly disclosed, but the *Washington Times* reported that "among the 36,000 released in 2013 were 193 homicide convictions, 426 sexual assault convictions,

303 kidnapping convictions and 16,070 convictions for driving under the influence of drugs or alcohol."[23]

Remember my description of the comic-book Bizarro World, where the Bizarro street sweeper would actually throw dirt and debris *back onto the streets* to make them dirtier rather than cleaning them up?

Isn't the Obama administration's annual release of at least thirty thousand illegal-alien convicted criminals back onto America's streets, rather than endeavoring to clean up our neighborhoods' violent crime problem, even more bizarre? Personally, I'd prefer the dirt.

Recall likewise the Bizarro Code, which banned doing "anything well" or making something "perfect or beautiful." I still vividly remember, like most Americans who were around in 1981, the thrillingly perfect three-point landing of NASA's original space shuttle *Columbia* as it touched down after its maiden voyage in outer space. It made everyone proud to be an American. But in the age of Obama, with the space shuttle program mothballed, NASA has a new mission, to inspire a new kind of pride—the pride of Muslim nations for being so great at math and science.

What?

Hard to believe, but here's how NASA chief Charles Bolden explains it:

> When I became the NASA administrator, [President Obama] charged me with three things. . . . One, he wanted me to help re-inspire children to want to get into science and math; he wanted me to expand our international relationships; and third, and *perhaps foremost*, he wanted me to find a way to reach out to the Muslim world and engage much more with dominantly Muslim nations to help them feel good about their historic contribution to science, math and engineering.[24]

Not bizarre enough for you? How about this?

There are now calls by environmentalists for punishment, even *imprisonment*, for "global-warming deniers" (now renamed "climate-change deniers," a label that still works even if the temperature goes down). One professor actually called for the death penalty for such intolerable "denial," but this increasingly totalitarian mind-set has been encouraged by the likes of Robert F. Kennedy Jr., who laments, "I wish there were a law you could punish [deniers] with," and Al Gore, who agrees "we need to put a price on denial in politics."[25]

Wow. But then, what do you expect from someone who insists we should spend *$90 trillion* to ban cars from every major city in the world?[26]

Of course, the problem with Al Gore's brilliant plan to eliminate the automobile's fossil-fuel carbon footprint is that the *gross world product* for 2014—that's the combined gross national product of every country on the planet—was $77 trillion.[27] So, Gore wants us to spend more money than the entire world earns annually to ban cars.

I don't think "bizarro" comes even close to describing Mr. Gore.

(And remember, all you Democrat voters, this is the candidate who came within a hair's breadth of the presidency in 2000, winning the popular vote against George W. Bush but losing the needed electoral majority.)

So goes the bizarre transformation of America in the age of Obama. Today we have summer camps for children whose parents want to encourage their little ones to change to the opposite gender.[28] We allow Satanic "black masses," featuring denunciations of Jesus Christ, spitting in holy water, and rituals that include urine, nudity, and sex to be publicized and held in public in the American heartland.[29] Four-year-olds who misbehave in preschool are now handcuffed and carted off to the police station.[30] Oh, and speaking of handcuffs, good old family-friendly Wal-Mart and Target have taken to promoting and selling sadomasochistic sex toys to cash in on the *Fifty Shades of Grey* craze.[31]

And let us not forget same-sex "marriage." It seems so familiar to us now, doesn't it? So warmly accepted and celebrated—and since the Supreme Court's decision, "the law of the land." But take a deep breath and consider that just a few short years ago, the idea of two men, or two women, marrying each other was regarded almost universally as not merely bizarre, but insane.[32] Yet today, dare express disapproval of same-sex marriage, and you risk being branded a bigot, an extremist, and a hater akin to a Ku Klux Klansman. Worse, for many Christian business owners, politely declining to actively participate in celebrating a homosexual wedding ceremony has exposed them to lawsuits, criminal prosecutions, huge fines, mandatory pro-LGBT "reeducation," death threats, and the loss of their businesses and homes.

In many ways, today's America makes Bizarro World of the *Superman* saga seem both tame and sane by comparison.

Yes, I know it all sounds very bleak, prompting the question, *Is there a way back?*

Of course there's a way back, and that's what this book is ultimately all about. Exploring the problems we've gotten ourselves into is not an end in itself, but rather a necessary step in arriving at genuinely enlightened solutions, which become apparent only when we've understood in a profound way what on earth has really happened to our beloved country—*and to us.*

Thus, in the next chapter, we'll explore exactly *how and why* America has so dramatically been morphing into a freakish version of its former self. But we will also discover, as we progress through that chapter and those that follow, that vital clues are coming into view, so that by the time we reach the end of our journey together, the way back—both for us as individuals and for our great nation—will be clear.

2

THE BLUR

America has changed so drastically in our lifetime that many say they can barely recognize the magnificent nation they once knew and loved.

When I was a child in the 1950s in suburban Washington, DC, it was a relatively innocent time. President Kennedy hadn't been assassinated, the great middle class was secure and prosperous for the most part, and the nation was unified, fundamentally decent, and altruistic. Divorce and family breakdown were rare compared with today. I barely even knew what abortion was. After safely walking or biking home from school, I would fix myself a snack and watch shows like *Leave It to Beaver* and *Father Knows Best* on a small black-and-white TV.

America was strong and flourishing, its culture unapologetically Judeo-Christian, and, despite its many flaws, it was simply the greatest and freest nation on the planet.

And the rest of the world knew it. People flocked here from all over, including my father, who, as a little boy, barely escaped along with his mother from the horrors of the Armenian Genocide. His physician father was murdered by the Turks, and his baby sister succumbed as well. In all, I lost dozens of family members, perhaps as many as one hundred, in the jihadist genocide of one and a half million Christian Armenians—the precursor to the Nazi Holocaust thirty years later. For people like my father and grandmother, America was the promised land. They were grateful to be welcomed here, and though they came with nothing and life was hard, they thrived, got an education, became successful, and had families—all because of the generosity of America and the liberty and opportunity this country freely offered them.

This is the America that was imprinted on me—and on you, if you're old enough. This is the America you love.

However, ever since the 1960s we've lived in a blur. And though we remember the long hair and flamboyant clothes, the British Invasion and ubiquitous rock music, and the obsession with psychedelic drugs, like LSD, the most important and consequential developments of that era were happening more out of view, particularly on America's college campuses. Unbeknownst to almost everyone at the time, our nation had come under withering assault from radical revolutionary movements with appealing names like women's liberation, black liberation, sexual liberation, gay liberation, animal liberation, and multiculturalism. But it was like a blur. We didn't really know what we were looking at, where it was coming from—or where it was taking us.

For decades, we blurred along like this. Even though our knowledge and technology were rapidly growing—indeed, were spectacularly transforming our world, imparting a sense of constant progress and growth—something was very wrong. Families, the bedrock institution of any healthy society, were imploding at an alarming rate. Perverse Supreme Court decisions banned prayer in our schools, yet forced states to legalize, virtually without limitation, the killing of unborn babies. There was a major upsurge in atheism and exotic religious cults, along with a rapid coarsening of our culture and ever-increasing sexual anarchy, led most prominently by an explosion of angry, well-organized homosexual activists demanding what ultimately turned out to be a fundamental reordering of Western culture, morality, and law.

Parallel to all of this was an ever-growing contempt—indeed, demonization—of Christianity, the faith that, along with Judaism, had for centuries provided the essential moral foundation for America and Western Civilization.

It seemed that as a people we were in a pitched battle with ourselves—literally at war with our own core founding values.

But again, all this was a blur. It was hard to pin down what was actually happening, where it was all coming from, and where it was heading.

Then, finally, in late 2008 something started to break the spell: Americans elected Barack Hussein Obama as president.

Pause for a moment and consider that America's most vexing geopolitical problems in the modern age have revolved around two malignant and virulently expansionist ideologies—Marxism and sharia Islam. And yet Americans elected as their leader someone with a strong affinity for both. It's a matter of public record that Obama was schooled as a Muslim in Indonesia, followed by decades steeped in Marxism and Far-Left radicalism—a worldview he has never renounced.

But we didn't hear about this from the big media, who instead anointed Obama as a political messiah, comparing him with Jesus and God.[1] In what became a full-fledged cult of personality, complete with people fainting right and left at his rallies, millions of Americans pinned all their hopes and dreams on Obama. But the political-messiah persona was something Obama had long cultivated, admitting in his second autobiography, *The Audacity of Hope,* "I serve as a blank screen on which people of vastly different political stripes project their own views."[2] Obama developed this appealing yet intentionally ambiguous mask by, for example, voting "present" an astounding 129 times[3] while a member of the Illinois state Senate to avoid taking a position that might alienate one side or the other—including on bills he had supported and even sponsored! Taking a position, you see, might have compromised the purity and universality of his "blank screen," which would one day serve to reflect the aspirations for "hope" and "change" of millions of Americans.

After Obama was elected, reality struck. Under the pretext of rescuing the economy, his socialist instincts took over immediately, with astonishing levels of spending, economic "stimulus," and bailouts. Just three weeks after Obama's inauguration in January 2009, *Newsweek*'s cover trumpeted the headline "WE ARE ALL SOCIALISTS NOW."[4] Before long, however, with recession still strangling the nation, Obama and congressional leaders Nancy Pelosi and Harry Reid abandoned efforts to fix the economy and instead maniacally pursued their plan to force the holy grail of socialism—government-run health care—down the throat of an unwilling America.

Multitudes openly revolted against Obama and the Democrat-controlled House and Senate, an awakening that led to the spontaneous generation of the Tea Party movement. By the time the Affordable Care Act was actually implemented, forcing millions to *lose* their health insurance and leading many to conclude the disaster could be resolved only by the eventual transition to a single-payer system, former New Left leader and best-selling author David Horowitz was openly characterizing Obama's healthcare takeover as nothing short of "communism."[5]

But that was just the beginning. As crisis after crisis and scandal after scandal piled up, each seemingly more outrageous than the one before, many people were forced to ask themselves a painful question: How could it be that hundreds of thousands of Americans fought and bled—and many died—on foreign shores to contain an evil and metastasizing ideology variously called communism, Marxism, socialism, collectivism, or statism, and yet now, just a few years later, we would gaze up at the pinnacle of power in our own country and behold leaders in thrall to essentially the same core ideology we fought and died to protect strangers from?

Of course, long before Obama's presidency, America's Judeo-Christian culture had been under attack, with patriotism, traditional morality, and strong family units replaced by "sexual liberation," disintegrating families, easy divorce, and a culture drenched in extreme violence and graphic sex.

Finally, in the age of Obama, the federal government itself had become as noxious as the culture that spawned it.

How did all this happen? In our search for answers, Americans scoured the Internet, read books and articles, listened to talk radio, held Tea Party rallies and meetings, and sought out honest news reporting and accurate historical accounts wherever the truth could be found.

And lo and behold, we started to discover our real history, including the long-term infiltration and subversion of Judeo-Christian America by people holding a profoundly un-Christian and un-American worldview.

We discovered the history of the "progressives"—a slippery and elusive label relatively unfamiliar to most Americans, certainly not a household word, like "liberal," "conservative," "libertarian," "constitutionalist," or even "Green." Those on the liberal left insist progressivism is the pursuit of progress, principally through more enlightened and compassionate social organization, while conservatives consider "progressive" to be just a sneaky catchall euphemism for socialists and Marxists. What is indisputable is that "progressives" have been taking over virtually all of America's key institutions for the last two to three generations.

We discovered that our public schools and colleges were, and continue to be, shaped by "education reformers" going back more than a century to the likes of progressives John Dewey, Edward Thorndike, and G. Stanley Hall. No wonder we never learned about this stuff in school!

We learned about other influential progressive "reformers," such as Planned Parenthood founder and eugenics proponent Margaret Sanger, and Roger Baldwin, the Communist Party member who later founded the American Civil Liberties Union. We heard about progressive presidents Woodrow Wilson and Theodore Roosevelt, and how they set the stage for the radical growth of government in the twentieth century.

Of special interest to us was Saul Alinsky, the Chicago leftist radical who developed and taught "community organizing" (code words for intimidation and naked extortion tactics used against those in "power") and whose methods exerted such a profound impact on the lives of both Barack Obama and Hillary Clinton.

But again, where did it all come from?

The progressive tree has many far-flung roots, but one of the most important—or at least the one that will most clearly bring into sharp focus what has happened to America during the blur—is the Frankfurt School. The story of this astonishingly influential group of Marxist

27

academics, who back in the 1930s during Hitler's ascendency moved from Germany to America, crystallizes the secret history of the nonviolent overthrow of America—first her culture, and later her government, as we finally witnessed with the election of Obama.

In his insightful book *The Death of the West*, Patrick J. Buchanan skillfully recounts the story: "The taproot of the revolution that captured the cultural institutions of the American republic goes back far beyond the 1960s," he writes, transporting readers back to the World War I era, and, ironically, calling to mind the abject *failure* of the international communist revolution Karl Marx had predicted.

"Marxists were stunned," he notes. "The long-anticipated European war was to be their time. 'Workers of the world, unite!' Marx had thundered in the closing line of his *Communist Manifesto*. Marxists had confidently predicted that when war came, the workers would rise up and rebel against their rulers rather than fight fellow workers of neighboring nations."

But it didn't happen. "Workers of the world" *didn't* unite, but instead, resonating with patriotism and devotion to their religion, fought for their beloved nations.

How could Marx have been so wrong? wondered the acolytes of communism's founder.[6]

As it turns out, at least a few of Marx's apologists figured out the problem: the working class was being poisoned by its religion, Christianity! As Buchanan explains, the new generation of Marxist purveyors realized that all those workers "had not risen in revolution because their souls had been saturated in two thousand years of Christianity, which blinded them to their true class interests. Unless and until Christianity and Western culture, the immune system of capitalism, were uprooted from the soul of Western Man, Marxism could not take root, and the revolution would be betrayed by the workers in whose name it was to be fought. In biblical terms," he quips, "the word of Marx, seed of the revolution, had fallen on rock-hard Christian soil and died."[7]

Let's meet a few of these "neo-Marxists" who had set up shop in America, and who were destined to so powerfully, albeit clandestinely, shape the hearts and minds of tens of millions of baby boomers.

For one, there was the Hungarian Georg (or György) Lukács, whose writings, Buchanan notes, had already made him a top Marxist theorist in the twentieth century:

> "I saw the revolutionary destruction of society as the one and only solution," said Lukacs. "A worldwide overturning of values cannot take place without the annihilation of the old values and the creation of new ones by the revolutionaries." As deputy commissar for culture in [Hungarian revolutionary leader] Bela Kun's regime, Lukacs put his self-described "demonic" ideas into action in what came to be known as "cultural terrorism."
>
> As part of this terrorism he instituted a radical sex education program in Hungarian schools. Children were instructed in free love, sexual intercourse, the archaic nature of middle-class family codes, the outdatedness of monogamy, and the irrelevance of religion, which deprives man of all pleasures. Women, too, were called to rebel against the sexual mores of the time.
>
> Lukacs' purpose in promoting licentiousness among women and children was to destroy the family, the core institution of Christianity and Western culture. Five decades after Lukacs fled Hungary, his ideas would be embraced by baby boomers in the "sexual revolution."[8]

Another big star among the neo-Marxist academics who would surreptitiously set the agenda for American culture and morals was Italian communist Antonio Gramsci.

Like Lukács, Gramsci realized it was the pervasive cultural and religious influence of Christianity that had impeded the Russian people from getting fully on board with Marx's communist revolution, complaining that "the civilized world had been thoroughly saturated with Christianity for 2,000 years."[9] Those deep roots had to be cut, concluded Gramsci.

Now comes the famous quote many have heard describing how America's institutions were captured. Writes Buchanan:

> Rather than seize power first and impose a cultural revolution from above, Gramsci argued, Marxists in the West must first change the culture; then power would fall into their laps like ripened fruit. But to change the culture would require a "long march through the institutions"—the arts, cinema, theater, schools, colleges, seminaries, newspapers, magazines, and the new electronic medium, radio. One by one, each had to be captured and converted and politicized into an agency of revolution. Then the people could be slowly educated to understand and even welcome the revolution.[10]

"WORSE THAN JOE McCARTHY"

Let's hit the pause button and deal with one nagging doubt in the back of some readers' minds: *Marxism? Are you kidding? No one believes that ancient and discredited ideology anymore, not even the rulers of China or Russia. How can we seriously be talking about Marxism in today's America?*

That's the question I ran into headfirst on Fox News' *Hannity* show when I was a guest on the Great American Panel with liberal Bob Beckel, with whom I had the following heated on-air exchange regarding Barack Obama:[11]

> ME: Sean, basically what we're looking at is an attempted socialist coup d'etat in Washington, DC. Here's a guy who has been steeped in Marxist ideology for the past 30 years—
>
> BECKEL: *(agitated)* The idea of suggesting socialism or Marxism . . . if you go back and look at what Marxism is, and what socialism is, there's nothing close to either one of them in the United States.
>
> ME: *(persisting)* Here's a guy who as a teenager was mentored by a card-carrying communist, Frank Marshall Davis; he goes to college, where he writes in his own book, *Dreams from My Father,* that he was attracted to the "Marxist professors"; out of college he goes into

community organizing, which was dreamed up by Chicago Marxist Saul Alinsky; and then . . . he started his political career in the living room of another Chicago Marxist and unrepentant, Pentagon-bombing terrorist William Ayers. And yet, if somebody comes on and says, "Well gee, I wonder if it's possible this guy is a socialist or even has Marxist ideas—"

BECKEL: *(fuming)* Let me tell you something: The idea of calling the president of the United States a Marxist, as far as I'm concerned, it's worse than Joe McCarthy calling people in the State Department communists, and you ought to apologize for it!

ME: I said socialist—and full of Marxist ideology, he's been marinating in it for thirty years.

OK, so what's the takeaway in this friendly little interchange (other than the fact that apparently I am "worse than Joe McCarthy")?

Beckel thinks Marxism means exactly what Karl Marx wrote in *The Communist Manifesto* in 1848. But expecting today's Marxists to regard as gospel everything Marx wrote more than a century and a half ago would be like expecting today's evolutionary scientists to accept every idea proposed in Charles Darwin's *On the Origin of Species*, written about the same time (1859). In both cases—Marxism and Darwinism—large portions of the originators' conception have been abandoned or updated to reflect greater knowledge that came later. Thus, today's Marxists no longer believe the oppressed worker proletariat will rise up in unison and smash the evil bourgeois factory owners, instituting a glorious workers' paradise while everyone robustly sings "The Internationale."

Even the website of the Communist Party USA affirms that Marxism has changed dramatically over time: "Marxism is not a rigid dogma, but relies on the scientific method to analyze and change society, so it is constantly developing and adapting as society itself changes."[12]

Marxists today embrace an *entirely new* version of Marxism—hence the terms "*neo*-Marxism" and "cultural Marxism"—while the core principles remain the same: the acquisition and radical redistribution of wealth and power (and on a deeper level, a radical rebellion against God, in order to play god).

So, now let's rejoin our story and discover how the *new* Marxism was injected into the cultural bloodstream of America's baby boomers.

Military historian William S. Lind, in his essay "Who Stole Our Culture?" cites one of Gramsci's famous colleagues, the Frankfurt School's Herbert Marcuse, dubbed the "father of the New Left." Lind picks up the story in the pivotal decade of the '60s:

> The student rebellion of the 1960s, driven largely by opposition to the draft for the Vietnam War, gave Marcuse a historic opportunity. As perhaps its most famous "guru," he injected the Frankfurt School's cultural Marxism into the baby boom generation. Of course, they did not understand what it really was. . . . Marcuse and the few other people "in the know" did not advertise that political correctness and multiculturalism were a form of Marxism. But the effect was devastating: A whole generation of Americans, especially the university-educated elite, absorbed cultural Marxism as their own, accepting a poisonous ideology that sought to destroy America's traditional culture and Christian faith. That generation, which runs every elite institution in America, now wages a ceaseless war on all traditional beliefs and institutions. They have largely won that war. Most of America's traditional culture lies in ruins.[13]

It turns out the Frankfurt School, and particularly Gramsci's notion of the "long march through the institutions"—takeover through gradual evolution, rather than violent revolution—was the only way to introduce Marxism into America.

While "Lenin's regime shook the world for seventy years, ultimately his revolution failed, and his regime collapsed," concludes Buchanan. "The Communist Party of Lenin and Stalin remained what it had been from the beginning, a conspiracy of political criminals who used Marxist ideas and rhetoric to disguise what they were really about: absolute power. Lenin's regime died detested and unmourned. But the Gramscian revolution rolls on, and, to this day, it continues to make converts."[14]

"To old Marxists," summarizes *The Death of the West*,

> the path to power was the violent overthrow of the regime, as in Paris
> in 1789 and in St. Petersburg in 1917. To the new Marxist, the path
> to power was nonviolent and would require decades of patient labor.
> Victory would come only after Christian beliefs had died in the soul
> of Western Man. And that would happen only after the institutions
> of culture and education had been captured and conscripted by allies
> and agents of the revolution.[15]

Got it? That's what Bob Beckel didn't understand: Marxism, American-style.

However, it gets even more surreal. These neo-Marxist academics, whose influence has been so pervasive in academia, determined that the best way to achieve total dominance over America's culture was "through psychological conditioning, not philosophical argument," explains Buchanan. Thus, "America's children could be conditioned at school to reject their parents' social and moral beliefs as racist, sexist, and homophobic, and conditioned to embrace a new morality." So, while most American parents have never even heard of the Frankfurt School, the ideas it promoted were very well-known throughout the teachers' colleges of the '40s and '50s.[16]

Oh, and just one more thing: While the great seducers of other past civilizations have captivated the masses with charismatic religious teachings, powerful appeals to national pride, mesmerizing emotional speeches, and the scapegoating of innocent minorities, the Frankfurt School guys, particularly Marcuse, found that sex and drugs would get the job done just fine.

In his book *Eros and Civilization*, Marcuse advocated universal adoption of the Pleasure Principle, arguing that by rejecting Judeo-Christian culture, a new world of—are you ready for this?—polymorphous perversity would come into being. And sure enough, when the baby boom generation went to college, Marcuse became a rock star. His books were widely read, and his slogan "Make love, not war" became the new *revealed truth* of the 1960s generation.[17]

Makes you wonder how many '60s hippies, antiwar protesters, and students who wore all those millions of Make Love, Not War buttons—and eagerly acted out its message—realized they were advancing the agenda of a dirty old Marxist revolutionary.

The online gay databank *glbtq: an encyclopedia of gay, lesbian, bisexual, transgender, and queer culture* describes Marcuse's pivotal role in the sexual revolution: "Marcuse had an enormous influence on theories of sexual liberation, particularly in the early post-Stonewall gay movement and on the left. Many young people in the 1960s adopted Marcuse-like sexual politics as the basis for the counter-culture's radical transformation of values."[18]

But now we come to the most disturbing—and for many, hardest-to-believe—part of the radical-left agenda, and that is the destruction of the nuclear family. "For cultural Marxists," writes Buchanan, "no cause ranked higher than the abolition of the family, which they despised as a dictatorship and the incubator of sexism and social injustice":

> Erich Fromm argued that differences between the sexes were not inherent, but a fiction of Western culture. Fromm became a founding father of feminism. To Wilhelm Reich, "The authoritarian family is the authoritarian state in miniature. . . . Familial imperialism is . . . reproduced in national imperialism." To [Theodor] Adorno, the patriarchal family was the cradle of fascism. . . . Like Lukacs, Wilhelm Reich believed the way to destroy the family was through revolutionary sexual politics and early sex education.[19]

Despite irrefutable proof, the notion that revolutionaries and ideologues *intentionally destroyed the family*—unleashing truly horrendous levels of misery, suffering, poverty, and despair on millions of parents and children alike—is, understandably, difficult to swallow. The core decency of most people causes their minds to reel at the suggestion that radicals, whatever their ideological persuasion, could really promote the destruction of the family—of innocence, trust, loyalty, and sacred marriage vows—which form the very warp and weft of happiness and security in our lives. We desperately want to believe some other explanation. Alas, the abolition of the family is indeed the necessary high price that must be paid for achieving socialist utopia—at least, in the minds of deranged neo-Marxists.

Let's back up just a bit and understand that the mission of the "old" Marxism (the hot, violent, revolutionary version spearheaded by Lenin) and the "new" Marxism (the cool, nonviolent, evolutionary version led by the Frankfurt School and advanced by the '60s "New Left," especially radical feminism) are the same.

First, the nasty, violent Marxism. As Soviet historian Mikhail Heller explained in his insightful book *Cogs in the Wheel:*

> One of the first things V. I. Lenin did when he came to power in the Soviet Union, after the revolution in 1917, was to have passed what amounts to our no-fault divorce statutes. Lenin, and later Stalin, determined that in order to maintain control of the people it would be necessary to completely destroy the family and restructure it. Thus, on September 16, 1918, a law was passed whereby one could obtain a divorce by simply mailing or delivering a postcard to the local resister without the necessity of even notifying the spouse being divorced. This statute, along with the communist encouragement of sexual immorality during marriage, approval of abortion, and forcing women out of the home into the workforce, accomplished its purpose of destroying the Russian family.[20]

Sound familiar? Or is today's "encouragement of sexual immorality" in America, along with widespread "approval of abortion" and the powerful cultural and economic factors "forcing women out of the home into the workforce," just a coincidence?

As attorney and author Phyllis Schlafly explains in her definitive book *Who Killed the American Family?* "The American family was destroyed by a combination of political activists, judges, economic theorists, self-proclaimed experts, and left-wing politicians," all guided by the utopian philosophies of the progressive left.

"The goal of the progressives," Schlafly broadly summarizes, "is to break down the American family, destroy parental authority, deny right and wrong, reduce family autonomy, and get as many people as possible dependent on government programs. That's why liberals, especially feminists, wage a persistent attack on the institution of marriage and the traditional family structure."[21]

Noting that top leaders in the feminist vanguard, including Betty Friedan and Bella Abzug, were trained in Marxism, Schlafly sums up Marx's view of marriage: "Karl Marx urged 'Abolition of the family!' in his 1848 *Communist Manifesto*. He argued that the family is based on 'capital' and 'private gain,' which were dirty words in his lexicon. He particularly objected to parents being able to educate their children, and he called the 'hallowed co-relation of parent and child . . . all the more disgusting.'"[22]

Arguing that the nuclear family constituted, in part, a system for "the orderly inheritance of property," Schlafly notes that Marx believed "social revolution would eliminate the need for private property, so marriage and family would no longer be needed." Hence the Russian Revolution's bold experiment in restructuring the family. "Revolutionary jurists," she noted, "believed children, the elderly, and the disabled would be supported under socialism by the state; housework would be socialized and waged; and women would no longer be economically dependent on men. The family, stripped of its social functions, would 'wither away.'"[23]

Fast-forward a hundred years. What do we see in today's America? While only 4 percent of this nation's children were born to unmarried mothers in 1950, today the rate is ten times higher, an astonishing 41 percent of US births being illegitimate (and 73 percent of African-American children). Schlafly reveals the shattering bottom-line costs of divorce, infidelity, and family breakdown that have resulted from the progressive policies and cultural attitudes that dominate today's America:

Father absence is devastating for children. Exhaustive peer-reviewed research confirms that the absence of a father is the single most reliable predictor for a whole roster of negative outcomes: low self-esteem, parental alienation, high school dropout (71 percent are fatherless), truancy, early sexual activity, promiscuity, teen pregnancy, gang membership, imprisonment (85 percent of jailed youth are fatherless), drug abuse, homelessness (90 percent of runaway children have an absent father), a 40 times higher risk of sexual abuse and 100 times higher risk of fatal abuse.

"Why haven't the facts around fatherlessness made a dent in the family law system?" she asks. "In a word, ideology."[24]

Unsurprisingly, the one major political party that espouses that very ideology—the Democratic Party—benefits enormously from the destruction of the American family. Polls repeatedly show married voters tend to vote Republican,[25] while unmarried people are shown to be (as a group) considerably more liberal than married people. And as recent elections have shown, single voters have favored Obama overwhelmingly—by a 30 percent margin![26] This, again, is hardly coincidental; taking over the Democratic Party has long been Job One of the Far Left.

Indeed, observes Schlafly, "the wreckage of the American family renders us incapable of having limited government because government must step in to perform tasks formerly done by the nuclear family."[27]

Get it? The bottom line, however difficult to believe, is that many decades ago, influential Marxist revolutionaries conspired to slowly extinguish Western culture, the religion that underpinned it—Christianity—and the nuclear family that cherishes, nurtures, and reproduces it, as the surest road to accomplishing their goal of "fundamentally transforming the United States of America."[28]

And transform they did. To disbelieve and scoff at what is written here is to disbelieve and scoff not just at history, but at the current reality staring us in the face. Just don't expect to find this spelled out in high school or college history books, most of which are written by progressives, because they're not about to tell on themselves.

SNEAK ATTACK

The evidence surrounds and overwhelms us. Over a relatively short period of time, virtually every major institution in America has been radically transformed: our public education system, our colleges and universities, our news and entertainment media, our foundations and philanthropies, many of our churches—even, as we have seen, our own families.

Why didn't we see this happening?

Oh, we had clues along the way—while we were living in the blur. We'd notice, for example, that our colleges were becoming rabidly left wing and immoral (many Ivy League schools now annually feature "Sex Week"). We'd notice that the powerful teachers' union, the National Education Association, was bizarrely Far Left as well, in no way representing the views of most of the nation's teachers. Even the National Council of Churches—the umbrella organization for many of America's "mainline" church denominations—for some mysterious reason (unlike the millions of churchgoers they claim to represent) was backing every communist revolutionary movement in the world.[29] "But communism is atheistic," you might well say, "so why would Christian churches support it?" Likewise we heard about *liberation theology*—Marxism disguised as Christianity—a particularly angry and deluded variation of which Barack Obama absorbed at the feet of his racist, America-hating pastor Jeremiah Wright for two decades.

We had lots of clues, but they were like odd puzzle pieces—intriguing, some foreboding—but we didn't know how to assemble them into one coherent picture.

Today, many Americans are finally discovering that decades ago, forces of the left realized that once you own the culture, it's just a matter of time before ultimate power (government) falls into your lap like a ripe fig. Americans witnessed the fig harvest in the November 2008 election of Obama, with another harvest in 2012, and yet another planned for 2016, with the possible election of Hillary Clinton.

Yet something still doesn't add up.

Why would a beautiful, noble country like America—a "shining city on a hill" as Ronald Reagan put it—fall prey to angry, largely atheistic, leftist ideology, especially when you consider that just a quarter century earlier, Reagan had presided over the dissolution of the communist "evil empire" of the Soviet Union? Don't you remember? We watched the USSR disintegrate and oppressed nations like Bulgaria, Hungary, Poland, Romania, Czechoslovakia, and East Germany celebrate their freedom. We beheld the glorious spectacle of formerly subjugated people taking sledgehammers to the Berlin Wall and knocking it to the ground. People of goodwill the world over wept and sent up shouts of joy.

How, then, could we win the war against an evil ideology—yet simultaneously lose that same war?

The answer is that in many respects this was—and remains—a two-front war: While we are busy repelling the enemy in open battle, he simultaneously conducts a long-term stealth operation. The battle that's out in the open is an immediate, life-endangering threat, demanding our full attention and drawing our return fire. Meanwhile, the other front in this war is slow-moving, seductive, sneaky, nonviolent, often even appealing and reasonable-sounding. And *that's* the one that gets us.

Until the dissolution of the USSR, America was preoccupied with the threat of Soviet expansionism and, worse, the fearsome specter of global nuclear war—thousands of nuclear-tipped intercontinental ballistic missiles raining down unthinkable mass destruction on our most populated cities, followed by decades of radiation, making survival seem more frightful than death. Scary stuff. Yet at the same time, largely unknown to us, there was a second front in this war being waged against America—quietly, in a much more civilized fashion and largely out of the limelight.

So that's the war strategy: While our attention is engaged in fighting a physical battle, we're distracted from dealing with the subtler, more seductive, but ultimately more dangerous ideological—and spiritual—battle.

STEALTH JIHAD

Not surprisingly, we have more recently witnessed the exact same two-front war strategy being used by Islamists intent on "fundamentally transforming" America in *their* image. While our homeland security, intelligence, and law enforcement assets are focused intently on the very real threat of terrorism—monitoring and analyzing thousands of potential terror flags in hopes of preventing mass-casualty events like 9/11 as well as lone-wolf attacks on the homeland—other Islamist campaigns, seemingly less threatening but pursuing the same long-term goal of total sharia dominance, are being carried out every day, right under our noses, and often with our blessing!

As federal prosecutors will attest, an advanced level of seditious Islamist infiltration and subversion exists within America's borders right now, including widespread jihadist indoctrination and even terror recruitment on college campuses. Islamic schools and mosques across America are promoting radical teachings and inciting terror. Jihad recruitment in our prisons, thanks to taxpayer-funded Muslim chaplains, is a long-established problem. In the digital-Internet age, the world's worst terrorists, including ISIS and al-Qaeda, use social media and other electronic means to recruit disaffected Westerners to join their ranks. And perhaps most alarming of all, there is well-documented Islamist subversion high up within our own government.[30]

Most major US-based Islamic organizations portray themselves as charitable, religious, and civil-rights groups, yet are dedicated to replacing the Constitution with the Koran and sharia. For example, Omar Ahmad, founder of the controversial Council on American-Islamic Relations (CAIR), which has been closely tied to the terror group Hamas, in an unusually candid interview, once admitted to a California newspaper that Islam isn't in America to be equal to any other faith, but to become dominant. The Koran, the Muslim book of scripture, he said, should be the highest authority in America, and Islam the only accepted religion on Earth.[31] Meanwhile, an FBI wiretap transcript quotes Ahmad as agreeing with Hamas financier Shukri Abu Baker when Baker asserted that they must "camouflage" their true intentions of Islamizing America. The conversation took place during an infamous secret meeting of terrorist suspects at Philadelphia's Marriott Hotel.

Unknown to the twenty-seven terror suspects, the FBI also attended the meeting, recording and photographing the participants.

Ahmad compared their planned stealth jihad with a "head fake" in basketball. "This is like one who plays basketball: he makes a player believe that he is doing this, while he does something else," Ahmad said, according to the FBI.[32]

Likewise, Ibrahim Hooper, CAIR's communications director, has publicly expressed his desire to overturn the American government in favor of an Islamic state. "I wouldn't want to create the impression that I wouldn't like the government of the United States to be Islamic sometime in the future," Hooper told an interviewer with the *Minneapolis Star Tribune*. "But I'm not going to do anything violent to promote that. I'm going to do it through education."[33]

"Education"? No thanks, we've already seen what the Left has done with America's education system.

THE LONG MARCH HOME

There's a dangerous psychology at play in this two-front war strategy, whether the adversary is Marxism, Islamism, or any other "ism," causing us to barely register any sense of alarm. After all, compared to the threat of all-out nuclear war and hundreds of millions of casualties, a few unhinged Marxist professors or subversive textbooks don't seem like a big deal. So we don't do anything. Likewise, compared with hijacking passenger jets and flying them into tall buildings as on 9/11 or detonating a nuclear or biological weapon in a major US city, a little fund-raising for Hamas, some anti-Semitic demonstrations on college campuses, even preaching anti-American and anti-Israel hatred inside US mosques, all seem comparatively tame.

Moreover, we imagine such subversion, however controversial and objectionable—even seditious—to somehow be permissible under America's expansive First Amendment rights of free speech, press, religion, and assembly.

In the end, there is one overriding factor that makes America, like

Europe and the United Kingdom, vulnerable to Islamization, and it's the exact same factor that has made us vulnerable to the seductive appeals of neo-Marxism. That is the growing level of societal self-doubt, self-hatred, and rejection of our own core Judeo-Christian beliefs and values—our most precious inheritance from our forefathers—thanks to several generations of near-total immersion in secular-leftist education, journalism, and entertainment. *That* is why we are ripe for subversion, for conversion, or as Obama boasted shortly before being elected president, for "fundamental transformation."

Can we yet win this war?

Ancient Chinese general Sun Tzu famously observed, "If you know the enemy and know yourself, you need not fear the result of a hundred battles."[34] But America's enemies, for the past several generations, have specialized in two big things: deceiving us about who and what they really are, but also, confusing us as to who *we* really are and what *we* really stand for—that being the primary purpose of the left's subversion of our educational system and news and entertainment media.

It's fair to say, after two or three generations of a secular (read: *atheistic*) leftist worldview being constantly implanted and reinforced throughout every level of our society, that tens of millions of us are just profoundly confused, conflicted, and corrupted. Worse, many of us, having been tricked into rebelling against our own values, now defend our confusion and corruption as though it were our God-given mission.

Thus are we confronted with the current civil war between two Americas. On one side we have those who basically still reverence God, common sense, reason, morality, natural law, and the laws of economics and of human nature—in general, the proven principles of Western civilization. On the other side are people who are confused, intimidated, or brainwashed—or else so covetous of power that they've abandoned all principle for the sake of that power.

The singular but very real blessing in all this madness is that suffering often causes people to finally wake up. And once we're awake and paying attention, we have a fighting chance, with God's help, of redeeming ourselves and our nation.

To put it plainly, what we must do is nothing less than what Gramsci and the other neo-Marxists did—except we need to head in the other direction. They took us *away* from reason, responsibility, morality, and reverence for life and for the Creator of life. We need to go back toward these foundational realities that underlie our great civilization, by embarking on a long march back through the institutions. We need to take back not just our government, but every one of our precious institutions that was stolen from us while we weren't paying attention to the secret battle being waged against us in broad daylight.

3

DISINFORMATION AGE

H aving now peeked behind the scenes to catch a glimpse of what was *really* going on in America during the transformative decades of "the blur," I'd like to pause momentarily and begin this chapter with a personal story that will dramatically illustrate just how profoundly America has changed. The story centers around one of our nation's top rocket scientists—my father, the late Vahey S. Kupelian.

As I noted previously, as a young boy my dad had barely survived the Armenian Genocide when he and his mother, Mary, by the grace of God, were able to escape to America, where they both thrived. It was hard—my father worked as a janitor at age thirteen while he was learning English—but not many years later he graduated from MIT and ultimately became one of this country's key aerospace pioneers.

As the Army's chief scientist for ballistic missile defense, and later, as deputy undersecretary of defense for strategic and theater nuclear forces under Ronald Reagan, my dad contributed greatly to his adopted nation's security, heading up the development of many cutting-edge ballistic missile defense projects, including the Army's HIT program—the original "spaced-based" missile interceptor in Reagan's visionary Strategic Defense Initiative. As we can see in today's world—especially in Israel, where that nation's spectacular Iron Dome air defense system knocks out thousands of rockets fired by the Hamas terror organization—the kind of technology my father helped develop decades ago has turned out to be vital for the protection of innocent civilian populations.

In fact, as I write this, I'm holding the original of a personal letter to my dad from President Reagan, which says, in part:

> You have been responsible for major steps forward in our ability to deter aggression and to meet the threats posed by our adversaries. I am particularly grateful to you for the outstanding leadership you have contributed to our strategic defense program. Because of your ideas and your labor, we are much closer to reaching the dream of a world free of the possibility of nuclear holocaust. Your work on ballistic missile defenses will have a profound and continuing effect on U.S. policies and strategic thinking for generations to come. God bless you. Sincerely, Ronald Reagan[1]

Yet there was a time during the 1970s that my father's four-decade career was in danger of grinding to a halt, when the government considered withdrawing his top-secret security clearance.

Why?

Well, it seems that decades earlier, during his teen years, his mother had driven to an Armenian church picnic (Armenia was then, however unwillingly, part of the Soviet Union) where apparently a pro-Soviet speaker gave a talk, and she had picked up a copy of the communist newspaper the *Daily Worker*. The FBI was surveilling the event as possibly subversive, took down my grandmother's license plate number, and somehow—years later—made the cross-connection with my dad's top-secret clearance and determined to find out whether he had any communist or Soviet loyalties.

This, we must remember, occurred during an era when, due to proven Soviet infiltration of the United States government, the FBI was understandably concerned about the loyalty of federal employees, especially those with security clearances and access to sensitive national security information.

Today, those on the left contemptuously scoff at the McCarthy era, the Red Scare, and the Hollywood blacklist as though they constituted the modern equivalent of the Salem witch trials, hysterically demonizing and destroying the lives of countless innocents.

Innocent? It's true that some Americans faddishly joined the Communist Party USA because it was the "cool" (if not stupid and deluded) thing to do at that time. (When Reagan headed the Screen Actors Guild, there were close to six hundred Communist Party members in Hollywood alone, including well-known actors and directors, some of whom later disavowed their previous communist infatuation.)[2] However, overshadowing this is the reality that the US government was host to many real-life Soviet agents, as proven definitively by the post–Cold War release of the decrypted Venona Project cables in 1995, transcripts of actual communications between the Kremlin and Soviet agents in the United States.

Let's be clear: we're talking about people in the US government, some in very senior positions, who were secretly loyal to our No.1 enemy—an evil empire dedicated to America's destruction—a threat ultimately manifesting in nuclear missiles targeted at American cities. It was not "cool" to have such people occupy trusted positions in our government.

Therefore, due to this official fervor to root out communists at that time, my father was in danger of losing his security clearance. Years later, my mother would tell me of my dad sitting on the side of their bed, tearfully breaking the news to her that he might lose his career and livelihood over this long-forgotten *Daily Worker* incident from decades earlier.

Crazy as this scenario may sound—high-level government concern over reported possession of a communist newspaper his mother picked up at a church picnic—my dad submitted a detailed written defense of his actions to the FBI.

In the aftermath of my mother's recent death, I had occasion to go through many of my father's papers and came across a partial copy of his defense. As my dad explained to the government, his mother was a trained social worker who dealt routinely with people of foreign nationalities and differing political ideologies, and she had an obvious special interest in helping Armenians. Therefore, explained my father, she was "bound to come into contact with . . . persons who were pro-Soviet Armenia."

"Since my mother was a social and Americanization worker with many ethnic groups, she would have had access to some of their nationality journals and papers," my dad continued, explaining:

> At one time or other I recollect seeing papers in Armenian, Turkish, Greek, and probably even the *Daily Worker*, which I presumed contained news of Soviet Armenia. However, I don't recall actually reading the *Daily Worker*, and I know that it has never had any bearing on my political thinking. . . .
>
> I cannot recall ever having attended, specifically, any meetings, picnic, or rally where any kind of political speeches were given. It is inevitable that I may have gone to an occasional Armenian picnic where Armenians of all political beliefs were present, but I cannot recall any such picnics or other meetings where political propaganda was distributed or the *Daily Worker* was distributed. I have never been a subscriber to the *Daily Worker* or the Sunday edition of that newspaper and I have never subscribed to any periodicals or papers that promoted Communism.
>
> I am not now nor have I ever been a member of or in any way affiliated with the Communist Party or any other Communist controlled or Soviet organization. To the best of my knowledge, I have never belonged to any organization designated by the Attorney General of the United . . .

That's all I've got—*United* being the last word typed on page 4, the only excerpt I have of my dad's defense of himself. Had the government not believed him, our nation would have lost one of its most important, creative, and *loyal* defense scientists.

Now let's contrast the government's level of concern over communism a generation ago with that of today.

The forty-fourth president of the United States, Barack Hussein

Obama—whose level of security clearance is far higher than my dad's, who indeed has access to *all* intelligence and *all* secrets, not to mention having his "finger on the nuclear button"—was during his college years a committed Marxist, advocating the revolutionary overthrow of America's capitalist system. His father was a Marxist. His mentor as a young teenager, Frank Marshall Davis, was a card-carrying member of the Communist Party USA (card no. 47544).[3]

Obama admits in his 1995 memoir *Dreams from My Father* that, during college, he was attracted to the "Marxist professors." Indeed, the Marxist student leader at Occidental College at the time, John Drew, says Obama was even more communistic than he was, actually believing that Marx's prophesied proletariat revolution to overthrow capitalism was imminent in the United States! As Drew recalls:

> The young Obama was a garden variety Marxist-Leninist. He . . . believed that social forces were creating an inevitable communist revolution in the U.S. and that it was important to have a highly trained elite of educated leaders guide this revolutionary process and oversee it once the revolution took place. Remember, this was at the height of the Cold War in 1980. Ronald Reagan had just been elected president and the U.S.S.R. was still our mortal enemy. In a lot of ways, the young Obama was more radical than me.[4]

Today Drew, having long since repudiated his former radicalism, says that even during his Marxist days he attempted to rein in Obama by trying to persuade him to work *within* America's political system to bring about the Marxist transformation they all desired.

After college, Obama followed in the footsteps of Chicago's leftist godfather Saul Alinsky and went on to practice and teach his revolutionary street-organizing methods. Obama famously kicked off his political career in the living room of Bill Ayers, a self-described "small-C communist" and founder of the terrorist Weather Underground. Moreover, the evidence is now overwhelming that Ayers played a major role in writing and editing Obama's much-fawned-over memoir.[5]

Obama's pastor for two decades, whom he described as his "spiritual mentor," was Jeremiah Wright, a perennially enraged, America-hating purveyor of the Marxist-inspired "black liberation theology." As president, Obama appointed as White House communications director Anita Dunn, who, in a videotaped speech to students, claimed mass-murdering Chinese communist leader Mao Zedong was one of her "favorite political philosophers,"[6] as well as "green jobs czar" Van Jones, who in his earlier years admitted to being a communist and, in fact, founded the communist group STORM (Standing Together to Organize a Revolutionary Movement).[7]

There is much more, of course. These few documented facts merely scratch the surface of Obama's long-term radicalism. But the point in juxtaposing my father's story with Obama's is as inescapable as it is troubling: My dad, a true American who was immeasurably grateful and loyal to his adopted country, could have lost everything because his mother went to a church picnic and picked up a Marxist rag.

That was then. In today's America, voters twice saw fit to elect as president a man who has spent most of his life immersed in Marxist ideology, influences, mentors, and benefactors. He has proven, as president, that he is still fully committed to dragging America—kicking and screaming if necessary—into a new era of unprecedented and lawless, government-coerced, radical redistribution of wealth, power, and privilege. That's a pretty good description of Marxism.

Of course, it would be folly to imagine that politicians like Obama, in the grip of dark utopian ideologies, just magically appear out of thin air to lead a nation of liberty-loving, responsible, moral, right-thinking grown-ups. Rather, during the decades of "the blur," America has been steadily moving in this sad direction. No, not under the "Marxist" label, or any of those other nasty words of yesteryear, like *socialism* or *communism* or *collectivism*. They've all been carefully replaced by warm-and-cuddly terms like *fairness, economic justice, redistribution, progressivism,* and *spreading the wealth around.*

MEET MY FAVORITE COMMUNIST SPYMASTER

Now, it so happens that this particular story of my father's run-in with the government over communism serendipitously led me to the awareness of one more crucial—albeit largely unknown—factor in America's current descent into chaos.

You see, shortly after I first told this story about my father in print, I received a message from Lt. Gen. Ion Mihai Pacepa, the highest-ranking official ever to defect to America from the Soviet intelligence community. The former communist spy chief—but now, by the grace of God, a proud American and naturalized US citizen—told me he was touched by reading my little tale, and we struck up a friendship that would profoundly increase my understanding of political evil, particularly the Far-Left subversion of America.

Having already written two books about high-level lying and manipulation, I thought I knew pretty much all the ways Americans have been influenced, seduced, misled, bullied, and brainwashed into abandoning all that is good and wholesome in favor of destructive ideologies and behaviors. But that was before I met "Mike" Pacepa.

Once the director of foreign intelligence for communist Romania and chief adviser to the infamous dictator Nicolae Ceaușescu, Pacepa was not only an eyewitness to some of the most extraordinary disinformation campaigns of our lifetime; he was in some cases an active participant!

Fortunately, God saw fit to disrupt Mike's brilliant career by instilling within him a strong conscience, so that eventually—despite the power and prestige, the seductive delusions of communism, and the luxurious lifestyle he enjoyed as a spymaster, replete with mountain villas, hunting lodges, and chauffeurs—his conscience won out. He mustered up the courage to turn his back on the evil empire and defect, taking a precarious leap of faith from the pinnacle of power.

He landed in the United States, where he spent years revealing to America's intelligence services precisely how their enemy counterparts conducted their most secret and nefarious activities. Now in his late eighties, Pacepa resides here in the United States, but due to long-term security threats and assassination plots against him, still lives under cover of an assumed identity.

That's because, when Pacepa broke with communism and single-handedly demolished an entire enemy espionage service (his own), Ceauşescu had a nervous breakdown. He put a $2 million bounty on Pacepa's head and dispatched multiple assassination squads, including the notorious terrorist Ilich Ramírez Sánchez ("Carlos the Jackal"), to the United States to find his former top adviser and kill him. Fortunately, all such efforts have been unsuccessful.

For those desiring to comprehend how America could possibly have fallen so far so fast, Pacepa is one of the few people on earth situated to expose the true breadth, depth, and sheer mind-numbing malevolence of a top-secret disinformation machine whose virulent mega-lies, some of them decades old, have taken on a life of their own and, as such, continue to poison the American mind to this day.

To shine a definitive light on all this, Pacepa recently wrote *Disinformation: Former Spy Chief Reveals Secret Strategies for Undermining Freedom, Attacking Religion, and Promoting Terrorism*, along with his coauthor, historian and law professor Ronald Rychlak. I was honored to be involved as the book's editor (and as a contributor to the companion film documentary, *Disinformation: The Secret Strategy to Destroy the West*).

It is rare to encounter a person like Pacepa who has lived and worked as a major participant in high-level evil, yet who somehow managed to leave it all behind due to an inner awakening. Most often, it seems, people enmeshed in the top tier of such dark enterprises just stay entangled in it until they die, being either too corrupted to wake up, or too paralyzed by fear of what will happen if they leave.

So, what did I learn from Pacepa that is so important to us today? After all, I already knew about the Marxist infiltration and subversion of our culture, institutions, and government, as discussed in the previous chapter. I knew the history of the mass atrocities of Lenin and Stalin, and about the nuclear "balance of terror" (the principle behind "mutual assured destruction"), having grown up with a father actively engaged in defending America against that very threat. I knew about Soviet agents high up in the US government, like Alger Hiss and Harry Dexter White. Most of all, I knew how the Marxist ideological virus had been reformulated into more appealing Western strains and introduced into the vast petri dish called America, and how, as the infection spread, millions of us had succumbed to it.

But what I knew very little about was the gargantuan lie-machine at the very beating heart of the Soviet monster, and the multitudes of people involved in literally re-creating reality, rewriting history, defaming noble people while glorifying despicable ones, setting one group viciously against another—all for the purpose of turning the world against Christianity, tricking Americans into hating their own country, actively promoting Islamic terrorism, and much more.

Here's how Pacepa briefly summarized his old job at the top level of the communist world's lie factory:

> World War III was conceived to be a war without weapons—a war the Soviet bloc would win without firing a single bullet. It was a war of ideas. It was an intelligence war, waged with a powerful new weapon called *dezinformatsiya*. Its task was to spread credible derogatory information in such a way that the slander would convince others that the targets were truly evil. To ensure the credibility of the lies, two things were required. First, the fabrications had to appear to come from respected and reputable Western sources; and second, there had to be . . . "a kernel of truth" behind the allegations, so that at least some part of the story could be definitively verified—and to ensure that the calumny would never be put to rest. In addition, the originator had to do his best to ensure that the story got plenty of publicity, if necessary, by having agents or leftist sympathizers in the West publish articles putting the desired spin on the alleged information.[8]

What sort of "information"?

For an object lesson in how to turn Americans against their own nation, Pacepa reveals how one particular KGB disinformation campaign

> launched the political career of the 2004 Democratic Party nominee
> for the White House, Senator John Kerry. On April 22, 1971, the
> former Navy lieutenant testified to the Senate Committee on Foreign
> Relations that American soldiers told him that in Vietnam they had
> "raped, cut off ears, cut off heads, taped wires from portable telephones
> to human genitals and turned up the power, cut off limbs, blown up
> bodies, randomly shot at civilians, razed villages in fashion reminiscent
> of Genghis Khan." Although Senator Kerry never fully revealed the
> source of those outrageous accusations, I recognized them as being the
> product of another KGB disinformation operation. In the 1960s and
> '70s, when I was a leader of the Soviet bloc intelligence community, the
> KGB spread those same vitriolic accusations, almost word for word,
> throughout American and European leftist movements. They were part
> of a KGB disinformation operation aimed at discouraging the United
> States from protecting the world against communist expansion.[9]

"During my years as an intelligence officer," adds Pacepa, "I was many times involved in creating anti-Americanism out of whole cloth, and I could see how *easy* it was to make young people hate the almighty America."[10]

Today, when you see students at Harvard, whose parents are shelling out astronomical annual tuition fees, telling journalists on national TV that "America is a bigger threat to world peace than ISIS,"[11] and when you hear high-profile former college professor Ward Churchill on television comparing the September 11, 2001, terror *victims* to Nazis, while claiming America is so evil she deserves to be bombed again,[12] understand that this bizarre and unprecedented self-hatred on the part of Americans toward their own country didn't develop by accident. From the days of Soviet *dezinformatsiya* right up into the present, when anti-American college history textbooks like Howard Zinn's irredeemably dark *A People's History of the United States* poison the next generation, seducing Americans into hating their country has long been a key strategic goal of the Far Left.

Another extraordinary secret Pacepa brought to light is the largely unreported role the Soviets played in promoting and fueling one of the biggest problems currently besieging America: Islamic terrorism. Indeed, reveals Pacepa, then-KGB chief Yuri Andropov was utterly obsessed with convincing Muslims that the United States Congress was conspiring to have "the Jews" take over the world: "If we whipped up Muslim anti-Semitism," Andropov would say, "then terrorism and violence against Israel and America would naturally follow."

Therefore, Pacepa's security apparatus, the Romanian *Securitate,* was given the following dark assignment:

> The *Securitate's* first major *dezinformatsiya* task in the new World War III was to help Moscow reignite anti-Semitism in Western Europe by spreading thousands of copies of an old Russian forgery, *The Protocols of the Elders of Zion,* in that part of the world. It had to be done secretly, so no one would know that the publications came from the Soviet bloc.
>
> *The Protocols,* which claimed that the Jews were plotting to take over the world, was a Russian forgery, compiled by a disinformation expert, Petr Ivanovich Rachovsky.[13]

But translating this infamous piece of anti-Jewish hate literature into Arabic and disseminating hundreds of thousands of copies throughout the Muslim world to encourage widespread Jew-hatred was just the beginning. The Soviets were also directly training and encouraging Muslim terrorism, beginning with their virtual creation of PLO leader Yasser Arafat, a committed Marxist who became the father of modern Islamic terrorism.

"The KGB had trained him at its Balashikha special-ops school east of Moscow and in the mid-1960s decided to groom him as the future PLO leader," recalls Pacepa. "First, the KGB destroyed the official records of Arafat's birth in Cairo, replacing them with fictitious documents saying that he had been born in Jerusalem and was therefore a Palestinian by birth. . . . The KGB gave Arafat an ideology and an image, just as it did for loyal communists in our international front organizations. High-minded idealism held no mass-appeal in the Arab world, so the KGB remolded Arafat as a rabid anti-Zionist."[14]

Arafat's successor, Mahmoud Abbas, was likewise educated in Moscow at a KGB-run school. Iran's Ayatollah Khomeini was also trained by Moscow. Even al-Qaeda top man Ayman al-Zawahiri was trained by the KGB, as revealed by KGB defector Alexander Litvinenko, who was assassinated by polonium poisoning.

As Soviet expert and political science professor Paul Kengor summarized in *Disinformation's* foreword:

> The authors chronicle Yuri Andropov's anti-Zionism campaign, support of Islamic terrorism, and dual promotion of virulent anti-Semitism and anti-Americanism among Middle East Arabs. By 1978, the Soviet bloc planted some four thousand agents of influence in the Islamic world, armed with hundreds of thousands of copies of the *Protocols of the Elders of Zion*—and military weapons. The seeds they planted in the Arab world decades ago still sow hatred and destruction in the form of violence and terror. Atheistic communism sought out a handmaiden in radical Islam, with extremist Muslims exploited by Soviet manipulators who hoped to besmirch Judaism and Israel and Christianity and America and the West—and too often with tragic success.[15]

Just to splash a little more color into this already nasty picture, here's how Pacepa describes one particular two-hour meeting he had with then-KGB chief (and later general secretary of the Communist Party of the USSR) Andropov. The ghoulish Soviet leader was counseling Pacepa on how to fool President Jimmy Carter into accepting the equally ghoulish dictator Ceauşescu as a "moderate" and "pro-Western" leader, one whom Americans "could do business with":

> Andropov's dark, cavernous office breathed secrecy from every inch of its thick walls. . . . The velvet window draperies were closed, and the only light came from the flickering flames of a fire inside the fireplace. The chairman's ascetic fingers felt cold and moist when he shook my hand. . . .

"Let the gullible fools believe you want to perfume your communism with a dab of Western democracy, and they will clothe you in gold," Andropov declared. The creation of the image of the "new Ceaușescu" should be planted like opium seeds—patiently but tenaciously, one by one by one. We should water our seeds day after day until they bear fruit. We should promise that more openness and Westernization will be forthcoming, if only the West helps our new "moderate" Ceaușescu to defeat his "hardline" opponents at home.[16]

Such gleeful high-level malevolence evokes an almost storybook-like quality, as though we were eavesdropping on the machinations of the evil lords of Mordor and Isengard, conspiring to stamp out freedom in Middle Earth in Tolkien's *Lord of the Rings* tales. Except this was real—and one of the "dark lords" was destined to switch sides.

Ultimately, after Pacepa's defection to America, the curse Ceaușescu placed upon his former spy chief for leaving "the dark side" was visited upon the dictator himself, along with his equally vile wife, Elena. Both were executed by a Romanian firing squad following a Christmas Day 1989 trial in which the accusations against them came almost word for word from Pacepa's first book, *Red Horizons: The True Story of Nicolae and Elena Ceausescu's Crimes, Lifestyle, and Corruption.* The book became an international best seller, and President Reagan came to refer to it as "my bible for dealing with dictators."

BURNING QUESTION

Another much more recent disinformation campaign—one that occurred *after* the breakup of the Soviet Union—will demonstrate just how effective this practice of spreading virus-like lies through "credible" sources still is in infecting America's national mind and soul. This example will particularly resonate in Obama's America, racked as it is by a mysterious upsurge in racial incidents, many of them stoked by leftist organizations and leaders who somehow thrive on promoting racial conflict.

Back in 1996, Pacepa and Rychlak recall,

a sensational story jolted the American conscience. The National Council of Churches (NCC) and the Center for Democratic Renewal (CDR), two secretly Marxist organizations headquartered in the United States, held a joint press conference to announce a "huge increase" in the number of arson cases committed against black churches in the United States.

On June 8, President Bill Clinton denounced those fires in a radio address, and he proposed a new federal task force to investigate them. The president spoke with emotion about his own "vivid and painful memories of black churches being burned in my own state [of Arkansas] when I was a child." Charging that "racial hostility" was the driving force behind the fires, he pledged to place the full power of the federal government behind the investigation. On June 15, the Federal Bureau of Investigation and the Bureau of Alcohol, Tobacco, Firearms and Explosives assigned two hundred federal agents to a new task force charged to investigate black church fires.

By July the accounts of arson committed against black churches had snowballed, with more than twenty-two hundred articles appearing in the press to condemn what the Center for Democratic Renewal called "a well-organized white-supremacist movement."[17]

The epidemic of arson attacks on black churches was one of the most widely reported and sensational news stories of that era, "inflaming decent people everywhere" against the monstrous racists who could commit such crimes, observes Pacepa.

Citing journalist Michael Fumento's exhaustive coverage of the scandal,[18] the *Disinformation* authors note that President Clinton, on July 13 of that year, "signed into law the Church Fire Prevention Act of 1996," making church arson a federal offense, and the following month, Clinton approved spending $12 million to combat fires at black churches. The National Council of Churches ran full-page ads in the *New York Times, Washington Post,* and other newspapers, asking for donations to its new "Burned Churches Fund," in response to which the *Wall Street Journal* reported the NCC had "managed to raise nearly $9 million," with contributions pouring in "at about $100,000 a day."[19]

"Then," says Pacepa, "the bubble burst. It was eventually established by a private group, the National Fire Protection Association, that in recent years there actually had been far *fewer* church fires than usual, and law enforcement officials in the South could not confirm *any* as having been racially motivated":

> No church burning had occurred in Arkansas during Clinton's child-hood, in spite of his "vivid and painful" memories, and the National Council of Churches was accused of fabricating "a great church-fire hoax."
>
> Average Americans looked upon the NCC/CDR hoax as simply a slip of the pen, and forgot about it. No one at home or abroad asked why the whole slanderous hoax had occurred in the first place. The political damage was done, however. The United States, which had paid with 405,399 American lives to save the world from the evils of Nazi racism and the Holocaust, now found itself slandered as a neo-Nazi, racist country.[20]

Astonishingly, not only is the National Council of Churches notorious for leaning far to the left, but as Pacepa and Rychlak have revealed, the NCC's parent organization, the World Council of Churches, "has been infiltrated and ultimately controlled by Russian intelligence since 1961":

> The *Mitrokhin Archive*, a voluminous collection of Soviet foreign intelligence documents smuggled out of the Soviet Union in 1992, provides the identities and Soviet intelligence code names of many Russian Orthodox priests dispatched over the years to the World Council of Churches for the specific purpose of influencing the politics and decisions of that body. In fact, in 1972 Soviet intelligence managed to have Metropolitan Nikodim (its agent "Adamant") elected WCC president. A 1989 KGB document boasts: "Now the agenda of the WCC is also our agenda." Most recently, Metropolitan

Kirill (agent "Mikhaylov"), who had been an influential representative to the World Council of Churches since 1971 and after 1975 a member of the WCC Central Committee, was in 2009 elected patriarch of the Russian Orthodox Church.[21]

Thus, concludes Pacepa, such a slanderous attack on the United States is really nothing new or surprising, but rather reflects how "the Kremlin has for centuries preferred to carry out its domestic and foreign policies by complicated deceptions." Religion is a frequent focus of such disinformation ops, he reveals, since the traditionally cynical Russian leaders "have considered themselves the only god mankind needs."[22]

THE LIE LAUNDERERS

There is still one more major player—absolutely essential for the success of most disinformation campaigns—that needs to be called out. How, for example, in the John Kerry case, could so many Americans come to believe the lie that large numbers of their own soldiers had somehow turned into unhinged, drugged-out "baby killers," routinely murdering and raping innocents in Vietnam? It is a defamatory slur that, to some degree, clings to Vietnam vets to this day—unlike veterans of all other American wars before or since. Why?

Remember, *dis*information is what you call it when intentional *mis*information is clandestinely conveyed to "respectable" sources—primarily the Western news media—to "launder" the misinformation and make it "clean" for public consumption. When the *New York Times* featured the story, most Americans assumed it must be true!

In fact, the concept of "laundering" (as in "money laundering") is such a good metaphor for understanding how disinformation works, let's just quickly recall what money laundering actually entails—basically three steps: (1) placement—tainted money is introduced into a financial institution; (2) layering—the institution performs a series of complex transactions designed to camouflage the original source; and (3) integration—the formerly dirty money, now clean, is free to spend.

One can readily see how this same process applies to the "laundering" of "dirty" information: (1) misinformation is introduced to a respected journalism organization; (2) the media organization showcases the misinformation in a "news report," camouflaging its original source; (3) the public receives the laundered misinformation in the form of apparently "clean" (credible) news, i.e., disinformation.

In short, every time our supposedly free and independent press broadcasts misleading propaganda from an undisclosed source as though it were originally researched, fair-and-balanced reporting—that's disinformation, just as in the days of Soviet communist treachery.

Believe it or not, what is being described here has long been, and remains to this day, standard operating procedure with the "elite media" in America.[23] And it occurs in two distinct ways.

The first is the classic disinformation campaign, whereby major US media—knowingly or unknowingly—carry water for foreign enemy powers. We already considered one: the Vietnam War–era narrative, widely propagated by the establishment press, that large numbers of US soldiers were drug-addicted, atrocity-committing barbarians. Without a sympathetic press, that Soviet disinformation narrative never could have taken root as it did in the American mind.

Another example of the US media being used in a classic communist disinformation campaign involved the *New York Times*' former Moscow bureau chief, Walter Duranty. In the early '30s, Stalin ordered his military to confiscate all of Ukraine's food and then sealed her borders to prevent any outside sustenance from getting in, thereby intentionally starving an estimated seven million men, women, and children to death.

How did the *New York Times* report this unprecedented genocidal famine? In his stories, Duranty not only denied the Ukraine famine was induced by communists—he denied anyone was dying of starvation at all! Idolizing Stalin and describing him as "the world's greatest living statesman," Duranty was thrilled to be granted the first American interview with this mass-murdering criminal psychopath.[24]

For his outrageously biased reporting, Duranty won a Pulitzer Prize. Decades later, spurred by widespread calls that the Pulitzer board revoke

Duranty's award, even the *New York Times* bemoaned their reporter's "largely uncritical recitation of Soviet sources" and confessed that Duranty's articles constituted "some of the worst reporting to appear in this newspaper." But his Pulitzer was never revoked, and the *Times* never had the class to give it up.[25] Revealingly, London's *Guardian* newspaper, in reporting on Ukrainians' understandable zeal to revoke Duranty's Pulitzer, began its story this way: "Drug addict, sexual predator on both sexes and apologist for Stalin, British reporter Walter Duranty still managed to win America's most coveted award for journalism, the Pulitzer Prize, for his coverage of Soviet life in the Thirties."[26]

Now let's leave the unseemly journalism scandals of yesteryear and fast-forward to the modern era, and see how the elite media are faring. And let's set aside US media channeling of the propaganda message of hard-edged communist disinformation purveyors, as illustrated in the previous two examples. We live in a more subtle world today.

For as we saw in the last chapter, there has long been a second front in this same war against Western Judeo-Christian civilization by atheistic Marxism. And whether we focus on Antonio Gramsci in the 1930s and his "long march through the institutions," or the 1960s "cultural revolution," when the radical left and its "liberation movements" spilled out onto America's streets, or the Obama administration's lawless attempts to convert the United States into a European-style socialist welfare state, the one institution whose cooperation is essential at all points is *the news media*.

America's predominantly left-leaning establishment press has long been the primary "launderer" and force-multiplier of all of these transformative leftist agendas.

Here's just one example—which utterly transformed America.

"WE FED LIES TO THE PUBLIC THROUGH THE MEDIA"
During the late 1960s, the pro–abortion-legalization group NARAL, cofounded by abortionist Dr. Bernard Nathanson, created a classic disinformation campaign by feeding statistical fabrications and other intentional lies to the news media, which in turn published and broadcast

the misinformation as though it were the result of their own journalistic research. The ultimate result was the legalization of abortion and well over 55 million dead babies in America.

In *The Marketing of Evil*, I include excerpts of my interview with Dr. Nathanson, who had by that time experienced a profound change of heart and had turned against abortion. But he revealed how he—just like Pacepa before his awakening and subsequent break with communism—had spent his earlier years exploiting a biased, lazy, and corrupt American press to advance a secret agenda. As Nathanson told me:

> In 1968, I met Lawrence Lader. Lader had just finished a book called *Abortion,* and in it had made the audacious demand that abortion should be legalized throughout the country. I had just finished a residency in obstetrics and gynecology and was impressed with the number of women who were coming into our clinics, wards and hospitals suffering from illegal, infected, botched abortions. . . . . We sat down and plotted out the organization now known as NARAL. With Betty Friedan, we set up this organization and began working on the strategy. . . .
>
> We persuaded the media that the cause of permissive abortion was a liberal, enlightened, sophisticated one. Knowing that if a true poll were taken, we would be soundly defeated, we simply fabricated the results of fictional polls. We announced to the media that we had taken polls and that 60 percent of Americans were in favor of permissive abortion. This is the tactic of the self-fulfilling lie. Few people care to be in the minority. We aroused enough sympathy to sell our program of permissive abortion by fabricating the number of illegal abortions done annually in the U.S. The actual figure was approaching 100,000, but the figure we gave to the media repeatedly was 1 million.
>
> Repeating the big lie often enough convinces the public. The number of women dying from illegal abortions was around 200–250 annually. The figure we constantly fed to the media was 10,000. These false figures took root in the consciousness of Americans, convincing many that we needed to crack the abortion law.

Another myth we fed to the public through the media was that legalizing abortion would only mean that the abortions taking place illegally would then be done legally. In fact, of course, abortion is now being used as a primary method of birth control in the U.S. and the annual number of abortions has increased by 1,500 percent since legalization.

NARAL's deceitful disinformation campaign, bolstered by fraudulent "research," was uncannily successful. In New York, the law outlawing abortion had been on the books for 140 years, and yet, recalled Nathanson, with the media's help, "in two years of work, we at NARAL struck that law down."

New York immediately became the abortion capital for the eastern half of the United States.

"We were inundated with applicants for abortion," said Nathanson. "To that end, I set up a clinic, the Center for Reproductive and Sexual Health (C.R.A.S.H.), which operated in the east side of Manhattan. It had 10 operating rooms, 35 doctors, 85 nurses. It operated seven days a week, from 8 a.m. to midnight. We did 120 abortions every day in that clinic. At the end of the two years that I was the director, we had done 60,000 abortions. I myself, with my own hands, have done 5,000 abortions. I have supervised another 10,000 that residents have done under my direction. So I have 75,000 abortions in my life. Those are pretty good credentials to speak on the subject of abortion."[27]

And speak he did: following his charge of heart, Bernard Nathanson worked tirelessly for the rest of his life to awaken America to the evils of abortion—just as my good friend, General Pacepa, has labored for decades to awaken Americans to the evils of Marxism.

In this chapter we've explored how power-mad ideologues created secret strategies to knock the Western Judeo-Christian world off its axis. It may all sound very far-off and exotic, but hang on—because the next chapter brings this same bizarre mind-set home to our own front door, as we explore the hidden mechanics of the destruction machine working relentlessly in today's America.

4

CHAOS THEORY

For millions of Americans beholding the chaos enveloping their country during the age of Obama, one of the biggest unanswered questions is whether the forty-fourth president has been destroying the nation intentionally—or destroying it out of incompetence and mind-numbing ideological blindness.

There's little serious dispute that, for whatever reasons, his influence on the country as president has been nothing short of catastrophic.

Some may argue it's irrelevant or unknowable whether the destruction is intentional or not. After all, if we're all passengers on a giant ship careening toward an iceberg, does it really matter what the captain is thinking? We need to veer sharply to avert disaster, or, failing that, get off the ship.

However, it's not only relevant and knowable, but crucial, that we understand why and *how* the current captain of our ship of state is—as former vice president Dick Cheney put it—trying "to take America down."[1]

Just consider Obama's track record:

- He has effectively eliminated America's borders, actively luring legions of illegal immigrants to flood into the United States across its wide-open southern border, while unconstitutionally granting through executive fiat de facto amnesty to millions of illegal aliens already here.

- He has presided over a perpetually stagnant economy, with an astounding 92 million Americans no longer in the workforce and 20 percent of households now dependent on government food stamps.[2]

- He has intentionally, through epic deceit ("You can keep your doctor"[3]), ravaged the most admired and advanced health care system in the world, causing millions of insured Americans to *lose* their health care coverage, premium prices to skyrocket, and many doctors to quit their profession in frustration.[4]

- He has daily displayed contempt for the Constitution he swore to uphold, exploiting the fearsome apparatus of the federal government—from the IRS to the Justice Department—to reward cronies and punish critics and political opponents, whom he calls "enemies."[5]

- He has, by refusing to leave the minimal stay-behind force in Iraq urged by every military expert, enabled a shockingly barbaric and rapidly growing terrorist army to declare statehood in Syria and Iraq, dishonoring the sacrifices of forty-five hundred American soldiers who died liberating Iraq, and resulting in a growing mass-terror threat to the US homeland; at the same time he released, during wartime, five top terrorist leaders detained at GTMO in exchange for a single US Army deserter he praised in a White House Rose Garden ceremony.

- He has actively attempted to bring down the elected leader of one of America's most valued allies, Israel, while making a Neville Chamberlain–like deal with Iranian leaders obsessed with obtaining nuclear weapons and intent on destroying not just Israel, but the United States; throughout the Middle East, from Iran to Iraq, Egypt to Libya, Syria to Yemen, he has turned the region upside down with his weak and perverse leadership.

I've just barely skimmed the record, but you get the idea.

Whether we regard Obama as someone well-intentioned but deeply misguided by leftist ideology (and perhaps manifesting, as well, a serious personality disorder, as some physicians and psychiatrists have publicly opined),[6] or as a genuine sociopath, devoid of conscience, aware that he is causing immense suffering and damage to the greatest nation on earth—the inescapable fact is, *he is doing it.* And what he is doing is transforming not only America as a nation, but *Americans.*

This last point is the focus of this chapter. It is ironic that a major aspect of Obama's "fundamental transformation of America"—in fact, the *most* important aspect long-term—is seldom discussed or even acknowledged.

So, here we go. Let's take a trip way past all the sensational headlines and analyses, and journey around to the far side of the moon of the Obama presidency—to the largely unexplored hidden side of "fundamental transformation," of progressive "hope and change," of "manufactured crisis," of "never letting a good crisis go to waste," of the Cloward-Piven strategy that so many have cited to explain the Obama presidency.

Once we see what lurks in that mysterious nether region, we'll have a much better appreciation of what we're really dealing with—and perhaps even get a stronger grip on how to reclaim our country.

CLOWARD-PIVEN 2.0

Once an obscure insider expression for the process of intentionally overloading and crashing a hated system or program to accomplish a hidden political goal, today Cloward-Piven is seemingly on everybody's lips: Governors, congressmen, and senators, as well as pundits, analysts, and politically aware Americans of many stripes have all described the nonstop crises and scandals that make up the very warp and weft of the Obama presidency as "the Cloward-Piven strategy" at work.[7]

First, a quick crash course in "crashing a system": Richard Andrew Cloward and Frances Fox Piven were Columbia University sociologists who in 1966 published, in the left-wing publication *The Nation*, their plan to collapse New York City's welfare system by intentionally overloading it with applicants. It was called "The Weight of the Poor: A Strategy to End Poverty."[8] Their assumption was that to resolve the resulting crisis and chaos, a new socialist system would eventually be instituted, guaranteeing a "livable minimum income" for everyone—whether they worked or not.

Journalist and author Richard Poe tells the amazing story of how Cloward and Piven's plan brought New York City to its knees:

> Their article called for "cadres of aggressive organizers" to use "demonstrations to create a climate of militancy." Intimidated by threats of black violence, politicians would appeal to the federal government for help. Carefully orchestrated media campaigns, carried out by friendly leftwing journalists, would float the idea of "a federal program of income redistribution," in the form of a guaranteed living income for all—working and non-working people alike. Local officials would clutch at this idea like drowning men to a lifeline. They would apply pressure on Washington to implement it. With every major city erupting into chaos, Washington would have to act.
>
> This was an example of what are commonly called Trojan Horse movements—mass movements whose outward purpose seems to be providing material help to the downtrodden, but whose real objective is to draft poor people into service as revolutionary foot soldiers; to mobilize poor people *en masse* to overwhelm government agencies with a flood of demands beyond the capacity of those agencies to meet. The flood of demands was calculated to break the budget, jam the bureaucratic gears into gridlock, and bring the system crashing down. Fear, turmoil, violence and economic collapse would accompany such a breakdown—providing perfect conditions for fostering radical change. That was the theory.[9]

This massive and aggressive extortion scheme worked like a charm. As Poe recounts, "Cloward and Piven recruited a militant black organizer named George Wiley to lead their new movement":

In the summer of 1967, Wiley founded the National Welfare Rights Organization (NWRO). His tactics closely followed the recommendations set out in Cloward and Piven's article. His followers invaded welfare offices across the United States—often violently—bullying social workers and loudly demanding every penny to which the law "entitled" them. By 1969, NWRO claimed a dues-paying membership of 22,500 families, with 523 chapters across the nation.[10]

The end result? According to the New York–based *City Journal*, "From 1965 to 1974, the number of single-parent households on welfare soared from 4.3 million to 10.8 million, despite mostly flush economic times. By the early 1970s, one person was on the welfare rolls in New York City for every two working in the city's private economy."[11]

As a direct consequence, the gargantuan levels of welfare spending forced New York City to declare bankruptcy in 1975.

Fast-forward to the present, and with this Cloward-Piven paradigm in mind, let's revisit one of Obama's many domestic crises: illegal immigration.

Consider first the unprecedented border crisis resulting from Obama's refusal to enforce federal immigration laws. Add to that his executive imposition of the DREAM Act (Development, Relief, and Education for Alien Minors) after Congress refused to pass it, plus his other presidential actions and statements, which together amounted to an engraved invitation to Central American youth to migrate to America in droves. Consider also that the flood of tens of thousands of illegal aliens crossing the United States–Mexican border has included many minors who were kidnapped, robbed, or preyed upon en route by sexual predators, "coyotes" (human smugglers), and drug cartels, according to news reports of astonishing numbers of both boys and girls being raped in transit.[12] Of those who have made it into America, many are secretly bussed and flown to communities all over the United States, whether the residents there want them or not, causing widespread anxiety and distress across the land.

Consider also the reports of medical doctors warning of a "public health catastrophe," one publicly predicting the wave of immigrants would likely bring "a number of infectious diseases that will spread like wildfire,"[13] and another warning, "A public health crisis, the likes of which I have not seen in my lifetime, is looming."[14]

There's more: Although most press reports on the waves of "unaccompanied minors" flooding across the southern border have included photos and video of infants and toddlers, "minors" means people under eighteen, and in fact includes teenage members of the ultraviolent MS-13 gang—whose initiation requires them to commit murder, rape, or other heinous crimes—also being welcomed into the United States under Obama's policy. Likewise, gangs reportedly have been recruiting new members from among the massive influx of unaccompanied immigrant minors.

Just to provide a sense of the scale of the problem: In Texas alone, during the first six years of the Obama presidency, illegal aliens were convicted of committing 640,000 crimes, including over 3,000 homicides.[15]

Consider also that after his final election cycle (the November 2014 midterms), Obama single-handedly granted what amounts to another executive amnesty, this time to 6 million illegal aliens already in the country, after having insisted publicly—on camera—twenty-two different times that he lacked the legal authority to do any such thing.[16]

On top of all this, in an age of rapidly growing Islamic radicalization in the United States, Britain, and Europe, Obama has stepped up the rate of allowing Muslim immigrants into the United States.[17] During the same period, he has released into the general US population more than sixty thousand illegal aliens who were convicted of crimes in the United States.[18]

It is absurd to regard all this as "incompetence," but rather the ideologically driven *intentional* overloading of a system—only this time, the system to be overloaded, broken, and transformed is America herself.

OVERLOADING MORE THAN THE "SYSTEM"

While Cloward-Piven has come to describe a major crisis manufactured for the purpose of bringing about a transformation, conversion, or revolution of some sort, such tactics and the chaos they produce, devastating as they are to the nation, constitute only part of the story.

You see, the crisis-creation strategy of radical transformation encompasses not merely stressing, overloading, and breaking "systems"—this entitlement program or that welfare system, this health care delivery or that border-security system. Rather, the creation of unbearable stress and crisis in our nation is, on a more fundamental level, all about stressing *Americans*, overloading *Americans,* about breaking down, rebuilding, and fundamentally transforming *Americans*.

If you don't understand this, you can't even begin to understand the radical left, how it operates, and what it's doing to America.

The key is to realize that stressing and breaking the exceptional and unique American system—grounded in Judeo-Christian morality, reverence for the Constitution, personal liberty, and individual responsibility—cannot possibly occur without first stressing and breaking *people.* That's where the *real* "fundamental transformation" takes place.

Therefore, what follows is a brief exploration of the world of everyday, garden-variety political and cultural brainwashing as it occurs in the United States.

We will discover why progressive change agents, consciously or unconsciously, find it necessary to overload not just systems, but people. Indeed, left-wing revolutionary tactics are all about overloading people until they break, which is, in large measure, why America is such a broken society today.

Let's pause and recognize a strange reality: The exploitation of crises—real, manufactured, or imagined—constitutes the left's primary mode of "governance," which for leftists always means the acquisition, exercise, and expansion of *power.* It's what former White House chief of staff Rahm Emanuel was obliquely admitting when he said, "You never want a serious crisis to go to waste. And what I mean by that is, it's an opportunity to do things you think you could not do before."[19]

The kind of all-powerful government Barack Obama wants is, quite literally, a condition of perpetual crisis. Of course, from the point of view of the hard left, the United States has long existed in a state of crisis, thanks to our intolerable level of so-called income inequality, our "broken" health care system, our supposed exploitation of other nations, the mythical war on women, and still-rampant racism, discrimination, Islamophobia, homophobia, transphobia, and so on.

But just imagine that progressives assumed total, unfettered control of American government and were able to completely reshape the nation in their image, implementing every single "change" their hearts desired. What then?

Life would be constant crisis. Leftists' idea of utopia—massive ongoing wealth confiscation and redistribution to enable cradle-to-grave security for all—*requires* ongoing and pervasive crisis. Socialism, or statism, being the parasitical system it is, thrives only in a nutrient base of dependency, which (for adults) is the evidence of some form of crisis.

What *does not* thrive in a state of crisis-induced, ever-expanding government is liberty—or happiness, or confidence, or independence. Businesses and entrepreneurs don't thrive or take risks under massive, enlarging government. Even worse, strong and intact families don't tend to thrive under a nanny state, with divorce so easy, single-parent dependence on government so perversely incentivized, and socialist government—being the jealous god it is—discouraging stable and God-centered families in a multitude of ways.

All of us, one way or another, tend to be pushed into crisis mode by ever-expanding government.

Veteran forensic psychiatrist Lyle Rossiter, MD, crystalizes the underlying psychology at work in his book, *The Liberal Mind*:

> What the radical liberal mind really longs for, as revealed in his political goals, is a child's relationship to a loving family whose caretaking compensates him for the injuries he suffered in his early years. He seeks all of this in the contemporary political arena. The major problem he faces is that a substantial portion of the population

is still competent: It is a population that deeply reveres individual liberty, readily accepts its responsibilities, and passionately opposes its destruction.[20]

Responsible, well-grounded adults, argues Rossiter, are happy to take care of their own families' needs through voluntary cooperation, and vehemently reject the nanny government's intrusions.

> What the competent citizen wants, in contrast to the modern liberal, is a coherent and dependable structure for ordered liberty, secured by a limited government that respects the autonomy and sovereignty of the individual and protects his property rights against the constant invasions of collectivism.
>
> The liberal mind rejects this prescription on principle and attempts to overthrow it in government policy. What the liberal seeks in order to feel secure is the modern welfare state with its endless guarantees and endless regulations. This *goal* is literally fantastic in its own right. But equally irrational is the *method* by which he attempts to achieve it. He is willing to use any kind of government power, including power which destroys the foundations of civilized freedom, in order to get what he demands: government-insured safety and security over the entire lifespan.[21]

So let's now examine how inordinate stress, anxiety, and anger—created and cultivated by radical change agents in and out of government—actually serve to transform the attitudes and beliefs of everyday citizens.

"THE DESIRED COLLAPSE"

"Whoever can be roused either to fear or anger by a politician . . . is more easily led to accept the desired pattern of 'cooperation,' even though this may violate his normal judgment."

So concludes William Sargant, MD, pioneering British psychiatrist and author of *Battle for the Mind: A Physiology of Conversion and Brainwashing*.

To put it plainly, Sargant documented that if you put people under enough stress, you can dramatically change the way they think—*just through pressure or excitement.* He wrote:

> The evidence . . . shows how various types of belief can be implanted in many people, after brain function has been sufficiently disturbed by accidentally or deliberately induced fear, anger or excitement. Of the results caused by such disturbances, the most common one is temporarily impaired judgment and heightened suggestibility. Its various group manifestations are sometimes classed under the heading of "herd instinct," and appear most spectacularly in wartime, during severe epidemics, and in all similar periods of common danger, which increase anxiety and so individual and mass suggestibility.[22]

Let's look at what he's saying through the lens of today: "Periods of common danger"—that is, serious national *crises*—"increase anxiety and so individual and mass suggestibility."

Do our current leaders resort to promoting "deliberately induced fear, anger or excitement" in the public mind? Yes, of course. But let's add in a couple more ingredients.

"Brainwashers," notes Sargant, "use a technique of conversion which does not depend only on the heightening of group suggestibility, but also on the fomenting in an individual of anxiety, of a sense of real or imaginary guilt, and of a conflict of loyalties, strong and prolonged enough to bring about the desired collapse."[23]

Fear, anger, excitement, guilt, anxiety, conflict—exactly the emotions today's "leaders" constantly create within us.

But let us pause momentarily and consider this whole business of "brainwashing," a seemingly exotic concept about which most of us are somewhat skeptical. Our few associations are vague and relate to far-flung examples, like the treatment of American POWs during the Korean War, the kidnapping and conversion of Patty Hearst, and the attempted bank robbery in Sweden that bequeathed us the psychological phenomenon called the "Stockholm syndrome."

Let's break it down. What I am suggesting is that the kind of conditioning Sargant observed, which occurs daily in "normal, civilized society," is in many respects just a very "lite" version of what occurs in real brainwashing. A preeminent scholar of wartime brainwashing is Robert Jay Lifton, the American psychiatrist most famous for studying the dynamics of POW brainwashing not only in the Korean War but in Chinese war camps. Lifton, now in his eighties, is a visiting professor of psychiatry at Harvard Medical School and Cambridge Hospital and the author of *Thought Reform and the Psychology of Totalism: A Study of "Brainwashing" in China.*

Lifton's analysis of heavy-duty wartime brainwashing identifies a sequence of ten factors that, taken together and in order, would reliably break down the victim's personality and then rebuild it in the image of the brainwashers:

TEN PSYCHOLOGICAL STEPS TOWARD THOUGHT REFORM

1. Assault on identity

2. Guilt

3. Self-betrayal

4. Breaking point

5. Leniency

6. The compulsion to confess

7. The channeling of guilt

8. Re-education: logical dishonoring

9. Progress and harmony

10. Final confession and rebirth[25]

These ten breaking-down and building-up processes can be further simplified into three basic stages:

1. Breaking down the person's sense of self

2. Introducing the possibility of salvation or redemption

3. Rebuilding the new self[26]

But everyday life is not a POW camp, and radical, immediate conversion for propaganda or intelligence reasons is not required by those dedicated to "fundamentally transforming" America. They can take their time. And make no mistake: *conversion* is still the endgame.

If you look carefully, you'll discern that the same basic dynamics of serious brainwashing—first promoting intense conflict and guilt, and then introducing a path to redemption, acceptance, and peace by giving in—are precisely what happens throughout society when revolutionaries are in charge, even if the intended revolution is a gradual one.

Let's consider a few examples:

RACISM: The left never tires of manipulating Americans' historical national guilt over slavery and segregation, persistently keeping the fires of guilt and shame alive in present-day Americans for sins committed generations ago by people long since dead. Remember: inducing guilt feelings is one of the brainwasher's first vital tasks.

In the age of Obama, racism is often portrayed as America's worst (or at least most ubiquitous and corrosive) national sin. In reality, of course—with the vast majority of citizens long ago having wholeheartedly embraced Martin Luther King's vision of a "color-blind America," and proven by the elevation of a popularly elected black president and a black attorney general—America is undoubtedly the *least* racist nation on earth.

Author Dinesh D'Souza tells the story of his debate with Jesse Jackson at Stanford University: When asked to identify any actual racism in today's America, Jackson "couldn't give any evidence that contemporary racism had kept his children down." However, adds D'Souza, Jackson countered "that precisely the *absence* of evidence is what worried him the most": "Jackson's argument was that racism, once overt, had now become covert. In other words, racism hadn't decreased in the slightest, but it now worked in ever-more-subtle ways to deny African Americans their share of the American dream."[27]

Got that? The less racism there is in America, the more racism there is.

Of course, for people like Jesse Jackson and Al Sharpton, America *must* be seen as racist, or they're out of a job. If their "victim" base is not constantly riled up, pumped full of perceived grievances and forever blaming others—and likewise, if the supposed "victimizer" class is not made to feel forever guilty and on the defensive for being "racist" (or at least "white privileged")—the whole "America is racist" spell rapidly wears off. Sadly, this shameful game of encouraging racial hatred has grown into a monster, as Obama, along with other key players, like Sharpton, attorney general Eric Holder, and New York City mayor Bill de Blasio have, figuratively, poured gasoline, lit matches, and fanned the racial flames in America, from Ferguson to Baltimore and beyond, igniting the most widespread racial strife in decades.

FEAR OF GOVERNMENT: One federal agency for which keeping Americans fearful and upset is its prime directive is the Internal Revenue Service. Everyone knows our "voluntary" federal income tax system works only if the IRS can keep taxpayers afraid. But did you ever stop to consider that maybe the entire *purpose* of the IRS, with its impossibly complex code (74,608 pages as of 2015) and excruciating audits designed to inspire dread in the rest of the population, is not raising revenue, but keeping people submissive to government? After all, Congress could easily transform the federal income tax into a "flat tax" or "fair tax," pegging either at a rate sufficient to bring in the same level of revenue as the income tax—or even *more* if need be. Both alternatives are widely acknowledged to be superior in every way—more equitable, more efficient, less invasive—when compared to the current income tax system ruled over by the IRS.

But it's not about the money. It's about maintaining a constant base-level of fear and anxiety—even contempt and disgust will work—as a means of conditioning the public to reflexively submit to government authority. Without the IRS, this major source of government fear-conditioning would vanish, and the American people would breathe more easily and deeply, would feel freer, more at liberty—almost as though the government existed to serve them! (Obviously, the ruling elite cannot allow *that* kind of crazy idea to take hold.)

The Obama-era IRS scandal, as outrageous and criminal as it is, does not really hurt the agency and arguably increases its effectiveness. Why? Do Americans now resent and fear the government agency more or less than before all the scandals? Remember: hate easily morphs into fear and anxiety, which in turn results in compliance at tax time.

SEXUALITY: Another key area where the public mind has proven extremely malleable under pressure is sexuality. A generation ago, the idea of two homosexuals marrying each other would *universally* have been considered so bizarre that its advocates would be regarded as deranged, or at least as unhinged moral anarchists operating far outside the realm of civilized society. Yet today, as noted in chapter 1, a business's refusal to participate in a same-sex "wedding" is increasingly regarded not just as bigotry and hatred—but as a crime.

How did this happen? Progressives tell us it is simply a matter of society "evolving" and embracing more "tolerant" and "enlightened" (i.e., not religiously based) attitudes toward previously discriminated-against "minorities." The Supreme Court, in redefining for the first time in American history the most basic institution of civilization—marriage—told us, "No longer may this liberty be denied" to gay couples.[28] And Barack Obama celebrated the court's decision by declaring, "We have made our union a little more perfect."[29] However, setting aside all the lofty, high-minded rhetoric, in reality this radical change is the result of a relentless, long-term campaign of intimidating, ridiculing, demonizing, suing, ostracizing, boycotting, threatening, prosecuting, and persecuting countless good people into finally abandoning their moral principles—or at least shutting up about them.

Recall Sargant's admonition that political "brainwashers" often rely on promoting "anxiety . . . a sense of real or imaginary guilt, and . . . a conflict of loyalties, strong and prolonged enough to bring about the desired collapse." (Again, this is just a "lite" version of full-strength brainwashing.) The "desired collapse" in this case would be the collapse of traditional biblical Judeo-Christian values—the very same values that have held up Western civilization for millennia.

Today, many "conservatives" and "Christians" openly embrace gay marriage, when just a few years ago those same people were repulsed by the very thought. What changed? Not the Christian faith or the Bible. Not common sense and basic morality. Not the core realities of biology and pathology. What changed is that for several decades the American public has been subjected to relentless pressure to embrace homosexuality and same-sex marriage.

In fact, here's the whole sad tale in just two words: *pressure converts.* Or as Sargant put it, applying pressure in a sufficiently "strong and prolonged enough" way will eventually "bring about the desired collapse."

In the age of Obama, of course, the "collapse" is better known as "fundamental transformation."

CHAOS THEORY

Who taught Obama to create chaos to usurp power? That's easy to answer—he has bragged about it.

In 2007, referring to his community-organizing years practicing and teaching the methods developed by Saul Alinsky and memorialized in *Rules for Radicals,* Obama told the Iowa Citizen Action Network, a left-wing "community organizing" group, "It was that education that was seared into my brain. It was the best education I ever had, better than anything I got at Harvard Law School."[30]

Let's see what Alinsky teaches in *Rules* and discover exactly what was "seared" into Obama's brain:

- "Any revolutionary change must be preceded by a passive, affirmative, non-challenging attitude toward change among the mass of our people. They must feel so frustrated, so defeated, so lost, so futureless in the prevailing system that they are willing to let go of the past and chance the future."[31]

- "A revolutionary organizer must shake up the prevailing patterns of their lives—agitate, create disenchantment and discontent with the current values, to produce, if not a passion for change, at least a passive, affirmative, non-challenging climate."[32]

Got that so far? All Americans must be made to feel frustrated, defeated, lost, and passive so these geniuses can step into leadership roles and create their socialist utopia. The fact that their plan has never worked before—*ever,* at any place or time in all of history—is not a problem to them. You see, all that was lacking in those other times and places was *the right people to run things*—namely, them, today's leftist utopians.

Here is some more timeless wisdom from Alinsky, in which he focuses on the key battle tactic:

- "Ridicule is man's most potent weapon. It is almost impossible to counterattack ridicule. Also it infuriates the opposition, who then react to your advantage."[33]

- "The major premise for tactics is the development of operations that will maintain a constant pressure upon the opposition. It is this unceasing pressure that results in the reactions from the opposition that are essential for the success of the campaign. It should be remembered not only that the action is in the reaction but that action is itself the consequence of reaction and of reaction to the reaction, ad infinitum. The pressure produces the reaction, and constant pressure sustains action."[34]

- "In a fight almost anything goes. It almost reaches the point where you stop to apologize if a chance blow lands *above* the belt."[35]

- "The real action is in the enemy's reaction."[36]

- "The enemy properly goaded and guided in his reaction will be your major strength."[37]

- "It should be remembered that you can threaten the enemy and get away with it. You can insult and annoy him, but the one thing that is unforgivable and that is certain to get him to react is to laugh at him. This causes an irrational anger."[38]

Pause button, please: A crucial and exceedingly dark principle is buried in these exhortations to pressure the "enemy" so that he "reacts" and keeps on "reacting." Alinsky even notes that "the reactions from the opposition . . . are essential for the success of the campaign." What he's saying is that it's not just the campaign tactics that deliver success. It is the reactions ("ad infinitum") of the enemy. And that word, "reactions," of course, is really code for anger, resentment, hostility, rage—which always takes you off your game and causes you to lose your cool, lose energy, lose happiness, lose the moral high ground, and lose your good judgment and ability to be effective.

Is there any doubt as to what Alinsky's rules and tactics are really all about? Making other people as angry, anxious, fearful, enraged, doubtful, guilty, and upset as possible.

Such tactics may be perfectly fine if you are truly at war with a dangerous and malignant enemy, but the problem is, the Far Left sees itself as being at war with traditional, Christian America!

Just how do you suppose hundreds of millions of people in China during Mao Zedong's Cultural Revolution came to believe in their leader's dark and demented teachings as expounded in his famous *Little Red Book*? Did they all magically see the light at the same time? No, but they all felt the heat at the same time—the heat of peer pressure and ruthless intimidation. And that, my friends, is a form of *brainwashing*, which causes you not only to accept the new "truth," but to embrace it heartily, to proselytize others, to rat out your "disloyal" neighbors, and to punish others who may stray from your newfound faith. That's how it works.

Decades ago, while traveling on a train through what was then communist Yugoslavia, I got into a conversation with a lady passenger about freedom and "basic rights." I explained that in America, we have fundamental freedoms of speech, the press, religion, association, travel, and so forth, as well as freedom of opportunity—to succeed or fail, but also to be able to keep the fruits of our labors and to be free of the tyranny of an all-powerful government.

She countered, with words very close to these: "I know that's what you believe in your country. But in my country, we believe basic rights include the right to a job, to housing, to health care, to the basics of life. We consider these to be our basic rights."

"OK," said I, "but what if you have to sacrifice your individual rights and liberties in order to provide such security for everyone?"

Her reply was that it was worth the trade-off.

Although that conversation occurred almost four decades ago, I remember it vividly. The lady passenger, an unashamed supporter of the communist system under which she lived, even said she thought it appropriate for her government to restrict freedom of speech and press to "protect" the citizenry from being confused and confounded by divisive information and opinions that might threaten the harmony of the nation!

Yet in no way did this woman seem particularly malevolent. She had simply internalized these anti-freedom beliefs, while elevating in her mind the supreme value of cradle-to-grave "security," all due to peer pressure and nothing else. Logic and reason never intruded into the process. She believed what everybody else believed, because if she didn't, she would be in serious trouble.

All it takes is pressure and, for many of us, our views are deftly remolded to conform to the pressure source.

But what about those who, despite the radical utopians' best efforts, stubbornly remain unconverted? They are to be blocked, demonized, punished, neutralized, and ridiculed. That's the gospel according to Saul.

Actually, Alinsky, an atheist, may have thought he was just being darkly whimsical in including, at the front of *Rules for Radicals,* a nod to Lucifer (whom he described as "the first radical known to man who rebelled against the establishment and did it so effectively that he at least won his own kingdom"). What he may not have realized, however, was that his teachings were very much from the dark realm.

BREAKING THE ALINSKY CODE

John Adams famously said, "Our Constitution was made only for a moral and religious people. It is wholly inadequate to the government of any other."

In much the same way, big-government socialism is fit only for an immoral, faithless, and broken people. It is wholly inadequate to the government of any other.

In the end, slippery political expressions like "fundamental transformation," "community organizing," "manufactured crisis," and "the Cloward-Piven strategy" all amount to the same thing: pressure and coercion to bring about "change."

To sum up: While the left is busy transforming the America we see, the most important part of that transformation is taking place inside the American mind. If you are continually pressured, stressed, and browbeaten—unless you discover the inner strength and grace to endure such pressure without being adversely impacted—*you change.*

And unfortunately, those who would usher in socialist paradise don't even need to convert you to win. They don't really have to change your worldview or values or morality or goodness. All they have to do to neutralize your influence is to stress you to the point that (1) you burn out, (2) you get so angry you end up doing something stupid that serves their interests, or (3) you give up and drop out, to avoid falling prey to 1 or 2.

As we shall see in the next chapter, one of the main arsenals of weapons these utopians use in fighting the war against common sense and individual freedom is language. As you proceed, bear in mind the oft-quoted words of the Soviet Union's first leader, Vladimir Lenin: "We can and must write in a language which sows among the masses hate, revulsion, and scorn toward those who disagree with us."

5

MAGIC WORDS

"*The deplorable word.*"

That was the colorful phrase used to describe an ancient incantation, which if spoken out loud had the terrible power to destroy every living thing in the world. At least, that was the scenario in *The Magician's Nephew*, C.S. Lewis's imaginative prequel to *The Lion, the Witch, and the Wardrobe* in his classic "Chronicles of Narnia" series.

The story transports readers to a desolate world called Charn, where the evil queen, Jadis, is locked in a bitter and bloody power struggle with her royal sister. With the tide of battle turning against her, Jadis exercises her last, desperate nuclear option and utters the deplorable word—a dark, secret power known only among royalty. In so doing, she annihilates all life on the planet—except her own, of course. (Jadis later becomes the White Witch, who would plague Narnia for a hundred years.)

The idea that special words, uttered a certain way, could somehow magically destroy an entire civilization is all good fun in fantasy literature and blockbuster movies. But of course, the idea that "the deplorable word" could somehow be operating in our own world would be absurd, right?

I mean, the notion that mere words could ever wield such powers of total annihilation in our world would be laughable.

Right?

As we're often reminded, truth is stranger than fiction.

For it is not only in the fantasylands of literature and entertainment, but right here on planet Earth that mere words—those simple noises and hieroglyphs we all constantly use—are secretly loaded with explosive power and a radioactive, mind-altering essence, which leads men and women down to hell, and causes cultures and societies to make war on each other, and ultimately disintegrate.

"Whoa," you might say. "How can words do all that? After all, they're just . . . words!"

Yes, but remember that the US Constitution and even the Bible are just words. And if you could *change the meaning* of certain words—not too many; just a few key words and phrases will do—you could succeed in reimagining America's founding principles as well as the laws of God laid out in the Holy Scriptures. You could redefine the rules of civilization, of human nature, of economics, of justice, goodness, and love, of reality itself. You could redefine it all.

What's more, if you could somehow also infuse words with secret meanings and associations, and hidden properties of emotional persuasion, you might well be able to lead entire populations in ways that appear to them to be good, but which are ultimately ruinous.

As we shall soon see, words have enormous power most of us neither understand nor suspect, and constitute one of the most devastating weapons being used against Americans today.

So let's take a little journey to the real-life world where "deplorable words" are employed to wreak untold havoc and destruction.

EMOTIONAL HAND GRENADES

Before starting out, let's first get our bearings by calling to mind one of the basic, self-evident truths of our life on earth: despite what much of our elite class might prefer we believe, there really is a God, good and evil are both very real, and each of them wants to possess us. Evil works primarily through deception, and the number-one means of deception is language—words.

Words are more than they seem. On the one hand, spoken and

written words are the primary means for expressing to one another not only knowledge, but truth and understanding, even the very truths that can save our souls and free us from bondage of every kind. On an even more transcendent level, Jesus Christ is described in the Bible as "the Word"—that is, the expression—of God: "In the beginning was the Word, and the Word was with God, and the Word was God. . . . And the Word was made flesh, and dwelt among us (and we beheld his glory, the glory as of the only begotten of the Father) full of grace and truth" (John 1:1, 14).

But what we are focusing on here is the dark side of words, something that desperately needs to be understood and transcended, since their use on behalf of evil is inflicting such profound harm on our society.

We like to think words are just symbols that correspond to tangible meanings; look up the word in a dictionary and you know what it means. Not exactly.

Words misused are more like little psychological explosive devices. Skillfully assembled, they can become very big explosive devices that destroy nations—not immediately as in *The Magician's Nephew,* but their ultimate result is devastation nevertheless.

A great many of the world's conflicting philosophies and religions are rooted in rebellion against reality—against God and His laws of life. How do they manage that? By the use of clever language, concepts, and suppositions, all tangled together to impress and captivate others, and make them doubt themselves in the face of supposedly superior knowledge of the "authority." Being in the grip of a deceitful ideology is to exist in an alternate reality—almost like an altered state of mind, such as drugs can induce.

Case in point: As we have previously noted, Americans elevated to the presidency Barack Obama, a Far-Left revolutionary manifestly hostile to free-market capitalism and American exceptionalism—in fact, to just about everything American—but who campaigned using powerfully evocative words of national restoration and reconciliation. *Hope, change, fairness, justice, reform,* and *transparency* would usher in a bright new era of *healing* and *unifying* America and the world through this charismatic young leader's *post-racial, post-partisan* presidency. What we got instead was a jarringly narcissistic, deceitful, reckless, and corrupt Chicago politician, lacking both in experience and wisdom, and displaying breathtaking contempt for America's Constitution and the magnificent system of government our nation's founders bequeathed to us.

Obama's election—twice—was epic proof that today's Americans can readily be sold something profoundly negative disguised as positive—through the power of deceptive words.

If this secret language war consisted solely of one man's use of emotionally compelling catchphrases, it wouldn't be difficult for the deception to be exposed and reality to prevail. But truth be told, the left has hijacked virtually our entire political and cultural language in the last couple of generations, redefining key words, phrases, and concepts. Indeed, changing not only the words we use, but the way we *think,* has been absolutely central to the transformation of America in our lifetime.

POLITICAL CORRECTNESS FOR "IDIOTS"

Today, a major engine for the left's insatiable quest for power goes under the strange name of "political correctness"—an insidious frontal attack on common sense and freedom through language manipulation.

Even the phrase *political correctness* sounds demented. Politics, like all areas of belief and values that emanate from one's worldview, is a matter of free choice and personal autonomy in America. Nobody can tell others the "correct" opinions to have! Yet that's precisely what political correctness does.

Many people mistakenly regard political correctness as just an exasperatingly nutty liberal fetish for not hurting people's feelings. Words and phrases are continually decreed to be insensitive to various minorities and therefore replaced with euphemisms to avoid real or perceived offense. So while wars rage and the world burns out of control, the progressive thought-leaders obsess endlessly over changing the supposedly insensitive name of the Washington Redskins football team—even though nine out of ten Native Americans polled said they were "not bothered" by the Redskins' name![1]

People who are mentally handicapped used to be categorized as "idiots," "imbeciles," and "morons"—clinical terms corresponding to varying IQ ranges (0–25 for idiots, 26–50 for imbeciles, 51–70 for morons). But as those words gradually came to be considered offensive, the euphemism "retarded" was adopted. When "retarded" was deemed insensitive, new and nicer euphemisms, like "mentally impaired," "intellectually disabled," "mentally handicapped," and "intellectually challenged" emerged, culminating with "special." It's hard to be offended over being "special."

In like manner, the deaf became "hearing impaired," the blind "vision impaired," and the crippled "mobility impaired." Bums became "homeless," gangs became "youth groups," jungles became "rain forests," impotence became "erectile dysfunction" (or "ED"), and "sex-change operation" transitioned into "gender reassignment surgery."

More subversively, however, bad or ignoble human qualities became disguised and excused: "Illegal aliens" became "illegal immigrants," then "undocumented immigrants," then "undocumented workers," magically transforming something bad into something good. (President Obama in 2015 started referring to illegal aliens in the United States as "Americans-in-waiting.")[2] Prostitutes became "sex workers," homosexuals "gay," atheists "brights," and abortion advocates "pro-choice," each euphemism converting a negative association into a positive. Today, increasing numbers of people refer to pedophiles as "minor-attracted persons" (or "MAPs") and child sexual abuse as "intergenerational sex." In Islam, the popular euphemism for raping children is "child marriage," just as adultery and even rape are commonly called "temporary marriage." Yes, really.

Indeed, the degree to which Islam has benefited from political correctness is rivaled only by the perverse language called "Newspeak" in George Orwell's *1984*. After nineteen Muslim terrorists, acting in the name of Islam, murdered almost three thousand Americans in an overt act of war on America on September 11, 2001, the US government and major media declared Islam a "religion of peace" to avoid offending Muslims. The horrendous Islamic jihad thus declared on us was delicately christened America's "war on terror," waged against a mysterious, unnamed enemy.

But even that awkward, near-meaningless expression was deemed too insensitive, so under Obama the euphemizing turned surreal when "war on terror" became "overseas contingency operations," while then Homeland Security secretary Janet Napolitano coined a friendly new phrase for mass-murder terrorist attacks. Announcing she was deliberately avoiding the term *terrorism* because "we want to move away from the politics of fear," Napolitano adopted the term *man-caused disasters*.

In this way, our leaders are able to squeeze every last drop of truth out of language so that, if we're not paying attention, we end up having no clue at all what is really going on all around us!

PAVLOV'S BELLS

But this is only the beginning. Far more than definitions, words are also carriers of all the feelings and associations that have been programmed into them—or more accurately, into *us*. Remember the famous experiments by Russian scientist Ivan Pavlov, who rang a bell while feeding his laboratory dogs? After sufficient repetition, simply ringing the bell caused the dogs to salivate as though food were present. The dogs, he discovered, had been "conditioned" to react to the ringing bell the same way they did to the presence of food due to the previous association of the two events.

For us, words are like Pavlov's ringing bells; we hear a word or phrase and it conjures up a constellation of associations that have been subtly programmed into us through repeated exposure. Often words and phrases, through this conditioning process, come to mean something worlds apart from what they originally meant. Consider some examples . . .

Equality has been totally redefined. To previous generations of Americans, equality—as crystalized by Jefferson in the Declaration of Independence, which affirms that "all men are created equal, and endowed by their Creator with certain inalienable rights"—meant equal in our God-given rights before the law. Then we adopted the socialist goal of equality—not just of opportunity, but of *results*. Today, however, in Bizarro America, a truly radical notion of equality is evolving, one necessitating the virtual repudiation of meaning, of morality, of God Himself, with good and evil basically being equals.

For example, the People for the Ethical Treatment of Animals (PETA), which claims three million members and supporters, epitomized today's radical notion of equality when its founder, Ingrid Newkirk, famously told *Vogue* magazine, "[T]here is no rational basis for saying that a human being has special rights. A rat is a pig is a dog is a boy. They're all mammals."[3]

Now *that's* equality! But how, we wonder, could anyone possibly equate a boy with a rat?

Animal liberationists claim they're elevating animals to champion their rights, but maybe in reality it's all about bringing humans down to the level of soulless animals.

After all, if we have no soul, logically there is no God to whom we're accountable, which means we're free—at least in an animalistic, atheistic sort of way. Which in turn means everything we do is moral and acceptable. Animals in the wild have total sexual freedom, and even kill each other, all without conflict or divine condemnation.

So, behind all their public moral posturing, those who equate boys with rats don't really care so much about rats, but rather, are in rebellion against the order and laws of God. By making man equal to animals, they've negated not only his transcendent humanity, but also his responsibility to a heavenly judge—and that's what it's really all about: just one more crazy form of freedom.

When we've descended sufficiently into notions of radical "equality" to the point that a human boy is considered by some to be equal to vermin (a rat), how far are we from the Nazis who called Jews "vermin" to justify the concentration camps and crematoria?

So you see, changing the meaning of *one word* can reprogram cultures and alter the destinies of human beings and entire societies. A foundation stone of civilized society—that is, a proper understanding of equality of opportunity and equality of protection under the law—can morph into a "deplorable word," an inversion of all values and a repudiation of all that is logical and wholesome, simply by redefining that term and using it as a weapon of war. (This has been the case with all of America's "liberation movements" of the last two generations.)

Justice too has been transformed into a "deplorable word." Terms like *social justice* and *economic justice* are euphemisms for the confiscation, by threat and brute force, of what belongs to others—in other words, *in*justice. More recently, many new left-wing "justice movements" are springing up, from "environmental justice" and "climate justice" to "reproductive justice" and "transgender justice." The object of these various new forms of "justice," again, is to twist actual justice into injustice. For example, "affirmative action" is imposed and defended in the name of justice, but what does it mandate? The most qualified applicant for a job is turned down in favor of someone else, because that other person has the preferred skin color. That used to be called "racial discrimination"—a great injustice—but now the exact same act is rationalized as a new breed of "justice."

"FREEDOM IS SLAVERY"

In Orwell's *1984,* the outside walls of the "Ministry of Truth" (head-quarters for propaganda and revisionist history) are adorned with three "Newspeak" phrases—slogans of the political party ruling the total surveillance state of Oceania. They are: WAR IS PEACE, FREEDOM IS SLAVERY, and IGNORANCE IS STRENGTH.

Reading this novel, we may be tempted to think, *Wow. How could people possibly be so stupid and deluded as to think something was its opposite?* Yet America today is rapidly becoming Oceania, where many key political and cultural concepts actually amount to the *opposite* of what their labels profess.

Reflect for a few seconds on these *1984*-style slogans and see if they fit today's America: THEFT IS JUSTICE. ENVY IS RIGHTEOUSNESS. FAITH IS IGNORANCE.

Or what about these? MORALITY IS BIGOTRY. SIN IS LOVE. CHARITY IS ENTITLEMENT.

A 180-degree inversion of reality has been codified within our political and cultural vernacular. Whereas the poor and disadvantaged once were the grateful recipients of *charity*, thanks to the generosity of individuals, churches, and altruistic organizations, today what used to be charity is an *entitlement*. The idea that charity—whether private-sector generosity or government "safety-net" programs—is something to which the recipient is *entitled* is presumptuous and discordant to all right-thinking people. It's almost as though the government is intent on encouraging charity recipients to become arrogant and ungrateful; after all, why would you be humbled and grateful to receive something to which you were already *entitled*, that you basically already owned?

Likewise, the word *tolerance* today means not only acceptance, but mandatory celebration of homosexuality—or at the very least, an agreement not to speak or write anything disapproving of it. However, LGBT activists condemning the "intolerance" of others are notoriously *in*tolerant of all who hold to the Christian moral code of the Western world.

Why are the most perverse, immoral, and confusing programs imaginable being instituted so easily throughout our nation's public schools under the banner of *anti-bullying*? Because gay activists figured out that the best way to intimidate people into embracing their agenda was to package it that way. This is pure conditioning. For most people, the very thought of opposing any "anti-bullying" program is chilling because we fear being condemned as haters of children.

Discrimination used to be a good word; it was important to be "discriminating." Now, the mere use of the word—in virtually any context—conjures up a powerful cloud of negativity and foreboding.

Here is how deranged the language manipulation gets: The Center for Reproductive Rights, a prominent, proabortion nongovernmental organization (NGO), presented a formal argument to the United Nations Committee Against Torture. The group's complaint? That antiabortion speech by the Catholic Church is a form of torture against women and girls.

Understand that increasingly abortions themselves, especially those performed beyond twenty weeks after conception, are seen as amounting to torture—twenty weeks being the current scientific consensus as to when the unborn child can feel pain, his or her brain development and neural pathways by then being capable of receiving pain signals from the body.[4]

Yet here is a proabortion organization going before the United Nations to denounce the Catholic Church as torturers—because the church strives to *prevent* the torture of children and mothers through abortion. Can they really be serious?

"Yes," confirms Jay Sekulow, chief counsel for the American Center for Law and Justice, "that was their argument: that efforts to save children's lives—to spare them from the horror of abortion—constituted 'torture' within the meaning of the United Nations Convention against Torture and Other Cruel, Inhuman or Degrading Treatment or Punishment."[5]

In indicting the Catholic Church before the UN's Committee Against Torture, the proabortion group pleaded, "The Holy See's canon law concerning abortion, specific actions taken to shame and condemn women who have undergone and doctors who have performed abortions, and interference in state efforts to permit abortion and prevent torture and ill-treatment, violate the Holy See's obligations under Articles 1, 2, and 16 [of the Convention Against Torture]."[6]

Look carefully and you'll see that such tortured redefining of words is the stock-in-trade of the Left, designed to confuse, bamboozle, and browbeat. Indeed, in a politically correct culture like ours, if you dare use certain words—and by logical extension, even *think* a certain way—you are considered ignorant, insensitive, intolerant, bigoted, or hateful.

Remember Saul Alinsky's famous Rule No. 5 from *Rules for Radicals*: "Ridicule is man's most potent weapon." Nobody wants to be scorned and mocked; therefore, many of us, consciously or unconsciously, avoid intimidating situations by refraining from standing up for what we really believe. Political correctness is nothing less than bullying others into thinking and speaking a certain way. It is literally the totalitarian demand that we refrain from speaking the truth as we see it. Unfortunately, of course, it is mind- and soul-destroying to be forced to believe absurdities.

"MARXIST IN ORIGIN"

Let us journey back in time to when political correctness first emerged into public consciousness in America. The December 24, 1990, edition of *Newsweek*, its cover title "THOUGHT POLICE," featured a jarring story titled "Taking Offense," focusing on what was then a new phenomenon on the nation's college campuses.

Subtitling its article "Is this the new enlightenment on campus or the new McCarthyism?," *Newsweek* introduced the exotic new "PC" campus culture in an astonishingly forthright way:

> There is an experiment of sorts taking place in American colleges. Or, more accurately, hundreds of experiments at different campuses, directed at changing the consciousness of this entire generation of university students. The goal is to eliminate prejudice, not just of the petty sort that shows up on sophomore dorm walls, but the grand prejudice that has ruled American universities since their founding: that the intellectual tradition of Western Europe occupies the central place in the history of civilization. In this context it would not be enough for a student to refrain from insulting homosexuals or other minorities. He or she would be expected to "affirm" their presence on campus and to study their literature and culture alongside that of Plato, Shakespeare and Locke. This agenda is broadly shared by most organizations of minority students, feminists and gays. It is also the program of a generation of campus radicals who grew up in the '60s and are now achieving positions of academic influence.[7]

Where PC reigns, explained *Newsweek*, "one defies it at one's peril." Among the examples it cited was that of Prof. Vincent Sarich of the University of California, Berkeley, who had written in an alumni magazine that Berkeley's affirmative-action program discriminated against white and Asian applicants, which of course is precisely the purpose of affirmative-action programs—to provide a special advantage for blacks.

In response, *Newsweek* reported, "Seventy-five students marched into his anthropology class last month and drowned out his lecture with chants of 'bullshit.' His department began an investigation of his views and chancellor Chang-Lin Tien invited complaints from students about his lectures. Sarich was left in doubt whether he would be allowed to teach the introductory anthropology course he has taught off and on for twenty-three years."

"There are subjects you don't even talk or *think* about," Sarich told *Newsweek*; among them, "race, gender [and] homosexuality."

With unusual candor, *Newsweek*'s report stated:

> PC is, strictly speaking, a totalitarian philosophy. No aspect of university life is too obscure to come under its scrutiny. . . .
>
> What are the underpinnings of this powerful movement, so seemingly at odds with what most Americans believe?
>
> Philosophically, PC represents the subordination of the right to free speech to the guarantee of equal protection under the law. . . .
>
> Politically, PC is Marxist in origin, in the broad sense of attempting to redistribute power from the privileged class (white males) to the oppressed masses. . . . The failure of Marxist systems throughout the world has not noticeably dimmed the allure of left-wing politics for American academics. Even today, says David Littlejohn of Berkeley's Graduate School of Literature, "an overwhelming proportion of our courses are taught by people who really hate the system."[8]

Some of the rationale being promoted through political correctness is so bizarre and nonsensical—and worse, so hostile to the very existence of moral values—that unless you have personally encountered it, you would probably go through your entire life never suspecting that anyone, however deluded, could possibly think this way. For instance, *Newsweek* illustrated the PC obsession with radical *equality*: "'If you make any judgment or assessment as to the quality of a work, then somehow you aren't being an intellectual egalitarian,' says Jean Bethke Elshtain, a political-science professor at Vanderbilt. At a conference recently she referred to Czeslaw Milosz's book *The Captive Mind* as 'classic'; to which another female professor exclaimed in dismay that the word *classic* 'makes me feel oppressed.'"[9]

Likewise, with such universal and nonpolitical aspects of life as age and beauty, no distinctions dare be made:

> A Smith College handout from the Office of Student Affairs lists 10 different kinds of oppression that can be inflicted by making judgments about people. These include "ageism—oppression of the young and old by young adults and the middle-aged"; "heterosexism—oppression of those of sexual orientations other than heterosexual . . . this can take place by not acknowledging their existence," and "lookism . . . construction of a standard for beauty/attractiveness." It's not sufficient to avoid discriminating against unattractive people; you must suppress the impulse to notice the difference.[10]

"SMALL IVY-COVERED NORTH KOREAS"

Unfortunately, the imposition of what amounts to an ideology of radical equality—especially on America's college campuses—inevitably results in totalitarianism and tyranny. It cannot be otherwise, as author and historian William Lind explains in "The Origins of Political Correctness."

Many of today's university campuses, says Lind, resemble "small ivy-covered North Koreas,"

> where the student or faculty member who dares to cross any of the lines set up by the gender feminist or the homosexual-rights activists, or the local black or Hispanic group, or any of the other sainted

"victims" groups that PC revolves around, quickly find themselves in judicial trouble. Within the small legal system of the college, they face formal charges—some star-chamber proceeding—and punishment. That is a little look into the future that political correctness intends for the nation as a whole.[11]

But why would such "North Korea"–style oppression be the logically inescapable result of political correctness on campus?

"All ideologies," asserts Lind, "are totalitarian because the essence of an ideology . . . is to take some philosophy and say on the basis of this philosophy certain things must be true—such as the whole of the history of our culture is the history of the oppression of women. Since reality contradicts that, reality must be forbidden." He adds, "It must become forbidden to acknowledge the reality of our history. People must be forced to live a lie, and since people are naturally reluctant to live a lie, they naturally use their ears and eyes to look out and say, 'Wait a minute. This isn't true. I can see it isn't true,' the power of the state must be put behind the demand to live a lie. That is why ideology invariably creates a totalitarian state."[12]

PATRON SAINT OF POLITICAL CORRECTNESS

"Not to have a correct political point of view is like having no soul."

Wow, really? No soul? Isn't that a little extreme?

Yes, but then, those are the words of Mao Zedong, the Chinese communist leader with the extreme distinction of having caused more deaths than any person in human history—50 to 70 million, more than Stalin and Hitler combined.

Mao was a rabid believer in "political correctness." In fact, he wrote the book.

Mao's 1967 book—officially titled *Quotations from Chairman Mao Zedong,* though better known in the West simply as Mao's *Little Red Book*—became the ultimate authority for political correctness during the 1960s. Carried around by millions of Chinese during the Great Proletarian Cultural Revolution of 1968, the small, red-plastic-bound book consisted of quotes from Mao's various writings, including "Significance of Agrarian Reforms in China," "Strategic Problems of China's Revolutionary War," "On the Rectification of Incorrect Ideas in the Party," "A Single Spark Can Start a Prairie Fire," and "On the Correct Handling of Contradictions Among the People."

A few quotes from Mao demonstrate just how obsessed he was with political correctness—a euphemism for the total reprogramming of the population:

> Once the correct ideas characteristic of the advanced class are grasped by the masses, these ideas turn into a material force which changes society and changes the world.[13]

> A Communist should have largeness of mind and he should be staunch and active, looking upon the interests of the revolution as his very life and subordinating his personal interests to those of the revolution; always and everywhere he should adhere to principle and wage a tireless struggle against all incorrect ideas and actions, so as to consolidate the collective life of the Party and strengthen the ties between the Party and the masses.[14]

> Be a pupil before you become a teacher; learn from the cadres at the lower levels before you issue orders. . . . What the cadres at the lower levels say may or may not be correct, after hearing it, we must analyze it. We must heed the correct views and act upon them. . . . Listen also to the mistaken views from below, it is wrong not to listen to them at all. Such views, however, are not to be acted upon but to be criticized.[15]

> In order to guarantee that our Party and country do not change their color, we must not only have a correct line and correct policies but must train and bring up millions of successors who will carry on the cause of proletarian revolution.[16]

THE "CORRECT" WAY

Like all sociopath leaders, Mao had a big job in front of him:

reprogramming hundreds of millions of people into thinking the exact same way—the "correct" way. His writings comprised the brainwashing manual whose precepts China's people were required to internalize and espouse. But what made that nation's uniquely bloody Cultural Revolution work was not the natural logic and virtue of Mao's words—for they had none—but the people's fear and dread of the consequences of failing to embrace them.

Contrast Mao's book, reportedly the second most widely printed book in history, with the Bible—the *most* widely printed and read book in history. Both books point to a "correct" way of being, thinking, speaking, believing, and behaving. But unlike Marxism and other bizarre ideologies that must be superimposed on us from the outside and thereby violate our minds and souls, the Bible's fundamental principles do not conflict with conscience and human nature.

To illustrate, the Bible's Ten Commandments say don't steal, don't lie, don't commit adultery, don't murder, don't covet, and so on. But our own conscience, a little bit of divine understanding tucked into each of us by our Creator, tells us exactly the same thing—that stealing, lying, adultery, murder, and covetousness (envy) are wrong. Unlike Marxist political correctness—whether promulgated by the tyrant Mao Zedong in China, or by left-wing activists in the United States—the Bible does not create some alien new moral code that makes no sense and forces us into conflict with our true nature; to the contrary, it beckons us to embrace an inborn standard already residing within us, and which we know deep down to be right. There is no conflict between the two.

According to Chairman Mao, lying and stealing for the glorious revolution is fine, as is murder—he did a whole lot of all three. Adultery is also fine with Mao, who led by example, according to accounts of his personal life,[17] including the extraordinary *Private Life of Chairman Mao* by the leader's personal physician of twenty-two years, who documented Mao's "extremely debauched" life and said he "regarded women as toys."[18]

What about the commandment against envy? That's the very cornerstone of collectivist philosophy, with the great Winston Churchill describing socialism as "the gospel of envy."[19] So, just as previous Marxist thinkers had, Mao bequeathed to the world an alternate, inverted "scripture," so to speak.

Fortunately, America is not China. We have a sacred heritage of liberty and independence that's part of our national DNA. Yet the left has injected a very different "genetic code" into the population, resulting in an ever-progressing transformation of our national mind.

The American founders' ideals still resonate with perhaps half of us, while the other half are either confused or thoroughly indoctrinated by the deplorable words of blind leaders and "experts." And the future of the most important nation on earth hangs in the balance.

WORDS OF DARK MAGIC

Ultimately, the most darkly magical language of all, the most deplorable words known to man are—very simply—lies. And that brings us right back to the present, because to super-ambitious, vainglorious leaders such as Barack Obama and Hillary Clinton, for whom personal ambition and ideology—however irrational—are their only reality, lying is a vital and creative power. *Lies open doors that would otherwise remain shut.* Thus in a very real sense, political lies are "magic words," the invocation of which represents the exercise of real power—power to impress voters, raise money, demonize critics, win elections, excuse failures, and transform a nation. Ordinary people don't possess this power, as they are constrained from such brazen lying by their conscience and/or fear of being caught. But highly narcissistic people like Obama and Clinton feel they have the freedom—indeed, the mandate—to reshape America by creatively *speaking into existence* an alternate version of reality, without regard for any higher standard of truth. In other words, to lie.

Here's how psychiatrist M. Scott Peck explains this in his classic best seller, *People of the Lie*:

> Malignant narcissism is characterized by an unsubmitted will. All adults who are mentally healthy submit themselves one way or another to something higher than themselves, be it God or truth or

love or some other ideal. They do what God wants them to do rather than what they would desire. "Thy will, not mine, be done," the God-submitted person says. They believe in what is true rather than what they would like to be true. . . . Not so the evil, however. In the conflict between their guilt and their will, it is the guilt that must go and the will that must win.

The reader will be struck by the extraordinary willfulness of evil people. They are men and women of obviously strong will, determined to have their own way. There is a remarkable power in the manner in which they attempt to control others. [20]

Bottom line: war is deception. The political-cultural left sees itself as engaged in an epic war with traditional, Judeo-Christian, capitalist America, which it regards as greedy, exploitive, bigoted, and corrupt. Language comprises the vast arsenal radicals use to wage that war by deceiving millions and continually redefining reality.

It's all about lying. Because for the unprincipled, deceitful person obsessed with implementing his will on earth, rather than God's, lies work—like magic.

6

URBAN WARFARE

"And they said, Go to, let us build us a city and a tower, whose top may reach unto heaven. . . . And the LORD came down to see the city and the tower, which the children of men builded. And the LORD said, Behold, the people is one, and they have all one language; and this they begin to do: and now nothing will be restrained from them, which they have imagined to do. Go to, let us go down, and there confound their language, that they may not understand one another's speech. So the LORD scattered them abroad from thence upon the face of all the earth: and they left off to build the city. Therefore is the name of it called Babel."

—GENESIS 11:4–9

I n today's America there is something a little strange about our big cities. And if we're talking about places like Detroit, there's something a *lot* strange.

The enigmatic biblical story of the tower of Babel revolves around this strange something that tends to occur when large numbers of people come together in one place and form a great hive.

It's not that something sinister *has* to happen—it doesn't, especially if the people governing that city are highly principled and grounded in reality. But how often does that happen?

What, then, is this strange "something"? At street level, it's what happens when power-hungry and corrupt people rise to positions of authority to rule over their own little "kingdom." On a more cosmic level, one might say it's the futility and inevitable disintegration of *anything*—even a great city—built as a monument to man's greatness rather than God's.

Such sentiments are, of course, foolishness to today's secular and sophisticated Western mind. But then, many of our cities *are* disintegrating—big-time. So why don't we take a closer look?

Today, the poster boy for sick cities is Detroit, with thousands of burned-out or abandoned homes, as of 2013 the highest violent crime rate in the country (1,052 per 100,000 people), over $18 billion in unpayable municipal debt, the biggest three-year drop in home prices in the United States (35 percent), a vanishing tax base due to stunning out-migration, and a remaining population that no longer bothers to call 911 in case of emergency—since more often than not, no one responds.[1] Utterly unable to pay its bills, Detroit is literally self-destructing before our eyes, with at least 40 percent of the city's streetlights broken and tens of thousands of residents failing to pay their water bills, causing the city to turn off the tap!

"It's frightening, because you think this is something that only happens somewhere like Africa," one Detroit resident told the *Los Angeles Times* six weeks after her water had been shut off.[2]

Detroit may appear to be in a class by itself, but there are so many other cities in crisis. Like Chicago, with its legendary murder rate and more legendary corruption rate (four of Illinois' last seven governors—Rod Blagojevich, George Ryan, Dan Walker, and Otto Kerner—went to prison), not to mention sky-high foreclosures and plummeting home prices. Or Stockton, California, the second-largest US city to go bankrupt (after Detroit), with the nation's highest foreclosure rate and among the five worst cities for unemployment and crime, according to *Forbes*.[3] Or even New York City, where taxes are higher than Manhattan's skyscrapers.

Meanwhile, dozens of other great American cities—from Modesto and Vallejo in the West to Rockford and St. Louis in the heartland to

Wilmington and Buffalo in the East and Miami and New Orleans in the South—are similarly afflicted.

However, overshadowing all these problems—the crime, degradation, racial hostilities, and ever-growing multitudes dependent on government assistance—is another parallel trend.

The last few elections have evidenced an extraordinary historic divide between liberal and conservative America. It is barely an exaggeration to say that, considered as a whole, America's cities are liberal, and the rest of the country is conservative. One glance at any recent electoral map makes that conclusion inescapable.[4]

The implications of this trend are nothing short of momentous.

"IT'S URBAN VERSUS RURAL"

In his report in the *Atlantic*, "Red State, Blue City: How the Urban-Rural Divide Is Splitting America," journalist Josh Kron describes the evolution of American cities since pre–Civil War times, when the nation's "political dividing lines were drawn along state and regional borders." Back then, residents of each state—city and country folk alike—shared a common worldview.

Not anymore. Today, writes Kron, "that divide has vanished":

> The new political divide is a stark division between cities and what remains of the countryside. Not just some cities and some rural areas, either—virtually *every* major city (100,000-plus population) in the United States of America has a different outlook from the less populous areas that are closest to it. The difference is no longer about where people live, it's about *how* people live: in spread-out, open, low-density privacy—or amid rough-and-tumble, in-your-face population density and diverse communities that enforce a lower-common denominator of tolerance among inhabitants.
>
> The voting data suggest that people don't make cities liberal—cities make people liberal.[5]

That last statement—"people don't make cities liberal—cities make people liberal"—has profound implications, as we will soon discover.

Using the 2012 presidential election as an example, Kron notes that of all the major cities in America, the only ones that went Republican were Phoenix, Oklahoma City, Fort Worth, and Salt Lake City: "With its dominant Mormon population, Mitt Romney was a lock in the Utah capital; Phoenix nearly voted for Obama. After that, the largest urban centers to tilt Republican included Wichita, Lincoln, Neb., and Boise."

So, just how great is this divide between cities and the rest of the population? Writes Kron:

> The gap is so stark that some of America's bluest cities are located in its reddest states. Every one of Texas' major cities—Austin, Dallas, Houston, and San Antonio—voted Democratic in 2012, the second consecutive presidential election in which they've done so. Other red-state cities that tipped blue include Atlanta, Indianapolis, New Orleans, Birmingham, Tucson, Little Rock, and Charleston, S.C.—ironically, the site of the first battle of the Civil War. In states like Nevada, the only blue districts are often also the only cities, like Reno and Las Vegas.[6]

The problem is that in every state except two, winning a simple majority of electoral votes, or even a plurality of less than 50 percent, means *all* of that state's electoral votes go to that candidate. With this "winner-takes-all" system, "a single city can change the entire game," writes Kron, noting that "blue cities in swing states that ended up going for Obama include Las Vegas, Philadelphia, Pittsburgh, Denver, the cities of Florida, and the cities of Ohio."

Consider Oregon, where I currently live. It reliably goes Democratic in every presidential election cycle. Yet of this beautiful state's thirty-six counties, by far the most—twenty-six or twenty-seven—are solidly red, and the other few blue.[7] But those few blue counties include the state's most populous cities, including Portland, Eugene, and the capital, Salem, liberal strongholds all. So Oregon as a whole goes blue every time.

It's the same in state after state across the country. As noted, if you look at a red-state–blue-state map of the United States, it's mostly red. And if you look at a red-county–blue-county map of the United States, the country is revealed to be *overwhelmingly* red.

Moreover, despite the traditional pendulum-like tendency of the American electorate to swing from one party to the other in successive presidential races, the "one part of the electoral map" that "has become a crystal clear constant," concludes the *Atlantic*, is that "cities, year by year, have become drenched in more blue. Everywhere else is that much more red."[8]

What explains this great mystery? Why the growing *urban-rural polarization* in America? Why does a recent Pew Research study reveal "conservatives would rather live in large houses in small towns and rural areas—ideally among people of the same religious faith—while liberals opt for smaller houses and walkable communities in cities, preferably with a mix of different races and ethnicities"?[9]

Of course, "there have always been differences between rural and urban America," notes the *Wall Street Journal*, "but they have grown vast and deep, and now are an underappreciated factor in dividing the US political system." Reaching the remarkable conclusion that all the "polling, consumer data and demographic profiles paint a picture of *two Americas*," the *Journal* adds:

> In many ways, the split between red Republican regions and blue Democratic ones—and their opposing views about the role of government—is an extension of the *cultural* divide between rural Americans and those living in cities and suburbs.
>
> As Democrats have come to dominate U.S. cities, it is Republican strength in rural areas that allows the party to hold control of the House and remain competitive in presidential elections.
>
> "The difference in this country is not red versus blue," said Neil Levesque, director of the New Hampshire Institute of Politics at Saint Anselm College. "It's urban versus rural."[10]

THE CITY MAKES LIBERALS

The notion that, as the *Atlantic* put it, "people don't make cities liberal—cities make people liberal," is haunting—mainly because it's so reliably true. Allow me to cite a personal example.

I grew up in the Washington, DC, metropolitan area, and my parents were Democrats (although a Democrat back in the '50s and '60s was roughly equivalent to a Republican today). I can distinctly remember the impression I had of the "Democrats versus Republicans" divide even as a six- or seven-year-old boy in elementary school in a "blue" area. If I put that child's mental impression into words, it would go something like: *Democrats are good, caring people who want to help others, while Republicans are selfish rich people who just want to preserve what they already have, but don't care about others.*

I don't remember anyone actually spelling it out for me in quite that way; it seems I just absorbed that belief "out of the air"— from the social atmosphere in which I lived, the only reality I knew.

My "liberal" childhood view of the two political parties could not be blamed on the usual culprits cited by conservatives for liberal "brainwashing," like attending a modern university and being indoctrinated by unhinged Marxist professors. I was seven. I was simply reflecting the mind-set of those around me, which at that age was primarily my family.

Indeed, research dating as far back as the 1950s has demonstrated that almost 70 percent of children identify with the political party of their parents.[11]

But that dynamic changes significantly as children grow up and their circle of influencers enlarges. Public school is strongly skewed secular left, and if that doesn't succeed in reorienting young conservatives, by the time they get to college—and away from their parents' influence— whatever their attitudes and beliefs upon entry to the hallowed campus are effortlessly remolded to mirror those dominating the modern university in many cases.

In my case, my childhood home was just outside of DC, in Montgomery County, Maryland, one of the most affluent and—especially today—ideologically progressive counties in the nation. To illustrate, Montgomery County was one of the very first, pioneering venues in the country to pass transgender bathroom ordinances permitting men to frequent women's public restrooms if they felt more comfortable thinking of themselves as women, and vice versa. Behaviors and "orientations" that just a generation ago would have been widely regarded as immoral, pathological, and possibly criminal are today enshrined in law and culture alike. And such upper middle-class suburban communities that serve as enclaves for the federal government's hundreds of thousands of well-paid employees—most of them liberal—serve as natural proving grounds for such wildly progressive policies.

I spent a lot of time in Montgomery County in recent years, following the death of my mother, to help settle her affairs. The area in which I grew up is today filled with many really nice, caring, liberal people. People who feel good about themselves and how caring they are. People whose friends and neighbors are liberals, who barely know any conservatives, and who still have Obama–Biden bumper stickers on their cars. People who not only reflexively dismiss conservative ideas, policies, and personalities, but who may mock or even demonize them. Much as during my youth in the 1950s, the message now permeating the ether is: *Liberals are good, generous, peace-loving, enlightened, tolerant, and forward-thinking people, while conservatives are selfish, ignorant, warmongering, bigoted gun-nuts!*

DC is a boom town. In the suburbs, half the cars on the road, it seems, are luxury cars—Mercedes, BMW, Lexus, Acura, Cadillac. Bethesda–Chevy Chase has the largest Mercedes dealership on the Eastern Seaboard. It even has a Bentley dealership. Bentleys! In my almost four decades in the Pacific Northwest, I don't think I've ever even seen a Bentley.

This prosperity, of course, is not hard to explain: The Washington metro area, including suburban Maryland and Northern Virginia, is one of the few regions of the country that is doing very well, thank you, even enjoying a red-hot real estate market. That's because the local industry in that area—the United States government—is thriving and expanding more than any other sector in the country.

To put it bluntly, economically speaking, the whole DC metroplex is like a gigantic bloated parasite—living off the life and energy (wealth and work) of the nation, while the rest of the country suffers. Sorry, the truth hurts.

IMPORTING DEMOCRATS

To understand the ever-increasingly left-wing orientation of America's cities, let's recognize that it's not just the inherent social pressure on residents to conform to the predominant values of the "hive." Another, far less mysterious phenomenon is at work, constantly turning major urban enclaves ever bluer: Waves of immigrants, encompassing millions of souls, tend to gravitate to our cities—mostly for economic reasons, as that's where most available jobs are.[12] And immigrants—whether legal or illegal—tend overwhelmingly to favor large government and liberal/ Democrat values.

An analysis by the Center for Immigration Studies reveals "the enormous flow of *legal* immigrants into the country—29.5 million 1980 to 2012—has remade and continues to remake the nation's electorate in favor of the Democratic Party."[13] For example, in 2012, Latino voters favored Obama over Romney by an almost three-to-one margin, 71 percent to 27 percent, according to the National Election Pool.

Likewise, a Pew Research survey found that "among Latino immigrants who are *not* US citizens or legal permanent residents"—in other words, illegal aliens—"about half of unauthorized Hispanic immigrants either identify with (31 percent) or lean towards (23 percent) the Democratic Party, while about two in ten identify with (4 percent) or lean towards (15 percent) the Republican Party."[14]

Moreover, since the political elite ruling America's cities understand the importance of preserving and enlarging their vast urban reservoirs of liberals and Democrats, many cities encourage lawbreaking, either implicitly or explicitly, by openly flouting or prohibiting enforcement of federal immigration laws. And while these so-called sanctuary cities embolden and *enable* lawlessness in the name of compassion, the real game is maintaining and enlarging the left's power base.

There are between one hundred and two hundred sanctuary cities—either officially (codified in government documents) or de facto (law enforcement and city employees instructed never to question anyone's immigration status)—including Phoenix, Los Angeles, San Diego, San Francisco, Denver, Miami, Chicago, Wichita, New Orleans, Cambridge, Portland (Maine), Baltimore, Detroit, Minneapolis, Newark, Trenton, Albuquerque, Albany, New York City, Oklahoma City, Portland (Oregon), Philadelphia, Dallas, Houston, Salt Lake City, Seattle, and Washington, DC. Unsurprisingly, Montgomery County, Maryland, where I grew up, is a sanctuary county.[15]

Not only has Obama left America's southern border even more wide-open to illegal entry than his predecessors; he has essentially invited Mexicans and Central Americans to come illegally in droves to America. His executive memorandum called "DACA"—the Deferred Action for Childhood Arrivals—explicitly sends the message to young people south of our border that if they can just make it to America, they will not be sent back. Many public officials and policy analysts conclude the real strategy at work here is one of turning powerhouse red-state Texas blue. It is, after all, the number-one destination of illegals after crossing the Rio Grande.

Former Texas representative Steve Stockman says it's "an open secret Obama is trying to flood Texas with illegals to make it into a blue state" with a Democrat majority.[16] Texas representative Louis Gohmert, vice chair of the House Judiciary Subcommittee on Crime, Terrorism and Homeland Security, agrees: "In the end, they have said they want to turn Texas blue and they want to turn America blue. If you bring in hundreds of thousands or millions of people and give them the ability to vote, and tell them if you want to keep getting the benefits, you have to go vote, that drives people to vote and it would ensure Republicans will never get elected again."[17]

If the Obama years have proven anything, it is that an administration that craves, above all else, a permanent Democrat/progressive voting majority will do just about anything to make that happen, no matter how ruinous to the country. In 2015, Obama openly advocated for instituting mandatory universal voting in the United States, a Far-Left idea that, if implemented, would almost certainly lead to permanent Democratic Party control of the United States government.[18]

CITIES AS HARBINGERS

In contemplating our cities' plight, Americans have been given a gift—a peek into the future, just like that afforded Ebenezer Scrooge in the Charles Dickens classic *A Christmas Carol.* We get to see what our future will be like if we don't change course: our future is our cities.

If you want to know what America will look like in the future under the "enlightened" leadership of progressive Democrats, look at our big cities, which have been run by progressive Democrats for the last century. The only reason you perhaps haven't heard this damning correlation is that the news media, for just about as long, have also been dominated by progressive Democrats, and progressives never like to publicize their failures.

Although there may be an inherent tendency for large urban areas to reflect a more collectivist outlook—that is, to lean blue—it doesn't have to be that way. Major cities can be extremely impressive, creative environments, magnificent centers of trade, culture, human cooperation and innovation—without self-destructing and fostering human degradation, but only if basic, proven principles of liberty remain foremost in those people we entrust to govern us.

Why does Detroit look like a war zone bombed by an enemy power? Because it has been run for so long by leaders like former mayor Coleman Young, who before reigning over Detroit for almost two decades, had secretly been a member of the Communist Party USA—an organization loyal to an enemy power!

This is what happens when, instead of elevating worthy statesmen as leaders, we instead turn our cities over to parasitic unions and plundering politicians dedicated to tearing down everything America has traditionally stood for, everything that has made this nation—including her shining cities—the envy of the world.

Consider Baltimore. As arson, looting, and race riots racked the city in mid-2015, Obama insisted the cure for what ails Baltimore is more progressive-style help: more taxpayer money for further "investments" so inner-city kids can get "the training they need to find jobs." As columnist Michelle Malkin reported, the president insisted "there's a bunch of my agenda that would make a difference right now," including more federal "school reform," "job training," and "investments in infrastructure" to "attract new businesses."[19]

Reality time: Baltimore, like most of America's major cities, is already suffering from decades of exactly such progressive solutions. According to *National Review*:

> Baltimore has seen two Republicans sit in the mayor's office since the 1920s—and none since the 1960s. Like St. Louis, it is effectively a single-party political monopoly from its schools to its police department. Philadelphia has not elected a Republican mayor since 1948. The last Republican to be elected mayor of Detroit was congratulated on his victory by President Eisenhower. Atlanta, a city so corrupt that its public schools are organized as a criminal conspiracy against its children, last had a Republican mayor in the 19th century. . . .
>
> Black urban communities face institutional failure across the board every day. American cities are by and large Democratic-party monopolies, monopolies generally dominated by the so-called progressive wing of the party. The results have been catastrophic.[20]

Question: What could be worse than turning our thriving metropolises, our engines of civilization, finance, and innovation, over to leftist "progressives"—a euphemism for neo-Marxists—with no clue how to run a candy store, let alone a great city? The only thing worse would be to make the same mistake with the entire country—which unfortunately is exactly what Americans did in 2008 and 2012 in elevating a corrupt Chicago politician and leftist revolutionary to the presidency.

"The Obama administration has won a triumphant victory," writes columnist Daniel Greenfield, "in imposing the irrational social and economic values of the city on the rest of the country."

The American city "used to serve as a center of transportation and industry," observes Greenfield. "Today the city holds a few knowledge industries and some secondary industries catering to them, but is mostly full of low-income immigrants whose big dream is to get a government job with good benefits. Until then there are government benefits that don't require government jobs."

Basically, Greenfield adds, "social welfare is the only thing that cities do anymore. Its broken school systems are forever trying to dig their students out of a hole while plunging their economy deeper into it. The alliance between community activists and public sector unions has created a runaway monster that no one from Arnold Schwarzenegger to Rahm Emanuel has been able to stop. Politicians have usually found it easier to pay off the representatives of human dysfunction and their caretakers than put up a fight."

No wonder the big blue cities voted for Obama and "carried him over the top," Greenfield concludes. "Unlike the rest of the country, there is no answer to the problems of the cities except more government money."[21]

Obama and the progressive left are totally obsessed with creating a redistributionist utopia wherein government rules supreme and all are dependent upon it, a great hive of needy drones that rely upon a benevolent and all-powerful government to right all wrongs, redress all grievances, provide for all needs—a testimony to the ruling elite's greatness and leadership. In short, a modern-day Babel.

Nevertheless, the intended "fundamental transformation" of America is by no means complete. What the nation is experiencing is much more like a cold civil war. Boston University professor of international relations Angelo M. Codevilla compellingly described the two warring sides in his book *The Ruling Class: How They Corrupted America and What We Can Do About It.*

In an analysis so cogent that Rush Limbaugh spent an entire hour on his radio show just reading from it, Codevilla calls the two sides of this great conflict the "ruling class" and the "country class." The ruling class comprises the political and cultural elite, including the "mainstream press," the entire Democratic Party, and way too much of the Republican Party, namely, "the Washington establishment." The country class comprises the totality of real-live, traditionally minded Americans.

Writes Codevilla:

> Nothing has set the country class apart, defined it, made it conscious of itself, given it whatever coherence it has, so much as the ruling class's insistence that people other than themselves are intellectually and hence otherwise humanly inferior. Persons who were brought up to believe themselves as worthy as anyone, who manage their own lives to their own satisfaction, naturally resent politicians of both parties who say that the issues of modern life are too complex for any but themselves. Most are insulted by the ruling class's dismissal of opposition as mere "anger and frustration"—an imputation of stupidity—while others just scoff at the claim that the ruling class's bureaucratic language demonstrates superior intelligence.

"The country class," observes Codevilla, "actually believes that America's ways are superior to the rest of the world's, and regards most of mankind as less free, less prosperous, and less virtuous." Noting that the country class "takes part in the U.S. armed forces body and soul," he asserts that "nearly all the enlisted, non-commissioned officers and officers under flag rank belong to this class in every measurable way. Few vote for the Democratic Party." There is no doubt "that you are amidst the country class," he says, "when the American flag passes by or 'God Bless America' is sung after seven innings of baseball, and most people show reverence."

One of the most jugular criteria for distinguishing the two classes from each other has to do with God and the Bible. Explains Codevilla:

> The ruling class's manifold efforts to discredit and drive worship of God out of public life—not even the Soviet Union arrested students for wearing crosses or praying, or reading the Bible on school property, as some U.S. localities have done in response to Supreme Court rulings—convinced many among the vast majority of Americans who believe and pray that today's regime is hostile to the most important things of all. Every December, they are reminded that the ruling class deems the very word "Christmas" to be offensive. Every time they try to manifest their religious identity in public affairs, they are deluged by accusations of being "American Taliban" trying to set up a "theocracy." Let members of the country class object to anything the ruling class says or does, and likely as not their objection will be characterized as "religious," that is to say irrational, that is to say not to be considered on a par with the "science" of which the ruling class is the sole legitimate interpreter.

Contrasting the two sides in the great civil war now engulfing America, Codevilla surveys the battlefield:

> The ruling class's appetite for deference, power, and perks grows. The country class disrespects its rulers, wants to curtail their power and reduce their perks. The ruling class wears on its sleeve the view that the rest of Americans are racist, greedy, and above all stupid. The country class is ever more convinced that our rulers are corrupt, malevolent, and inept. The rulers want the ruled to shut up and obey. The ruled want self-governance. The clash between the two is about which side's vision of itself and of the other is right and which is wrong.[22]

As in all wars, concludes Codevilla, "One side or the other will prevail. The clash is as sure and momentous as its outcome is unpredictable." He's right. Meanwhile, I'll take the country over the city any day.

7

THE REAL ZOMBIE APOCALYPSE

For all its difficulties, life should be something we enjoy, appreciate, and revere. Especially for those of us blessed to live in a uniquely free country like America, life can be a wide-open adventure, a journey of learning and discovery, and an opportunity to build and fight and sacrifice for great things, as it was for our forefathers.

But something has gone terribly wrong in today's America. So much conflict and corruption abound—and so many "experts" offer solutions that just make things worse—that hopelessness looms large for many. Tens of millions of us feel compelled to escape, to blot out reality, to seek solace in ways that alter our consciousness and numb our pain.

Thus it is that Americans today are in love with mind-altering drugs. There's just no other way to put it. Legal or illegal, drugs have become the go-to fix for most of our problems.

Of course, drug and alcohol abuse has always been a problem for all societies, and America's official response—the War on Drugs—has by most accounts been a spectacular failure. Still, we have trudged along for decades, targeting dealers, interdicting supplies, and arresting and incarcerating users.

In recent times, however, the complexion of the drug culture in America has changed dramatically. It started innocuously enough, with the legalization of medical marijuana. Despite legitimate medicinal uses, "medical pot" degenerated into a national farce, with people being encouraged to score marijuana prescriptions not just for oft-cited maladies like cancer and glaucoma, but for conditions ranging from headaches to diarrhea, whiplash, stuttering, and eczema. Also panic attacks, autism, bipolar disorder, schizophrenia, Alzheimer's, incontinence, nightmares, AIDS, tobacco dependence, and menopause. And genital herpes.[1] In other words, smoking pot, we're being told, is good for pretty much *everything* that ails us.

On January 1, 2014, flat-out legalization took center stage, with Colorado and Washington leading the way.

Immediately, stock prices for cannabis companies soared ("The demand for marijuana is insatiable," said one entrepreneur, "you have a feeding frenzy for the birth of a new industry");[2] the Manhattan-based publication *High Times* announced a new private-equity fund to "raise $100 million over the next two years to invest in cannabis-related businesses";[3] ad agencies geared up to support "an industry estimated to already be generating revenues in the billions of dollars";[4] and Jamaican reggae star Bob Marley was picked to become the "Marlboro Man of marijuana."[5]

Likewise, the entertainment industry has long been on board. While hit shows like *Glee*, *Parenthood*, and *Mad Men* portray cannabis consumption in a positive light,[6] Hollywood's "beautiful people" lead pot's de facto PR campaign. There's actor Morgan Freeman, who told London's *Guardian* newspaper that he'll "never give up the ganja," calling it "God's own weed." And Whoopi Goldberg, who was high when she accepted the Oscar for her role in *Ghost* (later saying, "I learned a great lesson, though. Never smoke pot before there's a possibility of having to talk to a hundred million people"). The list of admitted, proud pot-smokers runs the gamut from actresses like Jennifer Aniston, Cameron Diaz, Susan Sarandon, and Kirsten Dunst ("If everyone smoked weed, the world would be a better place") to director Oliver Stone (well, of course) and every pop singer imaginable—including Justin Bieber, Willie Nelson, Lady Gaga ("I smoke a lot of pot when I write music"), and Justin Timberlake ("Sometimes I have a brain that needs to be turned off. Some people are just better high").[7]

So let's put this into context: While modern America spins spectacularly out of control—as her culture, morals, laws, institutions, government, economy, and overall well-being disintegrate before our eyes, and as the forces of evil worldwide wax stronger and more menacing in the shadow of America's ever-growing feebleness in the age of Obama—for a large percentage of the population, the solution is: *get high!*

This disturbing trend was reflected in a CNN poll headlined, "Support for legal marijuana soaring."

"In a major turnaround from past decades, a majority of Americans support legalizing marijuana," trumpeted the network. With 55 percent favoring legalization (a similar Gallup poll showed 58 percent), support "has steadily soared over the past quarter century—from 16 percent in 1987 to 26 percent in 1996, 34 percent in 2002, and 43 percent just two years ago."

The poll's biggest surprise was the number of people who no longer consider smoking pot immoral. In 1987, seven in ten Americans believed it was, "making it a sin in the minds of more Americans than abortion or pornography," said the report.[8]

No more. Today, that number has been cut in half, with just 35 percent of Americans having any moral problem with pot smoking, a conclusion bolstered by Barack Obama when he equated pot with alcohol and tobacco, telling the *New Yorker*, "I don't think it is more dangerous than alcohol." Obama, who admits he "smoked pot as a kid," even told interviewer David Remnick he viewed marijuana as "not very different from the cigarettes that I smoked as a young person up through a big chunk of my adult life."[9]

Hit the pause button, please: Seeing "recreational" pot use as moral is much more consequential than it might seem. For many, legal *equals* moral. So not only does calling something moral lead to its legalization, but once legal—whether it's abortion, same-sex marriage, or marijuana—millions come to regard the once-forbidden as moral and wholesome. That, in turn, multiplies the numbers of participants. It happens every time.

This syndrome was exemplified when abortion was legalized. Americans were assured legalizing abortion would only mean that "back-alley," illegal abortions would become safe, legal abortions. In reality, since legalization, more than a million babies are aborted annually in America. Likewise, pot legalization immediately turned Colorado and Washington into havens for the outright celebration and encouragement of every aspect of marijuana cultivation, marketing, sale, and consumption. But that was just the beginning. In the 2014 midterm elections, recreational use of pot was legalized in Oregon, Alaska, and Washington, DC, and many other states are now in the marijuana legalization pipeline.

IT'S THE STUPIDITY, STUPID

Somehow, in all the hoopla, it apparently hasn't widely registered that pot use destroys young people's minds. Yes, really. A massive, four-decade study published in 2012 by the National Academy of Sciences, titled "Persistent cannabis users show neuropsychological decline from childhood to midlife," followed more than one thousand subjects from birth until they were thirty-eight years old. The researchers' core finding? Repeated marijuana use by teenagers lowers their IQ—permanently.[10]

And if irreversible "neuropsychological decline" and other long-proven hazards of cannabis aren't enough, a loud, discordant note was sounded right at ground zero by Dr. Christian Thurstone, professor of psychiatry at the University of Colorado. As head of an adolescent rehab center called STEP (Substance Abuse Treatment Education & Prevention), Thurstone said virtually all of the patient referrals to his program—95 percent of them—result from marijuana use.

"But wait," some might protest. "I thought marijuana was, you know, mellow, and not bad for you like alcohol and tobacco."

Not exactly, says the doc, who told ABC News, "We're seeing kids in treatment here who have paranoia and seeing things and hearing things that aren't there. Adolescent exposure to marijuana [raises] risk of *permanent psychosis* in adulthood."[11]

Indeed, a team of scientists has since revealed that "as many as a quarter of new cases of psychotic mental illness can be blamed on super-strength strains of cannabis," reports the *Daily Mail*.[12]

Just what a seriously troubled America needs right now—hordes of new psychotics!

UNDER THE INFLUENCE

Let's take in a quick aerial panorama of the American mindscape. First, the stats. According to the most recent such study by the federal Department of Health and Human Services, more than 24 million Americans use illegal drugs, comprising marijuana/hashish, cocaine (including crack), heroin, hallucinogens, inhalants, or prescription-type psychiatric drugs used without a prescription.[13]

A few highlights from the study:

- 24.6 million Americans aged 12 or older—that's 9.4 percent— were current illicit drug users.

- Marijuana was the most commonly used illicit drug, with 19.8 million users.

- There were also 1.5 million cocaine users aged 12 and up, plus 1.3 million using hallucinogens, another 595,000 using metham-phetamine, and 681,000 using heroin.

- 6.5 million people aged 12 or older used prescription-type psy-chotherapeutic drugs non-medically in the previous month.

- 9.9 million Americans aged 12 or older—3.8 percent—reported driving under the influence of illicit drugs during the past year.

Tragically, every single day, waves of new people—many of them minors—are starting their drug-use careers: The National Survey on Drug Use and Health documents that, as of 2013, some 1,647 new people *per day* used cocaine for the first time (in at least a year), 463 new users tried heroin for the first time each day, 395 newbies started on methamphetamine, 2,058 were initiated into Ecstasy, and a mind-boggling 4,110 new people twelve and up started using illegally obtained psychotherapeutics.[14] Remember, that's every single day.

In short: almost 25 million of us are using illegal drugs and 10 million of those admit to driving on the public roadways under the influence of drugs!

Now, when we think of driving "under the influence," our minds turn to alcohol, so fasten your seat belts:

- In 2013, nearly one-quarter of all Americans aged 12 and up participated in binge drinking, about 60.1 million people. ("Binge drinking" meant having five or more drinks on the same occasion on at least one day in the 30 days prior to the survey.)

- Heavy drinking was reported in 16.5 million people 12 and older. ("Heavy drinking" meant binge drinking on at least five days in the past 30 days.)

- Among young adults aged 21 to 25, the rate of binge drinking was an astonishing 43.3 percent, and the rate of heavy drinking 14.4 percent.

- An estimated 10.9 percent of persons 12 or older—that's an astounding 28.7 million people—drove under the influence of alcohol at least once in the past year.

Bottom line, according to the Department of Health and Human Services: "In an average year 30 million Americans drive drunk [and] 10 million drive impaired by illicit drugs."[15]

In case you're concerned about tobacco—and yes, nicotine is a drug (stimulant), and yes, every year tobacco kills more Americans than died in World War II—the same federal study showed that about one in four Americans 12 and older use it, with 55.8 million Americans smoking cigarettes, 12.4 million smoking cigars, 8.8 million using smokeless tobacco, and 2.3 million smoking tobacco in pipes.[16]

"FASTEST GROWING DRUG PROBLEM"

With well over *80 million Americans* thus stupefied on illegal drugs or excessive alcohol and 40 million of them driving under the influence, the nation undeniably suffers from a massive substance-abuse problem.

But there is another parallel drug problem, the devastation of which is arguably just as severe and detrimental to American society as that involving illegal drugs and alcohol abuse. Some would say it's worse.

And that is the astonishingly vast, and rapidly increasing, number of people taking medically prescribed but poorly understood, mind-altering psychiatric drugs.

Ironically, after marijuana (which is rapidly becoming legal), the most-abused drugs in America are psychiatric drugs, obtained and used "non-medically," that is, without a prescription from a doctor.

As revealed in a report from the Centers for Disease Control and Prevention, "approximately 27,000 unintentional drug overdose deaths occurred in the United States" over the course of one year, "one death every 19 minutes." Surprisingly, states the CDC, "prescription drug abuse is the fastest growing drug problem in the United States."[17]

The skyrocketing drug-overdose death rate "has been driven," says the report, "by increased use of a class of prescription drugs called opioid analgesics"—drugs like hydrocodone (brand names Norco, Vicodin), hydromorphone (Dilaudid, Exalgo), oxycodone (OxyContin, Percocet), and morphine (Astramorph, Avinza).

"Opioid analgesics suppress your perception of pain," explains WebMD, "and calm your emotional response to pain by reducing the number of pain signals sent by the nervous system and the brain's reaction to those pain signals."[18]

For the last decade, "more overdose deaths have involved opioid analgesics than heroin and cocaine combined," reports the CDC. In addition, "for every unintentional overdose death related to an opioid analgesic, nine persons are admitted for substance abuse treatment, 35 visit emergency departments, 161 report drug abuse or dependence, and 461 report nonmedical uses of opioid analgesics."

In other words, we're in a real epidemic.

Americans have traditionally thought of legal and illegal drugs in vastly different ways: On the one hand is what we think of as the respectable, legal, medical world, where enlightened doctors prescribe their patients wonder drugs that relieve their pains, symptoms, and stresses—OxyContin, antianxiety drugs (Valium, Xanax), sleeping pills, stimulants, mood stabilizers, and more recently, marijuana and even hallucinogens.

On the other hand, we tend to look down on what we think of as the sleazy, criminal world of dope pushers, who supply low-life users and addicts with drugs to relieve their pains, symptoms, and stresses—drugs like OxyContin and other illegally obtained psych meds, stimulants, cocaine, marijuana, and hallucinogens.

If the distinction between legal and illegal seems disturbingly indistinct and fluid—in some ways almost unreal—keep reading, because it gets *much* more bizarre.

CREATING "ZOMBIES"

A news story originating at *The Fix*, which specializes in reports on addiction and recovery, was topped with this interesting headline: "America's Number One Prescription Sleep Aid Could Trigger 'Zombies,' Murder and Other Disturbing Behavior."

The report includes true stories of murderers and other offenders who had taken the popular sleeping pill Ambien—classified as a "hypnotic" drug—and relates how their defense lawyers successfully argued that adverse drug effects from Ambien should be considered a mitigating factor. The drug achieved national notoriety in 2006 when then-congressman Patrick Kennedy had a bizarre nighttime car crash, telling police he was running late for a vote (which actually had occurred six hours earlier) and that, because he took Ambien, he had no recollection of the night's events.[19]

The current Ambien label reads as follows:

What is the most important information I should know about AMBIEN?

After taking AMBIEN, you may get up out of bed while not being fully awake and do an activity that you do not know you are doing. The next morning, you may not remember that you did anything during the night. You have a higher chance for doing these activities if you drink alcohol or take other medicines that make you sleepy with AMBIEN. Reported activities include:

- driving a car ("sleep-driving")

- making and eating food

- talking on the phone

- having sex

- sleep-walking[20]

Let's be clear: This is not fine print about "rare adverse events" (negative side effects that occur in fewer than one in one thousand people taking a medication). These are instructions given to new users of Ambien describing what they can and should expect.

So, drugging people into becoming sleepwalking, sleep-driving, sleep-eating, sleep-talking, and sleep-sexing zombies with no memory of what they have done while in a drug-induced hypnotic trance—this is a good thing?

In case that went by too fast (or in the event you're on Ambien and were sleep-reading), we are talking about *"sleep-driving"*! The frequency of motor vehicle accidents caused by people on Ambien is reportedly why the FDA has recommended that women take lower doses of such sleep aids, which were prescribed for Americans 60 million times in 2011.[21]

SUICIDE . . . AND HOMICIDE
Although psychiatric drugs take various forms—antipsychotics, antidepressants, hallucinogens, mood stabilizers, stimulants, anxiolytics (anti-anxiety drugs), hypnotics (for inducing sleep)—by far the most prescribed psych meds in America are antidepressants. In fact—and this will perhaps

be hard to swallow—according to the CDC, in 2010 some 254 million prescriptions for antidepressants were written for Americans.[22]

Of all the disturbing side effects of antidepressants—and the irony here is profound—the most notorious is that the medication can cause the user, who presumably is already depressed, to want to kill himself. Indeed, every single antidepressant sold in America today, regardless of manufacturer or brand, bears a mandatory "black box" warning label—the FDA's most serious drug warning—of "increased risks of suicidal thinking and behavior, known as suicidality, in young adults ages 18 to 24."[23]

Sadly, among US soldiers and veterans, there are on average twenty-two suicides *per day,* and astute physicians have been asking how big a role psychiatric drugs might be playing. After all, as *Time* reported back in 2008, "about 20,000 troops in Afghanistan and Iraq were on such medications," roughly half on antidepressants and the other half on Ambien and similar sleeping pills. Add to that the fact that antidepressants' suicidality warning label is aimed at "young adults ages 18 to 24"—the core age group for the Army—and the only reasonable conclusion is that the stresses and traumas of war, along with the proven effects of the drugs, can be a lethal combination.

Even more ominous is the fact that, where there are suicidal thoughts, homicidal thoughts may not be far behind, especially in a particularly angry or deranged person. Which brings us to one of the most disturbing correlations between psychiatric drugs and violent behavior.

It is well documented that perpetrators of many of the most horrendous school shootings and mass murders in our modern era were either on—or just recently coming off of—psychiatric medications, most commonly antidepressants.[24]

Andrea Yates drowned her five children in the bathtub after taking the antidepressant Effexor (the manufacturer, Wyeth Pharmaceuticals, later quietly adding "homicidal ideation" to Effexor's list of "rare adverse events"[25]). Columbine mass-killer Eric Harris was taking the antidepressant Luvox when he and fellow student Dylan Klebold murdered 12 students and a teacher before killing themselves. And John

Hinckley took four Valium two hours before shooting and almost killing President Ronald Reagan. Moreover, online databases like *SSRI Stories* have archived a huge collection of cases, numbering in the thousands, in which psychiatric medications were implicated or suspected in "a variety of adverse outcomes, including violence."[26]

Faced with myriad lawsuits over such catastrophic "rare adverse events," drug-company lawyers strive to avoid costly settlements and public relations nightmares (such as when GlaxoSmithKline had to pay over $6 million to the family of Donald Schnell who murdered his wife, daughter, and granddaughter in a fit of rage after taking Paxil) by paying out hundreds of millions to plaintiffs to quietly settle hundreds of such cases out of court.[27]

DRUGGING THE KIDS AT SCHOOL

While we stress over our kids' pot-smoking and binge drinking, at the same time we force millions of them—mostly boys—to take Ritalin or similar dangerous psychostimulant drugs for a medical condition that didn't officially exist a generation ago, attention deficit/hyperactivity disorder.[28]

Ritalin, a trade name for methylphenidate, is "a Schedule II substance [which has] a high potential for abuse and produces many of the same effects as cocaine or the amphetamines," according to the Drug Enforcement Administration, which notes that other Schedule II substances include cocaine, amphetamines, opium, methadone, oxycodone, morphine, codeine, and barbiturates.[29]

"The controlled substances in this schedule," the DEA adds, "have a high abuse potential with severe psychological or physical dependence liability, but have accepted medical use in the U.S."[30]

There is abundant evidence that Ritalin is simply dangerous. A federal advisory panel, concerned about the effects of psychostimulants on the heart, announced back in 2006 that it "wanted to slow the explosive growth in the drug's use" due to, among other things, dozens of suspicious deaths.[31]

Yet, despite twin controversies over the drugs' proven dangers and their wild over-prescription, the CDC reports a radical escalation in recent years.

Incredibly, 19 percent of high school–age boys in the United States are being diagnosed with ADHD, and about 10 percent are currently being prescribed drugs for it, while 10 percent of high school–age girls are being likewise diagnosed.[32]

"Those are astronomical numbers. I'm floored," says Dr. William Graf, a pediatric neurologist in New Haven and Yale medical professor, according to the *New York Times*. "Mild symptoms are being diagnosed so readily, which goes well beyond the disorder and beyond the zone of ambiguity to pure enhancement of children who are otherwise healthy." Adds CDC director Dr. Thomas R. Frieden, "Unfortunately, misuse appears to be growing at an alarming rate."[33]

Many more such examples of completely out-of-control psychiatric drug prescribing and use could be cited here, but focusing on just these few—and forthrightly acknowledging their often disastrous and heartbreaking results—should at least demonstrate that America has a serious *legal* drug problem.

MEDICAL PRIESTS AND SACRAMENTS

In 1979, famed pediatrician Robert S. Mendelsohn, MD, wrote the controversial best seller *Confessions of a Medical Heretic,* in which he likened the medical establishment to a religion and doctors to priests, complete with their own dogma, rituals, and sacraments.

To a disturbing degree, claimed Mendelsohn, what "doctors do is based on a conjecture, a guess, a clinical impression, a whim, a hope, a wish, an opinion or a belief. In short, everything they do is based on anything but solid scientific evidence. Thus, medicine is not a science at all, but a belief system. Beliefs are held by every religion, including the Religion of Modern Medicine."[34]

While one could argue that dazzling scientific and technological advances have filled in some of the gaps since Mendelsohn indicted his profession, drug-based psychiatry is still—truth be told—a murky, Dark Ages religion.

Although it has many enlightened and gifted practitioners, overall psychiatry has been transformed over time from a search for self-understanding and healing (via traditional talk therapy) into a massive drug-dispensing bureaucracy. Two parallel trends have brought this about.

One trend has been the gradual transformation of our society as a whole (and with it, psychiatry and psychology) away from the core Judeo-Christian values of earlier generations. There was a time when therapists generally understood that many mental-health problems were rooted in early traumatic experiences and seriously flawed family relationships, as well as possible deficits in the patient's own understanding, maturity, character, self-discipline, objectivity, and capacity for honest self-examination. This commonsense moral worldview stemmed, in turn, from an acknowledgment of the reality of God, of good and evil, of right and wrong, and of both a noble side to human nature and an ignoble one—an inheritance Christians describe as being "born in sin." However, over the past couple of generations, America has increasingly rejected these bedrock Western values and the understanding of human nature they affirm.

The other contributing trend has been, of course, the development of a great many ingenious and enormously profitable pharmaceutical drugs that could be marketed to doctors for relieving—which usually means *masking*—a host of clinical symptoms, with or without any understanding of what caused them.

So a new paradigm has evolved in our increasingly secular and mechanistic society, one characterized by an ever-expanding repertory of "personality disorders" and "mental illnesses" all in need of "drug therapy."

Many psychiatrists are openly rebelling against the latest version of their own diagnostic bible, the *Diagnostic and Statistical Manual of Mental Disorders,* or *DSM,* published by the American Psychiatric Association, whose most recent edition pathologizes—that is, labels as "disorders"—behaviors and conditions once considered just a part of life.

The new paradigm worked for quite a while. But recently, our modern "religious belief"—according to which psychiatric "priests" tell troubled souls, "You have a brain disorder; it's not your fault; take this wonder drug and you'll be OK"—is disintegrating under the weight of its own success.

Take, for example, the now-orthodox dogma that depression involves a physiological problem with the sufferer's brain chemistry, a notion that is comforting to patients who are thereby absolved of any stigma—or responsibility—associated with their condition. Yet today, with literally *tens of millions* of Americans taking antidepressants, the dogma—echoed by the National Institute of Mental Health when it proclaims "depressive illnesses are disorders of the brain"[35]—is recognized by more and more people to be a logical impossibility. After all, it would mean that one in four middle-aged American women (23 percent of all those forty to fifty-nine) suffer from an organic brain disease—physically defective brains. That's an obviously absurd proposition.

Thus it is that more and more doctors, peer-reviewed studies, articles, and books are exposing the blindness and irrationality that underlie much of modern drug-based psychiatry.

"THE UNMAKING OF PSYCHIATRY"

Here's how science writer and practicing psychotherapist Gary Greenberg, author of *The Book of Woe: The DSM and the Unmaking of Psychiatry,* summarized the current situation in the *New Yorker:*[36]

> It's been just over twenty-five years since Prozac came to market, and more than twenty percent of Americans now regularly take mind-altering drugs prescribed by their doctors. Almost as familiar as brands like Zoloft and Lexapro is the worry about what it means that the daily routine in many households, for parents and children alike, includes a dose of medications that are poorly understood and whose long-term effects on the body are unknown. Despite our ambivalence, sales of psychiatric drugs amounted to more than seventy billion dollars in 2010.

With all those tens of billions on the table, Greenberg poses a mystery: "In the past few years, one pharmaceutical giant after another—GlaxoSmithKline, AstraZeneca, Novartis, Pfizer, Merck, Sanofi—has shrunk or shuttered its neuroscience research facilities. Clinical trials have been halted, lines of research abandoned, and the new drug pipeline has been allowed to run dry.

"Why," he asks, "would an industry beat a hasty retreat from a market that continues to boom?"

Recounting the essentially accidental discoveries of most of today's superstar psych meds—"among them, mood stabilizers, antipsychotics, antidepressants, and anti-anxiety drugs"—Greenberg notes that the highly profitable drugs "lacked one important element: a theory that accounted for why they worked (or, in many cases, did not)."

Nevertheless, he writes, "That didn't stop drug makers and doctors from claiming that they knew. Drawing on another mostly serendipitous discovery of the fifties—that the brain did not conduct its business by sending sparks from neuron to neuron, as scientists previously thought, but rather by sending chemical messengers across synapses—they fashioned an explanation: mental illness was the result of imbalances among these neurotransmitters, which the drugs treated in the same way that insulin treats diabetes.

"The appeal of this account is obvious," explains Greenberg, as "it combines ancient notions of illness (specifically, the idea that sickness resulted from imbalanced humors) with the modern understanding of the molecular culprits that make us suffer—germs. It held out the hope that mental illness could be treated in the same way as pneumonia or hypertension: with a single pill."

The big drug companies, he confirms, "wasted no time in promulgating" the theory: "Merck, the manufacturer of Elavil, commissioned the psychiatrist Frank Ayd to write a book called *Recognizing the Depressed Patient,* in which he extolled the "chemical revolution in psychiatry" and urged doctors to reassure patients they weren't losing their minds, but rather suffering a "common illness" with a "physical basis" and a pharmacological cure.

So, a revolutionary and perversely counterintuitive theory—one utterly devoid of proof—was spread throughout the country, with Merck sending Ayd's book to fifty thousand doctors nationwide, followed by still more revisions to the flawed theory. And though each successive theory "was wrong," says Greenberg, "by the mid-nineties, antidepressants were the best-selling class of prescription medications in the country."

Noting that the current serotonin-imbalance theory is turning out to be "just as inaccurate" as all the others, Greenberg says it's becoming increasingly apparent that both "the causes of depression and the effects of the drugs" are far more complex than previously realized. Waxing philosophical, he observes: "The ensuing research has mostly yielded more evidence that the brain, which has more neurons than the Milky Way has stars and is perhaps one of the most complex objects in the universe, is an elusive target for drugs."

The disturbing bottom line? "Despite their continued failure to understand how psychiatric drugs work, doctors continue to tell patients that their troubles are the result of chemical imbalances in their brains," says Greenberg. "This explanation helps reassure patients even as it encourages them to take their medicine, and it fits in perfectly with our expectation that doctors will seek out and destroy the chemical villains responsible for all of our suffering, both physical and mental. The theory may not work as science, but it is a devastatingly effective myth."[37]

All of this is not to deny that psychiatric medications can have a genuine value; there are some people—a relative few—who, very simply, really require them. In fact, one of the reasons we tolerate the absurd overuse of psychiatric medications in America is our deep-down realization that we need these drugs to control, sedate, and manage the relatively few people who truly need them. We desire a better solution for the severely afflicted than the stark asylums of yesteryear that warehoused hundreds and sometimes thousands of seriously disturbed people. And finally, very frankly, we would rather not have anything to do with truly crazy characters, and so we kind of appreciate the fact that there are medications to chemically control them.

But all of that—combined with our overall acknowledgment of the vital role pharmaceuticals have played in our lives in the last century, from antibiotics to other genuine "wonder drugs"—is not a justification for the creation of a nation state where a massive part of the population, including much of the functional, productive middle class, is dependent on mind-altering drugs.

The desire for drug profits—combined with the profound blindness that results from a de facto atheistic orientation for rendering therapy to troubled human minds and souls—have taken our nation to a dangerous place. When our appointed "healers" do not understand the basics of human nature; when God, morality, and sin don't even enter into our thinking about how humans become entangled in mental-emotional-spiritual problems; when faith, repentance, and forgiveness are considered irrelevant to the healing process—then we compensate for this giant vacuum in understanding by creating our own quasi-"religious" beliefs and "priests" (experts), with their own peculiar "sacraments" and "salvation." All of which leads us, individually and as a nation, ever more into darkness.

"SPOTLESS MINDS"

Looking to the future of the American mind, it is shaping up to be—if we don't turn back—the stuff of the most terrifying science fiction novels and movies.

"How Scientists Are Learning to Shape Our Memory." That's the headline of a *Popular Science* article, ominously subtitled, "The next treatment for trauma could be spotless minds."

Noting that painful memories—"roadside bombs, childhood abuse, car accidents"—have the potential to "shape (and damage) us for a lifetime," the article cites new studies claiming "we're on the verge of erasing and even rewriting memories."

For example, since "both PTSD and addiction disorders hinge on memories that can trigger problematic behaviors," current research predicts future drugs that will cure such conditions by simply eliminating the problem memories: "Several studies have found chemical compounds that can be used to subdue or even delete memories in mice (and maybe someday in people)." One specific report it mentioned was "led by an Emory University researcher [and] showed that SR-8993, a drug that acts on the brain's opioid receptors, can prevent a fear memory from forming."

The article ends by acknowledging, "The idea of scientists manipulating memory does, naturally, sound a bit creepy. But it also points to some possible good: treatment for millions of people tormented by real memories."[38]

Meanwhile, groups like the Multidisciplinary Association for Psychedelic Studies (maps.org) are lobbying hard to legalize *all* of the psychedelic drugs of the 1960s—not just marijuana, but LSD, psilocybin mushrooms, mescaline, and so on, as well as the more modern "rave" drug Ecstasy.

"Psychedelic-legalization supporters say that the American public has been misinformed about the dangers of psychedelic drug use," claims the organization, "and . . . like marijuana, psychedelics have a medicinal benefit that may be a treatment option for groups suffering from mental health and psychological conditions such as autism, depression, post-traumatic stress disorder, schizophrenia, and alcoholism."[39]

Yes, you read that right: they want to "help" people who are depressed, schizophrenic, or drunk by giving them LSD or Ecstasy.

So you see, as America approaches the final stage of metamorphosis into a totally drug-dependent state, legal and illegal merge, the border line disappears, just as the line between normal consciousness and "drug-enhanced well-being" becomes almost indistinguishable. All becomes a new, drug-induced alternate reality in which tens of millions of Americans, unable to deal with life, are taking precarious refuge.

And as we'll discover in the next chapter, in the Internet age, the pitiable refuge of addiction has expanded into fantastic and ominous new forms.

8

ADDICT NATION

Americans' massive reliance on drugs, though alarming, is just one manifestation of the transformation of the American mind. Beyond the tens of millions who are outright addicted to legal and illegal mood-altering drugs, alcohol, and nicotine[1]—tens of millions more have become addicted to anything and everything else imaginable, and some things unimaginable.

No part of the population is immune. Believe it or not, reports abound of toddler iPad addicts who, according to the London *Telegraph*, "lack the motor skills needed to play with building blocks because of an 'addiction' to tablet computers and smartphones." The newspaper cites schoolteachers' observations that "many children aged just three or four can 'swipe a screen,' but have little or no dexterity in their fingers after spending hours glued to iPads."[2]

The digital revolution, of course, has produced far more ominous species of addiction, like Internet gaming disorder, a brand-new mental illness added to the psychiatrists' *Diagnostic and Statistical Manual*. "When these individuals are engrossed in Internet games," says the updated fifth edition, *DSM-5*, "certain pathways in their brains are triggered in the same direct and intense way that a drug addict's brain is affected by a particular substance."[3]

Previously, such addictions broke into the news cycle only when they led to appalling crimes—such as when sixteen-year-old Daniel Petric shot both of his parents in the head, his mother fatally, for taking away his Halo 3 game,[4] or when Rebecca Colleen Christie allowed her three-year-old daughter to starve to death because mom was so obsessed with playing *World of Warcraft* online.[5] More recently, a twelve-year-old Colorado girl was arrested for allegedly trying to "kill her mother after she took away the girl's iPhone."[6]

Internet-related addiction is so widespread, not just in the United States but worldwide, that "there are currently an estimated 24 million young 'web junkies' in China," reports the UK's *Telegraph*, "and a growing number of clinics and military-style 'boot camps' designed to rehabilitate them." The report cites an army psychologist who runs a rehab center for Internet addicts as saying, "They only do two things: sleeping and playing." One Chinese teen chopped off his left hand in an attempt to "cure" his addiction.[7]

Yet all of this—from toddler iPad problems and video game addiction to the mushrooming epidemic of online gambling[8] to the huge numbers reportedly addicted to the Internet itself ("nearly a quarter" of all American teens "go online 'almost constantly,'" says Pew Research)—pales in comparison to the truly gargantuan and society-ravaging problem of pornography addiction.[9]

In previous eras, an inclination to view hard-core porn might have required one to order it through the mail or drive to a sleazy "adult" store, providing plenty of opportunities along the way for one's "better angel" to whisper, in effect, *"Hey, idiot, what are you doing?"* But in the Internet age, it takes just a split second to instantly "beam" oneself, as via a *Star Trek* transporter, directly into pornographic quicksand. Thus, even a fleeting impulse to view porn can be acted on in mere moments, thereby slipping past one's moral defenses, with the end result that the most extreme hard-core porn routinely invades the once-safe inner sanctum of untold millions of American homes.

The statistics are truly mind-boggling:

- Eighty-five percent of young men and nearly half of young women watch porn at least once a month, while 1 in 8 online searches and 1 in 5 mobile searches are for porn. Twenty-four percent of smartphone owners admit to having pornographic material on their mobile handset, and 69 percent of the pay-per-view Internet content market is pornography.

- Children are not spared: Nine out of 10 boys and 6 out of 10 girls are exposed to porn before age 18, and 20 percent of 16-year-olds and 30 percent of 17-year-olds have received a sext, while nearly 1 in 5 young people 18–24 have sent a sext.

- It gets worse. Fifteen percent of boys and 9 percent of girls have seen child pornography, while 32 percent of boys and 18 percent of girls have seen bestiality online, 39 percent of boys and 23 percent of girls have seen sexual bondage online, 83 percent of boys and 57 percent of girls have seen group sex online, and 69 percent of boys and 55 percent of girls have seen homosexual sex online.[10]

By the way, lest you imagine that religious folk are somehow spared from porn addiction, a poll by the respected Barna Group found a staggering 77 percent of Christian men eighteen to thirty view porn monthly, and 36 percent view it *daily*.[11]

Ubiquitous, in-your-face, graphic sex. It is fundamentally transforming American culture, morals, and sanity, and is not only a major factor in family breakdown, divorce, and the resulting misery and bondage for millions of adults, but is likewise corrupting and reprogramming the next generation.

As psychologist Patrick F. Fagan, PhD, former deputy assistant Health and Human Services secretary, puts it: "Two recent reports, one by the American Psychological Association on hyper-sexualized girls, and the other by the National Campaign to Prevent Teen Pregnancy on the pornographic content of phone texting among teenagers, make clear that the digital revolution is being used by younger and younger children to dismantle the barriers that channel sexuality into family life."[12] That's a sanitized, clinical way of saying the next generation is being destroyed—set up for relational failure, heartbreak, misery, and disease.

Truth be told, America is becoming utterly obsessed with sex, pornography, and perversion. The "erotic novel" *Fifty Shades of Grey*, which celebrates BDSM sex (bondage and discipline, sadism, and masochism) sold over 100 million copies worldwide, 45 million in the United States.[13] When the film version debuted in February 2015, the opening weekend's box office take exceeded that of the previous record-holder for February releases, *The Passion of the Christ*.

NOT BY ACCIDENT

As we saw in the previous chapter, more than 70 million of us are currently taking powerful, mind-altering drugs—both legally from doctors and psychiatrists, and illegally from dealers and "friends"—and another 60 million have an alcohol problem. That's at least 130 million souls who feel compelled to chemically alter their consciousness just to get through life. In a nation of around 320 million, that's simply an astonishing number.

What about food? With more than one in three American adults and more than one in six youths clinically obese, food addiction is an ever-expanding problem—and it's not by accident.[14]

"Data suggest that hyperpalatable foods may be capable of triggering an addictive process," confirms a major Yale research paper published by the National Institutes of Health.[15] *Hyperpalatable* is the industry buzzword for highly processed foods ("junk food," "fast food") manufactured, critics contend, for the very *purpose of addicting consumers*.

Such foods, warn researchers, "are engineered in ways that appear to surpass the rewarding properties of traditional foods (e.g., vegetables, fruits, nuts) by increasing fat, sugar, salt, flavors, and food additives to high levels. Foods share multiple features with addictive drugs. Food cues and consumption can activate neurocircuitry (e.g., meso-cortico-limbic pathways) implicated in drug addiction."

In fact, conclude the study's authors, "foods and abused drugs may induce similar behavioral sequelae [resulting conditions] including craving, continued use despite negative consequences, and diminished control over consumption."[16]

Consider what David A. Kessler, MD, chief of the FDA for both the Bush 41 and Clinton administrations, says about food addiction. Kessler's book, *The End of Overeating: Taking Control of the Insatiable American Appetite,* was the subject of a *New York Times* profile provocatively headlined, "How the Food Makers Captured Our Brains":

> Dr. Kessler is perhaps best known for his efforts to investigate and regulate the tobacco industry, and his accusation that cigarette makers intentionally manipulated nicotine content to make their products more addictive.
>
> In *The End of Overeating,* Dr. Kessler finds some similarities in the food industry, which has combined and created foods in a way that taps into our brain circuitry and stimulates our desire for more.
>
> When it comes to stimulating our brains, Dr. Kessler noted, individual ingredients aren't particularly potent. But by combining fats, sugar and salt in innumerable ways, food makers have essentially tapped into the brain's reward system, creating a feedback loop that stimulates our desire to eat and leaves us wanting more and more even when we're full.[17]

And what could drive Kessler's point home more emphatically than a subsequent report by neuroscientists who concluded that Oreo cookies may be more addictive than cocaine?[18]

While drugs, alcohol, tobacco, gambling, food, and sex may comprise the familiar "traditional" addictive scourges, augmented in the digital age by new obsessions involving cell phones and the Internet, in truth there's precious little with which people are not becoming negatively and obsessively entangled. The focal point of addiction can range from normal activities like eating, exercising, and shopping, to criminal behaviors like kleptomania (compulsive stealing) and pyromania (compulsive setting of fires). Even self-injury ("cutting") is at epidemic levels, with a shocking one in twelve teens—and one in ten girls—engaging in repeated self-harm, usually in the form of cutting their bodies with a knife or razor blade.[19]

What is going on here? How did America become so conflicted and addicted? Most important, how can this alarming trend be reversed?

CO-OPTING THE BRAIN

For years, experts assured us addiction was triggered by particular psychoactive substances, like alcohol, nicotine, and certain powerful drugs crossing the blood-brain barrier. But their understanding was both flawed and misleading.

Current-generation research shows that addictions to pornography and other activities not involving substances nevertheless trigger the same changes in "brain reward circuitry" as those centered on heroin or other "addictive" substances.

"For many years," summarizes a Harvard Medical School bulletin, "experts believed that only alcohol and powerful drugs could cause addiction. Neuroimaging technologies and more recent research, however, have shown that certain pleasurable activities, such as gambling, shopping, and sex, can also co-opt the brain."[20]

Thus, reports the London *Independent*, "In a groundbreaking study, researchers used MRI scanners to reveal abnormalities in the brains of adolescents who spent many hours on the Internet, to the detriment of their social and personal lives."[21] Adds the *Telegraph*, "Internet users who become dependent on being online have showed signs of changes in the brain similar to alcoholics and cocaine addicts."[22]

All of which confirms the empirical reality of addiction in today's America: virtually *anything* can become the focus of an all-consuming, life-destroying obsession. Nowhere is this point made more clearly—and bizarrely—than in the TLC reality TV show *My Strange Addiction*. As the cable network describes it, the series "tells the compelling stories of people who are battling obsessive behaviors on the verge of taking over their lives. Follow these addicts as they reveal their strange addictions and meet with psychological experts."[23]

Or, as the *New York Daily News* describes it, it's the "most disgusting reality show on television." The paper's headline tells the whole story:

"'My Strange Addiction' has a gallery of weird cravings: eating tires, cat fur, VapoRub—TLC series delights in revolting obsessions, like a man sleeping with inflatable toys."[24]

Since 2010, the series has featured people with utterly weird addictions, including Kesha, from season 1, who eats half a roll of toilet paper every day; and Jazz (season 2), who has not cut her fingernails for the past twenty-two years (her longest is two feet long). "Everyday tasks such as typing on a keyboard, brushing her teeth or tying her shoes seem daunting," we're told.[25] No kidding.

With so many Americans becoming entangled in a multiplicity of obsessions, compulsions, and addictions—all of them unhealthy and stealing from them the happiness and contentment they were meant to enjoy—what kind of help are addicts getting?

"INVENTING ILLNESSES"

Since addiction is growing rampantly, particularly in the area of prescription opioid drug abuse, let's take a closer look at the world of addiction therapy, in which we'll see a fascinating microcosm of the same moral-spiritual divide racking the rest of America.

Today's addiction therapies are manifold and diverse, running the gamut from inpatient detox centers and halfway houses—including traditional twelve-step programs, like Alcoholics Anonymous, Narcotics Anonymous, Overeaters Anonymous, Chemically Dependent Anonymous, and Marijuana Anonymous—to the therapeutic use of drugs like methadone and naloxone.[26]

For really hard cases, there are newer, exotic treatments, like "deep brain stimulation," or DBS, which involves implanting electrodes within certain parts of the brain to electrically regulate abnormal impulses, as well as development of vaccines to neutralize the effects of highly addictive substances like heroin, cocaine, and methamphetamine before they ever reach the user's brain.[27]

When it comes to the problem of addiction, today's experts are divided into two distinct camps, with competing paradigms for understanding and treating it: the traditional "moral model" and the newer "disease model." Let's look at them.

"Over the past decade," explains PBS, "there has been a debate over the fundamental nature of addiction, which has resulted in very different models for effective treatment programs."[28]

Here's how Harvard Health pitches the "disease model" in its "Understanding Addiction" report: "In the 1930s, when researchers first began to investigate what caused addictive behavior, they believed that people who developed addictions were somehow morally flawed or lacking in willpower." However, Harvard reassures readers, "the scientific consensus has changed since then. Today we recognize addiction as a chronic disease that changes both brain structure and function. Just as cardiovascular disease damages the heart and diabetes impairs the pancreas, addiction hijacks the brain."[29]

The "disease model" is the centerpiece of a massive five-year study released in July 2012, over five hundred pages in length, and considered by some to be the definitive contemporary survey of the addiction issue. Researchers for the National Center on Addiction and Substance Abuse at Columbia University reviewed more than seven thousand publications, analyzed five different national data sets, and interviewed 176 leading experts in preparing their report, titled *Addiction Medicine: Closing the Gap between Science and Practice.*[30]

Believe it or not—just in case you're one of those people still inclined toward the old-fashioned "moral" worldview—this new mega-study has determined not only that addiction is a "disease," but that it is caused, to a great extent, not by any moral failure, but by genetics! Defining addiction as "a primary, chronic disease of brain reward, motivation, memory and related circuitry," the report concludes that nicotine addiction is "75 percent" caused by genetics, that alcohol addiction "48 to 66 percent" determined by genes, and that "up to 78 percent of the risk for developing addiction involving illegal or controlled prescription drugs" is likewise the result of genetic factors largely out of your control.

Stop for a moment and reflect on what a revolutionary notion this is: According to today's ascendant medical philosophy, more than three-fourths of the "blame" for people's addiction to heroin or cocaine rests with their genes. That's disturbingly close to asserting they were born that way!

And what about the "moral model"? One high-profile proponent would be Dr. Keith Ablow, Fox News Channel's go-to psychiatry expert, who claims a high success rate in treating addiction in private practice. In "Obesity Is Not A Disease—and Neither Is Alcoholism," Ablow attacks the continual "invention" of new illnesses by the medical establishment:

> The American Medical Association has decided to classify obesity as a disease. This decision is another example of inventing illnesses— a favorite pastime of the American Psychiatric Association—and another step towards eroding people's autonomy and making them passive participants in their health. It is also an example of how the medical establishment is laying the groundwork to bill Medicare and Medicaid for every bad choice anyone makes, ever. . . .
>
> The solution to obesity is to empower the individual to make choices that won't lead to weight gain. This is made significantly more difficult for psychiatrists like me when organizations like the AMA and APA suggest to folks that their weight is beyond their control because an anonymous illness has descended upon them, blowing them up like balloons.[31]

Charging that the mental health intelligentsia has "gone way too far down the road of suggesting that addictions, in general, are beyond the control of individuals," Ablow brings the responsibility for addiction right back to the addict:

> When an alcoholic chooses alcohol over being available to his or her family and friends, that person is making a decision. When a heroin addict chooses heroin over financial stability and performing well at work, that person is making a choice, too.

> And the choice is not beyond that person's control. It is a measure of how much discomfort the person is willing to endure, in service to himself and others.[32]

By classifying addictions, including obesity, as "diseases," concludes Ablow, the AMA simply "furthers the dependency, disempowerment and entitlement culture that is eroding scientific truth and personal autonomy in America."[33]

Even more blunt is Los Angeles–based clinical and forensic psychologist and author Stephen A. Diamond, who in *Psychology Today* summarizes the "moral model" with refreshing candor: "Psychologically speaking, addiction is all about escapism. Avoidance. Denial. Addicts run from reality, and, in some cases, have been running all their lives. The addict cannot tolerate reality and its vicissitudes. Neither internal reality nor external reality. They find reality repugnant, uncomfortable, overwhelming, and prefer, like the psychotic, withdrawal into fantasy, bliss or oblivion over reality."

"Reality," observes Diamond, "inevitably includes suffering, pain, loss," and thus entails "consciously acknowledging, not just intellectually but emotionally, both what was hurtfully done to us in the past (by parents, peers or others) and what we have hurtfully done to others."

The problem with escaping into addictions to avoid facing reality, he adds, is that "the addict has to keep getting high, because these 'demons' never go away." They're always close by, he says, waiting to bite the addict as soon as he comes off his current high. After all, "what goes up must always come down."

Indeed, Diamond concludes, when our consciousness "comes crashing back to earth, reality and withdrawal from fantasy painfully set in. The psychological and emotional demons and demands of reality return with a vengeance. Reality cannot be run from indefinitely."[34]

The problem with the current genetics-based "disease model" is that it is tantamount to whispering into the ear of a troubled, self-destructive, denial-steeped person in the grip of very dark forces: *Don't bother being introspective. Even if you're full of perverse cravings, blame for others, and absurd excuse-making; even if you're serially dishonest and manipulative with your loved ones; even if you have very little forgiveness for others who have wronged you, and virtually no tolerance for discomfort and unpleasant truth: Never mind all that. Your addiction has nothing to do with any character defect or refusal to face reality. It's just a chronic illness like cardiovascular disease and diabetes—and you were just unlucky enough to get the wrong genes.*

Really? And exactly how are alcoholics and addicts to heroin, opioids, and other drugs supposed to find genuine healing if they embrace such "expert" assurances that defy common sense and absolve them of responsibility for their problem?

Fortunately, many addiction therapists, counselors, and other professionals engaged in the front lines of battling addiction are far too steeped in street-level reality to pay much attention to the fantastic new disease models being churned out in the ivory towers of medical priestcraft.

"Whether you embrace or deny the 'disease' model is beside any practical point," writes Candy Finnigan, a nationally recognized addiction interventionist featured on the Emmy-winning A&E documentary TV show *Intervention*, which profiles addicts and the monumental struggles they and their families undergo to get clean. In her book, *When Enough Is Enough,* Finnigan shoves the whole "moral versus disease" debate aside, asserting simply, "I always ask families whether they prefer their loved one to be addicted or mentally ill: pick one and let's get started."[35]

What all addictions—whether involving drugs, alcohol, food, sex, gambling, shoplifting, or "cutting"—have in common is the intense feeling, excitement, and relief they bring, however temporary. Underlying all of this is an overwhelming urge to *escape.*

But escape from what?

From pain, anxiety, fear, anger, guilt. From remembering painful traumas—childhood abuse, parental divorce, betrayal, loss, death, cruelty, the bad things others have done to us, the bad things we have done to them. But that's just the beginning. The more we run away, the more guilty we become for running away, the more intense our need for escape, and the more toxic substances and toxic relationships we're drawn into—as we lose more and more of our true selves and a dark identity grows ever stronger within us.

Have you wondered why addicts tend to crave ever greater doses to obtain the same level of relief? In previous eras, experts assured us the body developed a physical tolerance to the addictive substance, requiring progressively more to cross the blood-brain barrier to re-create the same "high." Yet non-substance addictions mimic this progression—like gambling, for instance, which requires ever bigger bets to create the same high.

For compulsive gamblers, you see, the experience isn't as much about money as about *excitement,* which equals *escape* and *relief.* That's why sustaining the thrill gambling provides usually involves taking increasingly bigger risks and placing larger bets.[36] Food addiction is the same, with ever greater amounts of the target food required to reproduce the earlier thrill. Same with pornography; addicts often crave progressively more explicit, bizarre, and degrading images to feed something dark growing inside of them. At the extreme are practices like so-called erotic asphyxiation (perversely euphemized as "breath control play"), the increasingly frequent cause of accidental deaths across America[37]— sometimes mistaken for murders—when one sexual partner strangles the other, or himself, to increase pleasure by limiting oxygen to the brain.

If you can "get high"—escape from the pain of life into excitement, distraction and temporary relief—by choking or strangling yourself or someone else, what *can't* you get high on?

Clearly there is no limit to how low human beings can sink in their efforts to get high.

To fulfill this primal if unholy purpose, we can become addicted to literally *anything*—even hate. Hatred of Jews is a full-fledged addiction for many in the Arab-Muslim Middle East—and make no mistake, it delivers a powerful high. In fact, any hatred, sufficiently intense, focused, and sustained, can fulfill the requirements of an addiction, making the "user" feel excited, alive, righteous, empowered—and most important, entirely forgetful of his or her own failings. The "drugs" available to us are limited only by our prodigious capacity for escape and denial.

HOW AMERICAN CULTURE ENCOURAGES ADDICTION

Addiction has been a problem in all nations, cultures, social classes, and historical eras. But today's America "is in the grip of an epidemic," writes Finnigan. "Overstating the enormity of the addiction crisis is impossible. The reality defies imagination or exaggeration."

Although Americans taking mood-altering substances number well over 100 million, Finnigan says currently the nation has about 25 million hard-core, end-of-their-rope, drug-or-alcohol addicts. And "the conventional wisdom," she says, "is that each of those 25 million affects seven other people through familial, social, or professional associations." That would be 200 million Americans personally touched by addiction. Even being "super-conservative" and "cut[ting] that number in half," says Finnigan, "twenty-five million in thrall times three people affected equals 75 million involved."[38] So, depending on which multiplier you choose, America has somewhere between 75 million and 200 million people whose lives are impacted by soul-crushing, body-destroying addictions.

Why so many?

"The nature of the epidemic is systemic," says Finnigan, "and it is an indictment of our ability as a culture and a country to respond."

Let's consider our culture and our country's role in the addiction epidemic currently engulfing us.

Often, addictions have their roots in childhood trauma and family dysfunction, and are not in themselves directly related to politics, ideology, or any other factor outside of the addict's family and social sphere. Other times, however, culture and ideology play a central role, as in Russia, which notoriously maintains one of the highest alcoholism rates in the world. According to the World Health Organization, in Russia and neighboring countries, "every fifth death among men and 6% of deaths among women are attributable to the harmful use of alcohol."[39]

Let that sink in: *alcohol addiction causes one in five male deaths in Russia!*

What about America?

Consider this: If a nation is basically moral and decent, and if its morality and decency are reinforced by widely shared cultural, religious, and educational values that are, metaphorically, "in the air we breathe," this constitutes a powerfully stabilizing force for each of us. It's like a gyroscope—an external one, but one largely in sync with our God-given internal gyroscope we call *conscience*. The America of my youth was a good, if imperfect, example of this.

However, our society is so troubled today that, as previously noted, one in ten girls becomes addicted to "cutting," which is both painful and disfiguring. Why do they do it? Because, as any former cutter will affirm, the physical pain of making razor cuts in her arm is preferable to the intolerable emotional pain she is experiencing. These young people at some point discover they can obtain a measure of temporary relief by injuring themselves.

What, then, is it about our contemporary society that is driving astronomical numbers of us, young and old, to suicide, drug abuse, addiction, and other compulsive, self-destructive behaviors?

Let us reason together.

Do you think telling children, in a multitude of ways as today's culture and education system consistently do, that God does not exist has no effect on their mental health and happiness?

Do you think the legalization of marijuana in state after state, creating a celebratory atmosphere around pot and other drugs, doesn't contribute to drug dependency, not to mention growing psychosis—especially when today's marijuana is known to be many times more potent than in decades past?

Do you think aborting almost 60 million American children in the four-plus decades since the Supreme Court legalized it in 1973—and the not-subtle message this sanitized slaughter sends throughout society about the lack of sacredness of human life—has no effect on people's mental health? Do you think a mother's sudden realization that she has ended the life of her own child—a realization that often dawns immediately *after* the "procedure" is over, and it's too late—exerts no negative impact on the health and happiness of the tens of millions of mothers who have experienced this trauma?

Do you think, in the Internet age, that ubiquitous graphic images and videos of intimate body parts and hard-core sex—images that intrude and are indelibly burned into the minds and souls of tens of millions of young and old alike—does not awaken and feed a very dark nature, and exacerbate all manner of personal, relational, marital, and mental health problems?

Do you think, for America's military members, that having a president who—let's just say it—hates America and therefore logically cannot have American soldiers' best interests at heart in his decisions as commander in chief, wouldn't cause tremendous stress and morale problems in the armed forces, possibly even contributing to growing levels of alcohol and prescription drug abuse a Department of Defense study says have exploded into a "public health crisis"?[40]

Do you think the miserable economy that results when a Far-Left, capitalism-hating president tries to reshape the world's most powerful and successful free-market economy doesn't drive some people toward drug dependency? When we hear of dismal economic news quarter after quarter[41] and a labor participation rate at its lowest in almost four decades,[42] we don't immediately register the human cost of these staggering numbers. The impact is not merely "economic"—the struggle, hardship, and dislocation of the chronically unemployed and their families—but equally mental, emotional, and spiritual. Not being employed when one *needs* to work causes great stress, fear, guilt, insecurity, and feelings of inadequacy and desperation that can easily lead to escape into drugs and alcohol.

Do you think indoctrinating and pressuring young children to affirm that two men kissing or getting "married" is normal and wholesome has no long-term effect on their mental health and happiness? Allow me to spell it out: When a young child sees two men kissing, the "ick factor" he or she automatically experiences (*"Oh, that's so gross!"*) is from God. It *is* gross. That is obvious to every soul who has not yet become confused, corrupted, or desensitized by a culture that celebrates perversion with the force of law. When, as happens today in America, openly homosexual schoolteachers emotionally manipulate classrooms of four-year-olds to embrace the idea that two men or two women marrying each other is wonderful[43]—and make these same children feel ashamed, as though they're somehow bigoted and *hateful* if they don't embrace this—those teachers are literally brainwashing these little ones.

Clearly, the deck seems stacked against sanity and happiness in today's America.

In one sense, widespread addiction is understandable when you reflect on human nature. Much has been written about the so-called addictive personality, but here's my simple take: a major component of the syndrome is a person's strong tendency to want to *escape* from pain, anxiety, and guilt—which means that most of us, to one degree or another, suffer from an addictive personality.

Do you easily rationalize your bad behavior? Does your sense of well-being depend on other's approval and validation? Are you subtly dishonest, manipulating people's opinion of you? Do you blame others for your problems, but fail to take an honest look at your own failings? Are you quietly angry a lot of the time? Do you frequently reach for escape, relief, pleasure, or distraction? Is there a demanding "voice" inside of you that isn't really you, and doesn't have your best interests at heart? Welcome to addict nation.

So the question is, how do we all resolve our core addiction problem—namely, the compulsion to run away from, rather than face, our painful anxiety and whatever lies beyond it?

Allow me to frame this in somewhat religious terms. It's part of the human condition that there's always a certain friction between us and God, thanks to the "sin" nature we inherit—a nature which, like gravity, tends to pull us down and entangles us in all sorts of troubles. To escape from our self-consciousness of this uncomfortable rift between us and our Creator, we are easily tempted to lose ourselves in distraction, excitement, and addictive substances and relationships.

As if that weren't challenging enough, add to the mix a culture addicted to encouraging and celebrating everything wrong with us, and a government dominated by people addicted to exercising power and control over us, and these influences make things immeasurably worse.

But God's plan is still operating and beckoning to us, whether we realize it or not. Eventually, if we're willing, our suffering may finally bring us to our knees and cause us to realize our need for a genuine and ongoing relationship with our Creator. But how does that come about?

Faith and hope visit us effortlessly on the heels of genuine, sincere repentance. And that requires honest introspection, infused with a little trust in God. Without that trust, self-examination becomes self-condemnation and a spiral of morbid thinking and feeling that leads back to the comfort of distractions and addictions. But faithful introspection, where we realize God loves us, and that the wrong we're looking at within us—the sin nature and its tangled web—is not really and truly even us, but rather, something that exists within us, sort of a spiritual parasite. After all, if we are the ones *observing* the sin and disagreeing with it and wishing to be free of it, how then can *it* also be *us,* the observer? Are there two of us?

As the apostle Paul famously expressed this paradox, *"Now then it is no more I that do it, but sin that dwelleth in me"* (Romans 7:17). In other words, the angry, prideful, selfish, escape-prone nature that exists within us—within you—that's the sin self. The part of you that disagrees with and repents of the sin nature within you and just wants to face reality and live unto God from now on, whatever it takes—that's the real you. We just need to keep that straight. Because for many lost souls, including seemingly hopeless addicts, dramatic change for the better comes when they simply stop listening to the "addict voice" within them and start listening again to the *real* self—the quiet inner "voice" of God we experience as conscience and common sense—that got lost so long ago in the chaos and confusion of life.

9

GENDER MADNESS

"When I looked in the mirror, I just saw disgusting fat." Those words, spoken by a dangerously skinny teenager named Emma Stewart, are typical of girls suffering from anorexia nervosa.

"I was convinced I needed to be skinny to look good in a bikini," Emma told the UK's *Daily Mirror*. "I started obsessing about my weight and what I'd look like sunbathing. I was convinced I was too heavy, so I started skipping meals and making myself sick."[1]

Emma, literally wasting away, as shocking photos document,[2] resembled an emaciated concentration-camp survivor. And yet, the effect her anorexia had on her mind and emotions was to make her see herself as disgustingly fat.

Emma's delusion is far from unusual. Between half and 1 percent of all American girls—that's hundreds of thousands of young women—suffer from anorexia nervosa, a key symptom of which is experiencing strong feelings of being fat, while in reality being skinny. Or, as the National Eating Disorders Association puts it, making "frequent comments about feeling 'fat' or overweight despite weight loss."[3]

Hold that thought. Now let's look into the mirror of people suffering from another condition, one increasingly fawned over by the news and entertainment media, widely hailed as the next "civil rights movement" and legitimized through passage of special laws all over the country—namely, gender dysphoria.[4] That's the new name for what used to be called gender identity disorder, referring to the plight of transgender (or transsexual) people who so strongly identify with the opposite sex that they often undergo major surgery in an attempt to change genders.

"When I look in the mirror in the morning, before having shaved, it's certainly a painful experience. . . . The immediate reaction I get from my reflection is a feeling of very strong disassociation, accompanied by a kind of shock, confusion, or mental jarring. I have the strong, gut-level sensation that whoever is behind the mirror is not me," says one "trans" individual.[5]

"Whenever I look in the mirror it's like I'm looking at a stranger or something," says another.[6]

"Transsexuals," explains one commentator, "report feeling out of place, feeling awkward, and to get others to understand their inner struggle, transsexuals will ask: 'If you're a woman, imagine that every morning when you awaken and look in the mirror, you see a man. And if you're a man, imagine that when you awaken, you see a woman in the mirror. That's how a transsexual feels.'"[7]

Increasingly, Americans are being inundated with sympathetic, media-driven stories showcasing this unfortunate and perplexing condition, like ABC's two-hour prime-time interview with reality TV star Bruce Jenner, during which the legendary Olympic champion told a nation and world that have long revered his masculine athleticism: "I am a woman."[8] Weeks later, Jenner sensationally "came out" on the cover of *Vanity Fair*, featuring a pinup girl-style Annie Leibovitz glamour shot of the newly minted "Caitlyn."[9]

"WHY WOULD YOUR BRAIN LIE?"

The human mind is an amazing thing. Just like computers, they're awesome when they work properly, but vexing when they don't.

Yet there it is: whether it's the anorexic or transgender individual staring intently into the mirror and seeing the exact *opposite* of reality, or millions of others in similar straits tormented from within with myriad obsessions, compulsions, addictions, and delusions, our minds and emotions are—very simply—capable of lying to us, to the point of seriously disrupting our lives.

Take OCD, or obsessive-compulsive disorder, which currently afflicts one in one hundred American adults (between 2 and 3 million), plus one in two hundred children and teens (that's another five hundred thousand), according to the National Institute of Mental Health.

Here, courtesy of the International OCD Foundation, is a vivid description of what obsessive-compulsive disorder feels like from the inside:

Imagine that your mind got stuck on a certain thought or image . . .

Then this thought or image got replayed in your mind, over and over again, no matter what you did . . .

You don't want these thoughts—it feels like an avalanche . . .

Along with the thoughts come intense feelings of anxiety . . .

Anxiety is your brain's warning system. When you feel anxious, it feels like you are in danger. Anxiety is an emotion that tells you to respond, react, protect yourself, DO SOMETHING!

On the one hand, you might recognize that the fear doesn't make sense, doesn't seem reasonable, yet it still feels very real, intense, and true . . .

Why would your brain lie?

Why would you have these feelings if they weren't true? Feelings don't lie . . . Do they?

Unfortunately, if you have OCD, *they do lie.*[10]

How many Americans have problems like these, where their thinking and feeling (or whatever lurks behind their thinking and feeling) profoundly deceives them? Fasten your seat belt, because in addition to the 2 to 3 million with OCD, the National Institute of Mental Health reports that almost 14.8 million American adults have a major depressive disorder, 21 million have a mood disorder, 5.7 million suffer from bipolar disorder, 2.4 million have schizophrenia, 40 million have an anxiety disorder, 6 million have a panic disorder, 7.7

million are dealing with post-traumatic stress disorder, 6.8 million have generalized anxiety disorder, 15 million have a social phobia (fear of any situation where escape may be difficult, like traveling in a car, bus, or airplane), and another 19 million have some type of specific phobia (marked, persistent fear and avoidance of a specific object or situation).[11]

There are multitudes of phobias, running the gamut from A (ablutophobia, fear of washing; achluophobia, fear of darkness; acousticophobia, fear of noise) to Z (zelophobia, fear of jealousy; zeusophobia, fear of God or gods; zoophobia, fear of animals), with hundreds more in between. Yet what most if not all phobias have in common is a root in some traumatic experience (or experiences) generating a syndrome of unwanted, irrationally fearful thoughts and feelings.

By the way, the mental health statistics cited earlier, which appear to account for around half of Americans, don't even include attention deficit/hyperactivity disorder, or ADHD, one of the most common diagnoses in children and adolescents, or autism spectrum disorder, which now afflicts as many as *one in fifty American kids*, according to the CDC.[12]

Makes you wonder: Is there anybody left who is not afflicted?

AMPUTATION OF HEALTHY ORGANS "THE NEW NORMAL"
Having made this quick survey, something very strange now comes into view.

All of these conditions, whatever their symptoms or level of severity, are named and described in the psychiatrists' bible—the *Diagnostic and Statistical Manual of Mental Disorders,* the most recent being the fifth edition (so-called *DSM-5*)—and all are considered "pathological" (that is, "relating to, or caused by, disease") and classified as "disorders."

Well, all except one.

Ironically, one the most extreme of all of these conditions—at least in terms of its preferred treatment, which often involves the amputation of healthy body parts, and whose sufferers have one of the highest suicide-attempt rates of any population on earth[13]—is for some reason in the process of being *de*-pathologized; that is, reclassified as normal.

Indeed, the recent renaming of gender identity disorder as gender dysphoria, thanks to pressure from the powerful LGBT lobby, means the condition itself is no longer considered abnormal or "disordered" at all, but only the *anxiety* one may feel over it—anxiety that LGBT apologists blame largely on public ignorance and intolerance.

Actually, this "dysphoria" business is a strategic half measure; the unabashed, publicly stated goal of the LGBT world is to get gender identity disorder completely de-pathologized so it is officially and legally declared to be an absolutely normal variant of human identity and behavior. It is, after all, the *T* in the LGBT coalition, which represents itself as a minority community exactly like blacks and Jews—so, no room for mental illness in the mix.

Ironically, there is some criticism toward the latest edition of the *Diagnostic and Statistical Manual* among mental health professionals, who claim the manual makes it *too easy* to diagnose people as "disordered." For example, as one clinical psychologist wrote in *Slate*, "DSM-5 will change . . . the criteria for 'generalized anxiety disorder,' a disorder that involves excessive and persistent worrying. Whereas the criteria in DSM-4 required three out of six symptoms of worrying, only one symptom is needed in DSM-5."[14]

How, then, when today's mental-health trend is to categorize more and more marginally problematic human behaviors as diagnosable "disorders," does the mental/emotional state that craves having healthy body parts amputated in a pathetic and utterly impossible quest to change genders become magically transformed into something "normal"?

NBC News, like many in the big media, trumpeted the good news in this headline: "Being transgender no longer a 'mental disorder': APA." As the network reported:

> The American Psychiatric Association has revised its *Diagnostic and Statistical Manual of Mental Disorders* and it no longer lists being transgender as a mental disorder, among other changes announced this past weekend.

Transgender people will now be diagnosed with "gender dysphoria," which means emotional stress related to gender identity. "Gender identity disorder" had been listed as a mental disorder since the third edition of the *DSM* more than 20 years ago.

In an interview with *The Advocate*, APA member Jack Drescher explained the new revision, saying, "All psychiatric diagnoses occur within a cultural context. We know there is a whole community of people out there who are not seeking medical attention and live between the two binary categories. We wanted to send the message that the therapist's job isn't to pathologize."[15]

Drescher's comment that "all psychiatric diagnoses occur within a cultural context" is just code, of course, for admitting that the American Psychiatric Association cravenly caved in to LGBT demands to remove the "disorder" label.

One organization that successfully lobbied for the change, the World Professional Association for Transgender Health, confirms that it "conducted a consensus process in order to make recommendations for revision of the *DSM* diagnoses of Gender Identity Disorders. . . . The [work group] recommended changing the diagnosis to one based on distress rather than on identity, on which the current diagnosis is based."[16]

"There was consensus," the group reported, "that a transgender identity is not pathology. Gender variant individuals are not inherently disordered; rather, the distress of gender dysphoria is the psychological problem."[17]

If that line of thinking seems confusing, just wait: a report in the peer-reviewed journal *Clinical Child Psychology and Psychiatry* uses opaque academic lingo and tortured multicultural logic to rationalize why there's nothing at all wrong with people who want to cut off healthy breasts or genitalia in pursuit of "gender transition":

> As a diagnostic category, gender identity disorder remains problematic with ongoing debates concerning etiology, definition and ethics of treatment. Inherent in the current *DSM* definition is a Western

model of the relationship between sex and gender which epitomizes the tension existing between essentialist and constructivist accounts of gender development. This model determines that gender-aberrant behavior and gender variation are, by definition, pathological, and reinforces a binary gender model. Studies of non-Western cultures reveal variations in models of gender and in the understanding of gender deviance. Cultures vary in their definition of gender roles and show varying degrees of tolerance for atypical gender behaviors and gender change. An understanding of cultural context is important in the clinical assessment of atypical gender development and challenges current models of sex and gender.[18]

Translation: If you think there's something wrong with people who want to amputate parts of their body, it's only because you are biased in favor of oppressive Western culture, and hung up on the outdated notion that there are just two genders. If you were more multiculturally enlightened, you would realize it is just your own prejudice and narrow frame of reference that is the real problem here.

But back in the world of reality, transgenderism (or transsexualism) is *not* normal. In fact, it's so abnormal and unnatural that a staggeringly tragic 41 percent of all transgender individuals living in the United States have attempted to commit suicide, according to a 2010 study.[19]

And more recently, "sex change regret" is emerging as a huge reality, as the *Federalist* documented in its "Trouble in Transtopia" report, concluding: "Biological truth has a way of outing itself. The hard reality of it is written right into our DNA as 'male' or 'female.' In the end, transgender activists and their media enablers won't be able to drown that massive iceberg."[20]

In fact, former psychiatrist-in-chief at Johns Hopkins Hospital, Paul R. McHugh, MD, confirms that transgenderism is indeed a "mental disorder."[21]

Writing in the *Wall Street Journal,* McHugh, who is currently Hopkins' distinguished service professor of psychiatry, cites a long-term Swedish study that followed transgendered people for up to thirty years, revealing that "beginning about ten years after having the surgery, the transgendered began to experience increasing mental difficulties. Most shockingly, their suicide mortality rose almost twenty-fold above the comparable non-transgender population."[22]

What about those special transgender camps now springing up in the United States,[23] where parents of young children who like to play or dress as the opposite sex take their kids, presumably to affirm and celebrate these poor youngsters' supposed "transgender identity"? Yet, reveals McHugh: "When children who reported transgender feelings were tracked without medical or surgical treatment at both Vanderbilt University and London's Portman Clinic, 70 to 80 percent of them spontaneously lost those feelings." How tragic, then, that some parents, cheered on by irresponsible journalists and agenda-driven "experts," would set their children on the path of a lifetime of profound confusion and needless suffering.

Meanwhile, the same politically influenced psychiatric elite that see fit to diagnose millions of fidgety schoolboys with the "mental disorder" of ADHD (and then "treat" them with powerful and poorly understood drugs), are recategorizing the undeniably extreme transgender disorder as normal.

Why has the American Psychiatric Association given in to activist pressure with regard to transsexuals?

For the same reason the same psychiatrist organization, coming under similar pressure, declassified homosexuality as a mental disorder in 1973, while its sister organization, the American Psychological Association, followed suit two years later.

Stunningly, the former president of the American Psychological Association—indeed, the man who actually introduced the motion to declassify homosexuality as a mental illness in 1975—is now sounding the alarm. Dr. Nicholas Cummings says the psychologists' organization has become dominated by "ultraliberals" under the thumb of the "gay rights movement." Since the mid-1990s, warns Cummings, the group's positions have become based on "political stances" that "seemed to override any scientific results," adding, "Cherry-picking results became the mode. The gay rights movement sort of captured the APA."[24]

How far will the official normalization of pathological sexuality go? So-called genetic sexual attraction (adult incest) is intruding into the mainstream with ever greater frequency, with news stories of fathers marrying their daughters and having children together.[25] No word as to whether the American Psychiatric Association's stance on incest is "evolving." However, believe it or not, the APA actually altered the classification of pedophilia in the latest edition of its *Diagnostic and Statistical Manual* from a "disorder" to a "sexual orientation."

But wait! "Sexual orientations" are protected classes of Americans according to the current generation of "anti-discrimination" laws. That would make pedophiles a protected class!

After a deafening public outcry, the APA released a press statement claiming it was all just a big mistake: "'Sexual orientation' is not a term used in the diagnostic criteria for pedophilic disorder," the psychiatrists' group clarified, "and its use in the *DSM-5* text discussion is an error and should read 'sexual interest.'"[26] The group promised to correct the error in its manual's next edition.

RECLAIMING REALITY AND SANITY

Part and parcel of the decision to reclassify conditions once considered mental illnesses—like homosexuality and transsexuality—as normal, benign, healthy sexual or gender "orientations," is a determination that these proclivities are largely determined by genetics.

But a generation ago, before the search for the elusive and hypothetical "gay gene" ever began, psychologists and psychiatrists believed aberrant sexual attractions and obsessions often were rooted in childhood trauma.

Is it true? Certainly it's undeniable that little children, being so exquisitely impressionable, are powerfully shaped by the environment in which they grow up. Early sexual abuse, for example, can be devastating, and it's a sad fact that our prisons house many child molesters who were themselves molested as children.[27]

Objective consideration of true causes is also complicated by the fact that today's psychiatric priesthood just doesn't seem that interested. Ever-increasing weight is instead placed on biological factors, like genetics, infections, brain defects or injury, prenatal damage, substance abuse, and poor nutrition. Moreover, even when factors such as childhood abuse (physical, emotional or sexual), divorce, death in the family, and so forth, *are* considered, the "therapy"—almost always drugs—doesn't deal with the trauma. How, for example, can psychiatric drugs undo a young woman's hatred and feelings of betrayal toward her father for having abused and/or abandoned her when she was a little girl?

The evolving medical philosophy that says our mental health problems (like our drug and alcohol addictions, as we saw earlier) are determined largely by genetics and other mysterious biological factors is increasingly at war with reality.

To dramatize the problem, let's engage in a sort of thought experiment: Consider how some unfortunate children in the Arab-Muslim Middle East develop a bad case of (let's give it a clinical name) "jihad martyrdom syndrome." I think it's fair to say that the compulsion to kill dozens of innocent people *and yourself,* while simultaneously believing the creator of the universe will reward you for mass murder with endless sex with six dozen beautiful women in the afterlife, is at least as serious a disorder as some of the newly minted "mental illnesses" in the latest *DSM,* like "mild cognitive impairment" and "binge eating disorder."

So how exactly do innocent little kids come to be possessed by such all-consuming emotions and delusional beliefs that lead them to blow themselves up while slaughtering innocent strangers?

If one were to suggest genetics, biochemical imbalances, or environmental toxins were responsible, everyone would laugh. Little jihadists are created when, from an early age, they are indoctrinated to hate "infidels" and see them as less than human—when they are continually intimidated, degraded, frightened, tempted, brutalized, brainwashed, lied to, punished, threatened, and rewarded (for reinforcement)—until their little developing minds and emotions no longer belong to them. They internalize and act out a completely new implanted identity, utterly foreign to the one with which they were born.

If the forces in one child's life can thus transform him so totally that, when he looks in a mirror, he sees someone with an overwhelming desire to kill "infidels" in a glorious "martyrdom operation," couldn't the forces in another child's life (perhaps far more subtle, but nevertheless powerful) transform him or her into a person with feelings, thoughts, and desires he likewise was not born with—including homosexual or transgender feelings? Many lesbians have confessed that their hatred for their cruel, abusive fathers blocked them from bonding to men later in life. Why is this so hard to understand?

At the extreme, consider the sad story of "female-to-male" transsexual Nancy Verhelst of Belgium, who was legally euthanized by lethal injection after a botched sex-change operation. The back story? Her parents hated and rejected her because she was a girl, and they wanted another boy. So this poor girl tried to become a boy, and when it didn't work, she took her life.[28]

Many other types of unseen (from the outside) but devastating family dysfunction, along with various forms of child abuse and sexual molestation, are indisputably powerful factors in causing sexual deviance later in life. In particular, it's scandalous that childhood sexual abuse as a well-known pathway into homosexuality is virtually ignored in our culture's rush to glorify aberrant sexual practices.

A multitude of peer-reviewed studies corroborate the fundamental truth that childhood trauma plays a huge role in later homosexuality:

- A 2012 study by scientists at Brown University reveals that "research has indicated a high prevalence of childhood sexual abuse among men who have sex with men in the United States."[29]

- University of Pittsburgh researchers in a 2011 meta-analysis likewise conclude, "The higher rates of abuse experienced by sexual minority youths may be one of the driving mechanisms underlying higher rates of mental health problems, substance use, risky sexual behavior, and HIV reported by sexual minority adults."[30]

- A 2012 study out of Harvard Medical School and Boston Children's Hospital documented that "gay/lesbian respondents had higher odds of exposure to child abuse" than heterosexuals, and "bisexual respondents had higher odds of exposure to child abuse . . . and intimate partner violence" than heterosexuals.[31]

- These studies and others corroborate earlier research, like the 2007 study by Boston College researchers, which found that "childhood sexual abuse was associated with alarmingly high rates of men who were HIV infected and antecedent risk behaviors."[32]

- In 2008, researchers from Boston Children's Hospital documented "prevalent and persistent abuse disproportionately experienced by lesbian and bisexual women."[33]

- And in a comprehensive 2013 study, titled "Does Maltreatment in Childhood Affect Sexual Orientation in Adulthood?" and published by the National Institutes of Health, researchers at Harvard and Columbia documented definitively: "Epidemiological studies find a positive association between childhood maltreatment and same-sex sexuality in adulthood, with lesbians and gay men reporting 1.6 to 4 times greater prevalence of sexual and physical abuse than heterosexuals."[34]

Confirming that "numerous studies document an association between childhood physical and sexual abuse, neglect, and witnessing violence in childhood and same-sex sexuality," this highly revealing study identifies several "pathways" for such early-childhood engendering of same-sex feelings:

1. abuse of boys perpetrated by men causes boys to believe they are gay;

2. abuse of girls by men leads them to be averse to sexual relationships with men;

3. abuse survivors may feel stigmatized and different from others and may, therefore, be more willing to behave in ways that are socially stigmatized, including acknowledging same-sex attraction or having same-sex partners.[35]

Yet, however clear, compelling, and heartbreaking the evidence, none of this apparently matters. Fewer and fewer people seem to care anymore about actual causes and effects, about the true nature of things. Instead, too many of us care only about what we want to believe, what we wish to be true. We *want* homosexuality to be a healthy lifestyle, even though, as the *Wall Street Journal* has documented, "Projections have shown that if current trends continue, *half of all gay and bisexual men will be HIV-positive by age 50.*"[36] We *want* transgenderism to be normal, even though reason, experience, and biology all shout otherwise.

After all, if transgenderism is normal, amputations and all, then what about "transabled" people who, like the transgendered, experience powerful feelings that their true identity is other than what they appear to be? In this case, we're talking about people craving disability.

"We define transability [also known as body integrity identity disorder] as the desire or the need for a person identified as able-bodied by other people to transform his or her body to obtain a physical impairment," Alexandre Baril, a Quebec-born academic knowledgeable on the transabled community explained to Canada's *National Post*. "The person could want to become deaf, blind, amputee, paraplegic. It's a really, really strong desire."[37]

One "transabled" individual, for example, who now goes by the name of "One hand Jason," amputated his own right hand above the wrist and now claims he is very happy with his stump, or "amp," as he told a popular body modification website.[38] Both groups—transgendered and transabled—are obsessed with changing their bodies to recreate themselves in accord with strange, persistent inner feelings they have determined represent their "real" self.

Yet while the transabled (who want to cut off various parts of their bodies so they can feel whole) are considered mentally ill, the transgendered (who likewise wish to amputate healthy breasts and sex organs so they can feel whole) are being lionized not only as normal, but as a protected and courageous minority.

Unfortunately, sooner or later there is always a very big price to pay when a society willfully denies reality. The LGBT movement has not only succeeded in mainstreaming behaviors all previous generations considered pathological and immoral; it also insists that the rest of society not only accept these behaviors, but affirm and *celebrate* them—or be punished.

BURGEONING TOTALITARIANISM

Today, what started in the '60s as "gay liberation," later called "gay rights," then "LGBT" (and more recently "LGBTQIA," for lesbian-gay-bisexual-transgender-questioning-intersex-asexual), has metastasized into an ever-expanding form of totalitarianism and persecution of religious conscientious objectors.

Since long before the Supreme Court's imposition of same-sex marriage on all fifty states, a wave of legislation has been sweeping the country, outlawing counseling help for minors who wish to overcome unwanted same-sex attractions; decreeing that boys and young men must be allowed to use girls' restrooms and locker rooms if they claim to identify with the opposite sex (and vice versa); mandating pro-homosexual/pro-transgender indoctrination of children at kindergarten and even preschool age; requiring the integration of open homosexuals into the military; and, perhaps most shockingly, leading to the outright persecution of individuals and businesses that simply oppose the LGBT agenda on moral and religious grounds:

Some of the cases are high-profile, like that of Brendan Eich, the tech prodigy who created JavaScript and co-founded Mozilla, maker of the popular Firefox browser, who committed the unpardonable sin of donating one thousand dollars to California's Proposition 8, upholding traditional marriage. For that he was forced out as CEO of his company.

HGTV pulled the plug on its highly anticipated reality show, *Flip It Forward*, starring David and Jason Benham. The problem? The Benham twins are Christians, with mainstream, traditional values, including a belief that homosexuality and same-sex marriage are neither moral nor biblical. Their show was killed in the cradle.[39]

Duck Dynasty's Phil Robertson, an evangelical Christian, started a firestorm of protest after he told *GQ* magazine that he believed homosexuality is a sin. The show's creator, A&E, announced it was indefinitely suspending Robertson from its most lucrative show, until a massive public backlash caused the network to realize its colossal stupidity and it reinstated Robertson.

Media reports that Chick-fil-A CEO Dan Cathy opposed same-sex marriage and donated to traditional-values groups prompted gay activists to call for protests and a national boycott, with Chicago mayor Rahm Emanuel banning Chick-fil-A from the city and several universities barring Chick-fil-A from their campuses. Although the boycott effort backfired in the short term—when "Chick-fil-A Appreciation Day" and grassroots goodwill resulted in a dramatic increase in the chain's income—in the longer run, the intimidation had its desired effect: Dan Cathy later said he made a "mistake" and had become "wiser."[40] Perhaps part of what weakened his prior resolve was the August 2012 attempted mass-murder attack on the Family Research Council, when an angry homosexual activist named Floyd Lee Corkins entered FRC's Washington, DC, headquarters carrying fifteen Chick-fil-A sandwiches and a 9 mm handgun, shooting a security guard before being overcome by the courageous staffer. After his arrest, Corkins—who told FBI agents he was inspired to commit the terror attack on the Christian organization by the Far-Left Southern Poverty Law Center's "hate map"—confessed he had planned to "kill as many people as I could . . . then smear a Chicken-fil-A sandwich on their face."[41]

Now, that's tolerance for you.

A major win for homosexual activists was over the Boy Scouts of America, which they relentlessly pressured year after year, putting enormous financial, legal, boycott, and media pressure on the private group until enough members of its governing body finally weakened—and then broke—admitting open homosexuals. In the process, they severely wounded the century-old "morally straight," Christian-inspired organization for boys.

Remember Carrie Prejean, Miss California USA, who during finals of the Miss USA Pageant was ambushed by homosexual pageant judge Perez Hilton, who asked for Prejean's opinion of same-sex marriage? Her kind, respectful, and utterly normal response—"I believe that marriage should be between a man and a woman, no offense to anybody out there, but that's how I was raised and I believe that it should be between a man and a woman"—was considered so outrageous that the evangelical Christian contestant was widely mocked.

More recently was the firestorm surrounding the family-owned Indiana restaurant, Memories Pizza. The owner's twenty-one-year-old daughter, replying to a hypothetical question posed by a local TV news reporter, said her family was devoutly Christian and wouldn't in good conscience be able to cater a homosexual wedding. This resulted in a mountain of obscene abuse and death threats, including threats and incitement to burn down the family's business, which was forced temporarily to close.

"CEASE AND DESIST" BEING A CHRISTIAN

But these high-profile news events don't even begin to paint the true picture. The exact same sorts of totalitarian, "you-aren't-allowed-to-even-*think*-that-way" assaults are occurring all the time, throughout America. Here (courtesy of Americans for Truth) are just a few more everyday examples:[42]

Did you hear about New Mexico Christian photographers Jon and Elaine Huguenin, who were sued by two lesbians under the state's "sexual orientation" law after declining to photograph the lesbians' "commitment ceremony"?

Or the New Jersey case of the Ocean Grove Camp Meeting Association, convicted of "discrimination" after two lesbians, Harriet Bernstein and Luisa Paster, decided to hold their "commitment ceremony" on the Methodist-run association's popular family-friendly boardwalk? After that, Ocean Grove quit the wedding-hosting business.

What about the Aloha Bed & Breakfast in Hawaii, a Christian business forced to "accommodate" two Southern California lesbians after a judge ruled the B&B violated state law when the owner told Taeko Bufford and Diane Cervelli she wasn't comfortable having them stay together in her home, due to her religious beliefs? Aloha has since been ordered by the state "to provide a room to any same-sex couple that wishes to stay there."

Similar cases are mounting up with disturbing frequency, including: Illinois Christian bed-and-breakfast owners Jim and Beth Walder who, for expressing their religious convictions regarding homosexuality, have been sued by LGBT activist Todd Wathen, who demanded monetary damages, attorneys' fees, and "an order directing [the Walders] to cease and desist from any violation" of the state's Human Rights Act. And Vermont's Wildflower Inn, which paid a settlement to lesbians and shut down its wedding reception business after the ACLU won a ten-thousand-dollar civil penalty for two lesbians. The settlement also requires the inn's owners to place twenty thousand dollars in a charitable trust for the lesbians.

You may have heard about Oregon's Sweet Cakes by Melissa bakery, which was fined $135,000 after declining to bake for a "gay wedding." But what about the owners of Indiana's Just Cookies, who, for refusing to fill a special order for "rainbow cookies" for an LGBT group, were charged with "discrimination" under the city's "sexual orientation" law. Or Colorado's Masterpiece Cakes, which became the target of a formal complaint by the state's attorney general for refusing, on religious grounds, to make a "gay" wedding cake. Or Iowa's Victoria's Cake Cottage, whose owner, Victoria Childress, refused to provide a wedding cake for a homosexual couple out of "convictions for their lifestyle," and is being boycotted and threatened with lawsuits. Oregon's Fleur Cakes, which joined Sweet Cakes in refusing to bake a wedding cake for a same-sex couple, stands accused by the *Huffington Post* of being part of a "disturbing trend."[43]

How many cases must pile up before we recognize the *real* "disturbing trend" toward harassment and legal targeting of America's Christians? In Washington State, the owner of Arlene's Flowers, Barronelle Stutzman, declined to provide flowers for the wedding of a same-sex couple who had long frequented her shop, because of her "relationship with Jesus Christ." She later faced two lawsuits. In New York, Liberty Ridge Farm, which refused to allow its property to be rented out for a lesbian "wedding," was fined thousands of dollars.

Do I need to keep going?

Craig James was fired by Fox Sports Southwest after a GOP debate tape showed him expressing Christian beliefs in opposition to "homosexual marriage." A Christian T-shirt maker in Kentucky was targeted by the Lexington-Fayette Urban County Human Rights Commission for refusing to print "gay pride" designs for a local homosexual group.

And think about this one: Chris Penner, owner of the Twilight Room Annex bar in Portland, was fined $400,000 under the Oregon Equality Act for excluding transgender men who, dressed as women, had been alienating other customers by using the women's restroom. According to the *Seattle Times*, eleven people—calling themselves the "T-girls"— "will get the money, with awards ranging from $20,000 to 50,000."[44]

There are mountains of other examples—the Catholic Church being forced to shut down successful adoption agencies in several states because it opposes adoption by homosexual couples; Christians kicked out of college counseling programs because they oppose homosexuality; therapists prohibited by law from helping young people overcome unwanted same-sex attractions; "ex-gay" and pro-change therapists forced out of business by lawsuits; people fired from their jobs solely because they oppose same-sex marriage; school districts forced to positively affirm homosexuality; "anti-gay" 501(c)(3) organizations having their nonprofit status challenged; even a proposal to ban Christians from serving in government if they had ever demonstrated "bias" against homosexuals.

On and on it goes, increasing, not diminishing, with each passing year.

Many thought same-sex marriage would be the crowning achievement of the LGBT movement and that the juggernaut would finally wind down. But then, suddenly the focus shifted to "transgender rights," with *Time* magazine's "The Transgender Tipping Point" issue trumpeting the headline, "America's next civil rights frontier,"[45] and Vice President Joe Biden likewise proclaiming transgender discrimination "the civil rights issue of our time."[46] And then—brace yourself—there were reports of *three-year-old children* being required to sign a contract promising they will not use "transphobic language" in nursery school![47]

The secret of this never-ending, always-expanding revolutionary movement, in case you haven't realized, is that it has the full support of the Far Left. Not because the Left loves homosexuals, bisexuals, and transsexuals for themselves, but because finally the Left has found its spear tip, with which—as it has dreamed of doing for decades—it can effectively attack, wound, marginalize, demonize, and criminalize its greatest enemy: the Christian religion.

Indeed, the LGBT sexual anarchy movement has the unique potential to permanently corrupt our civilization's core institution, *marriage and family,* as well as our core "operating system," *Judeo-Christian values.*

Yet ironically, it is the one issue almost everybody is afraid to confront.

Like Voldemort, the arch-villain so feared by everyone in the Harry Potter stories that they "do not speak his name," almost no one—not Democrats, not Republicans, not Libertarians, not the news media, not even most churches—dares speak openly about it. Indeed, many have succumbed and joined forces with it.

However, when considering the increasing assault on the American mindscape we've explored in this book, ask yourself this: How can the simultaneous glorification of sexual perversion, the revolutionary redefinition of "marriage" and "family," and the criminalization of the religion that for centuries has served as America's moral foundation, *not* compound the epidemic of stress, anxiety, depression, addiction, and suicide today plaguing our nation?

Is it not time for us to face reality and give up the illusions now tearing our nation apart? Can't we understand why, after thousands of years of human history, letting five unelected lawyers in black robes suddenly and radically redefine the most foundational institution of the human race—marriage—is a bad idea? And is it not madness to think we can transform a man into a woman by surgically fiddling with his plumbing and feeding him hormones—when every single one of his body's 37.2 trillion cells is permanently coded *"male"* with Y chromosomes? Paul R. McHugh, Johns Hopkins Hospital's former top psychiatrist, affirms it simply is "biologically impossible" to change the sex you were born with, and that those who advocate "sexual reassignment surgery" are thus *promoting* mental illness.[48]

We Americans are in desperate need of serious self-reflection, of awakening, and a radical course correction. Perhaps more than ever, we need to take a good, long, hard, uncompromisingly honest look at ourselves in the mirror.

But what will we see staring back at us?

Will we—like the starving anorexic girl who saw in the mirror only "disgusting fat," or the man with transgender feelings who saw the reflection of a woman beckoning—continue to be drawn into a deceptive fantasy world, one where intense emotions of unclear origin drown out reality? Will we continue to embrace a brave new world of constantly mutating sexual anarchy, one so disconnected from science, faith, reason, and the lessons of history that it can lead us only into societal ruin?

Or, will we finally be able to see past the illusions generated by ceaseless propaganda and pressure? Will we be able to break free and catch a glimpse of our true self once again—a people uniquely blessed by God and safely grounded (as George Washington admonished) in the twin virtues of "religion and morality"? For our children's sake, let us fervently hope our nation can once again reclaim this great blessing.

In the next chapter we will focus on the growing war for the American mind, and will survey the extraordinary battlefields now shaping up between the forces of sanity and madness, the outcome of which will determine who ultimately runs the American asylum—the sane people, or the lunatics.

10

WAKING UP

Living in a time of rapid disintegration of so much that has made America the greatest nation in history, many have commented they feel almost as though they're trapped in a "bad dream," waiting to wake up. It turns out, there's a lot more truth to that sentiment than we may realize.

Let's start at the top, with a president who has reshaped America according to his own strange inner dreamscape.

In Dinesh D'Souza's popular documentary, *2016: Obama's America,* based on his book *The Roots of Obama's Rage,* the author/filmmaker argues that Obama's shockingly anti-American mind-set and policies can best be understood in light of the grievances, resentments, and utopian ambitions—in a word, the dreams—he absorbed from his Kenyan father.

Barack Obama Sr., explains D'Souza, was a fierce champion of anticolonialism, "the doctrine that rich countries of the West got rich by invading, occupying and looting poor countries of Asia, Africa and South America."

A Far-Left economist, Obama Sr. insisted Kenya needed "to eliminate power structures that have been built through excessive accumulation so that not only a few individuals shall control a vast magnitude of resources as is the case now." That's right; President Obama's father was so enamored of Marxist wealth distribution as a remedy for "colonialist exploitation" that he even argued that "theoretically there is nothing that can stop the government from taxing 100 percent of income so long as the people get benefits from the government commensurate with their income which is taxed."[1]

Taxing "100 percent of income," of course, is straight-up communism, and such radical and rage-rooted attitudes became deeply embedded within the mind and soul of the forty-fourth US president, contends D'Souza:

> We are today living out the script for America and the world that was dreamt up not by Obama but by Obama's father. How do I know this? Because Obama says so himself. Reflect for a moment on the title of his book: It's not *Dreams of My Father,* but rather, *Dreams from My Father.* In other words, Obama is not writing a book about his father's dreams; he is writing a book about the dreams that he got from his father.
>
> Think about what this means. The most powerful country in the world is being governed according to the dreams of a Luo tribesman of the 1950s—a polygamist who abandoned his wives, drank himself into stupors, and bounced around on two iron legs (after his real legs had to be amputated because of a car crash caused by his drunk driving). This philandering, inebriated African socialist, who raged against the world for denying him the realization of his anti-colonial ambitions, is now setting the nation's agenda through the reincarnation of his dreams in his son. The son is the one who is making it happen, but the son is, as he candidly admits, only living out his father's dream. The invisible father provides the inspiration, and the son dutifully gets the job done. America today is being governed by a ghost.[2]

But the radical left's ruinous utopian fantasies, to which Obama has long been in thrall, by no means constitute the only dark dream world plaguing Americans today.

Just as the World War II generation was confronted with Nazis proclaiming they were destined to rule the world (and who insisted "the Jews" were the cause of the world's problems and deserving of annihilation), today we are confronted with rapidly growing armies of Islamic jihadists, who, just like the Nazis, proclaim they are destined to rule the world (and insist "the Jews" are the cause of the world's problems and deserving of annihilation). Radical Islam attracts thousands of lost souls in the West, mostly young people full of hate, frustration, blame, and hopelessness, and seduces them into believing they are becoming shining warriors for God, part of a powerful brotherhood and dazzling revolution, when in reality they are just being recruited into a murderous international mind-control cult.

However, let's move beyond all the big "isms," the totalitarian ideologies that metastasize across our world, wreaking havoc, misery, and war wherever they spread. This same phenomenon of embracing a delusional alternate reality to justify evil deeds, or escapism, or lust for power, advantage, or revenge, can be seen everywhere, in endless variations large and small. If you love smoking pot or crack, you adopt a philosophy of life that rationalizes that. If you join a gang—whether a local street gang or the biggest, "baddest" gang of all, ISIS—there's also a powerful worldview waiting to absorb you. The purpose of such philosophies is *always* to justify something bad.

For example, French philosopher Michel Foucault, celebrated as one of the most influential intellectuals in modern times, championed a philosophy some heralded as brilliant, daring, and profound (and critics considered barely comprehensible gibberish). By redefining morality, normality, madness, and human nature itself so as to eradicate every vestige of right and wrong, Foucault's true, albeit hidden, purpose was to justify his personal obsession with drugs, sadomasochistic homosexuality, and pedophilia. (Foucault was arrested for sex with an underage boy, publicly called for legalized child sex,[3] and, before dying of AIDS, notoriously proclaimed, "To die for the love of boys—what could be more beautiful?")[4]

Think of it: a supposedly "great philosopher" constructs an entire alternate reality—a dream world, into which he invites millions—all to secretly justify his perverse personal sins, and in the process, portray normal society as ignorant and oppressive. Like Foucault, multitudes of people similarly embrace irrational worldviews, which we human beings seem so effortlessly able to concoct.

Having thus set the stage for the next leg of our journey, let us now closely examine one particular form of mass delusion that has widely taken hold of modern America.

Fortunately, as we proceed we will also discover what happens when people start waking up en masse from such a mass delusion. Fascinating and wildly unexpected things sometimes occur.

Also, let us bear in mind that while America is certainly full of troubles, there is always at least one redeeming aspect to great suffering such as we are now enduring as a country—and that is, suffering has a powerful way of *awakening* people.

So, get ready for a wild ride along the razor's edge between madness and reality, between terminal delusion and blessed awakening.

WHEN WORLDS COLLIDE

For most of us, the death of a child is our worst nightmare.

The Sandy Hook Elementary School massacre was so singularly gut-wrenching because the victims were mostly young children. Likewise, news reports about the Boston Marathon bombing emphasized the fact that, of the three people killed, one was an eight-year-old boy—as if to highlight the uniquely great loss of a child.

In the world of crime, one of the most incomprehensible acts is baby-murder. We're outraged at the widespread sex-selective infanticide of newborn girls in China. And news headlines like "Georgia boys face murder charges after cold-blooded killing of infant being strolled by mother"[5] and "Black teens murder white baby for the fun of it"[6] cause us to shake our heads and wonder, *How could anyone possibly sink so low?*

Many murders of babies—almost half, according to the Justice Department's National Criminal Justice Reference Service—occur within the first twenty-four hours after birth, so-called neonaticide.[7]

Of course, appalling crimes like these have always have been a part of life in this fallen world—a world of good and evil, of decent and indecent people, where moral outrage is kindled within all good souls by the murder of the innocent.

However, parallel to this moral, rational world exists yet another world—an amoral, irrational one rooted in deepest denial, and constructed over several decades with great effort and ingenuity. We're talking about the realm of . . . well, what shall we call it? Every official label—"abortion," "choice," "women's health," "reproductive freedom," "pregnancy termination," "voluntary miscarriage"—is a fragile euphemism designed to obscure a dark reality.

That reality, stated objectively, would be: the premeditated killing of human babies residing inside their mother.

In this strange parallel world, the same killing of a baby that in the real world outrages us and results in prosecution, prison, and possibly execution, is mysteriously transformed into a "medical procedure" and "constitutional right," provided for and fiercely defended by a multibillion-dollar industry and all the powers of government—and funded by taxpayers.

These two worlds collided spectacularly in the trial of Philadelphia abortionist Kermit Gosnell.

As everyone who followed the 2013 trial knows, Gosnell's clinic, despite its dignified-sounding name—Women's Medical Society—was actually a house of horrors more reminiscent of the Nazi doctor Josef Mengele than a legitimate medical practice. Here's the grand jury's summary:

> This case is about a doctor who killed babies and endangered women. What we mean is that he regularly and illegally delivered live, viable babies in the third trimester of pregnancy—and then murdered these newborns by severing their spinal cords with scissors. The medical practice by which he carried out this business was a filthy fraud in which he overdosed his patients with dangerous drugs, spread venereal disease among them with infected instruments, perforated their wombs and bowels—and, on at least two occasions, caused their deaths.[8]

The grand jury's report is horrifying not just for what it reveals about Gosnell's crimes, but because it documents that a lot of what was later universally condemned about Gosnell's abortion business had been known throughout the Pennsylvania regulatory agencies for years—but no one lifted a finger to stop it.

The sun started to shine on all this when the case went to trial. Eyewitness testimony painted an otherworldly picture of a Nazi-like torture clinic, with one Gosnell employee saying, "It would rain fetuses—fetuses and blood all over the place," and another recalling one baby expelled alive into a toilet and observing the infant "was swimming" and "trying to get out."[9]

For a "mainstream" press overwhelmingly skewed toward "reproductive rights," it was stunning when top news organizations from the *New York Times* to the *Washington Post* suddenly proclaimed their outrage over Gosnell's abortion crimes and the lack of news coverage.

"Infant beheadings. Severed baby feet in jars. A child screaming after it was delivered alive during an abortion procedure," wrote liberal Democrat and Fox News contributor Kirsten Powers in an impassioned and widely read *USA Today* column. "Haven't heard about these sickening accusations? It's not your fault," she explained. "Since the murder trial of Pennsylvania abortion doctor Kermit Gosnell began March 18, there has been precious little coverage of the case that should be on every news show and front page. The revolting revelations of Gosnell's former staff, who have been testifying to what they witnessed and did during late-term abortions, should shock anyone with a heart."[10]

Likewise, the *Atlantic*, as "mainstream" and elite as media organizations get, headlined its report decrying lack of national press coverage "Why Dr. Kermit Gosnell's Trial Should Be a Front-Page Story." Its dramatic subhead summarized the whole sordid tale: "The dead babies. The exploited women. The racism. The numerous governmental failures. It is thoroughly newsworthy."[11]

There was just one problem with this journalistic outrage over Gosnell's abortion crimes: Virtually everything Gosnell was accused of doing occurs routinely in other abortion clinics throughout America.

Everything. Routinely.

"The dead babies," intoned the *Atlantic*'s headline. Yes, the dead babies—close to 60 million of them so far since *Roe v. Wade*, including hundreds of thousands of late-term abortions just like those babies "murdered" by Gosnell and his employees.

"The exploited women." Sorry, but exploiting women—frightening and pressuring them, pretending to care about them so they'll buy the abortion, withholding life-and-death medical information about both the unborn child's development and the adverse physical and psychological consequences for the mother, essentially conning them from start to finish—is the central operating principle of the abortion industry. If women were counseled with absolute honesty and full disclosure, the number of abortions would plunge overnight. Moreover, abortionists' routine exploitation of women when the "procedure" goes awry, as it often does, has resulted in death for many and permanent injury, trauma, sterility, and soul-scarring heartache for countless more.[12]

"The racism." The left-leaning press, which somehow is more offended by racism than almost anything else in this life, complained about Gosnell's "racist" double standard in treating poor minority women worse than he treated rich white women from the suburbs. Reality check: The abortion industry is one of the most racist enterprises in the Western world. Margaret Sanger, founder of the nation's number-one abortion provider, Planned Parenthood, was an unapologetic racist and eugenics proponent who openly advocated for discouraging blacks from breeding. To this day, US abortion clinics are set up predominantly in areas with a disproportionately high black population, a fact documented repeatedly over the years.[13]

"The numerous governmental failures." Seriously? It's not just the "failures" of the Pennsylvania regulatory authorities. Government at all levels, but especially at the federal level, for decades has overtly supported, enabled, and protected the abortion industry in myriad ways ranging from providing taxpayer support to enacting laws prohibiting pro-life

demonstrators from congregating anywhere near abortion clinics, legislation flagrantly violating the First Amendment's right to assemble.

"So," asked Mark Crutcher, founder and president of the Denton, Texas–based organization Life Dynamics, "why is everyone so upset over Kermit Gosnell?"

Along with other pro-life activist groups engaged in undercover work like Operation Rescue and Live Action, Life Dynamics has long specialized in exposing criminal abortionists.

"For years," Crutcher told me during the Gosnell trial, "we've exposed one criminal abortionist after the other. But abortion proponents always say the offender is just a 'bad apple' and an 'aberration.' But when we expose *hundreds* of similar offenders, every one of them is still just a 'bad apple' in a barrel of good apples. At what point do we realize they're *all* bad apples?"

One chapter of Crutcher's book, *Lime 5: Exploited by Choice,* details *three dozen cases* of abortionists (and references many more) who raped or otherwise sexually molested their "patients." One of the abortion doctors, called a "predator in a white coat" by California's deputy attorney general, was accused of sexually assaulting more than 160 women.[14]

"MORALLY IRRECONCILABLE"

The collision of these two warring worlds in the Gosnell case—the real world, where killing a baby is a capital crime, and the dream world, where killing the exact same baby at the exact same age is a "woman's fundamental right"—forces us to confront a peculiar question: *Where did the killing occur?*

Understand, the babies Gosnell was convicted of murdering were no older, larger, more viable, more human, or more precious than other late-term babies aborted routinely over the past forty-plus years. It's just that Gosnell *pulled them out of their mother* before killing them. Had he done exactly the same horrendous things (like snipping infants' spinal cords) while the baby was still inside the mother, many who today express horror would have regarded it as just another late-term "women's health procedure" that mother and doctor determined to be in her best interest.

How is this possible? Aside from legal restrictions imposed (but routinely ignored) by a few states, abortion in America under *Roe v. Wade* is legal from the moment of conception until the moment of birth, if the mother's life *or health* is determined to be endangered. And "health"—here's the giant loophole—is broadly interpreted to include both physical *and mental* health. That means late-term abortionists (with a cooperating second doctor) can, and routinely do, sign authorization forms claiming the mother risks becoming, oh, let's just say, "depressed" if denied the "procedure" or "therapy."

To her credit, Powers forthrightly confronted this now-institutionalized mass delusion: "Whether Gosnell was killing the infants one second after they left the womb instead of partially inside or completely inside the womb—as in a routine late-term abortion—is merely a matter of geography. That one is murder and the other is a legal procedure is morally irreconcilable."[15]

The existence of these two competing worlds, one based on self-evident truth and valuing human life, and the other on monumental selfishness and denial, is easy enough to explain—just as slavery was easy to explain (in terms of its supposed economic "necessity" in maintaining the South's giant tobacco and cotton plantations) when it was an established practice in the United States.

America's mass acquiescence to abortion is rooted in our devotion to what has become a near-sacred belief in *total sexual freedom*. However disastrously, we have determined as a modern, secular, post-Christian society that we have the absolute right to engage in sexual relations with whomever we want, whenever and wherever we want, and we repudiate any notion that we must take responsibility for the natural result of sex—which is children. Having committed so deeply to this proposition, it matters not how barbaric and inhuman abortion is, how many gorgeous children we see with their throats cut, heads cut off, chemically burned alive, brains sucked out, or spinal cord snipped with scissors.

THE SNAPPING OF THE AMERICAN MIND

We *must* allow for abortion-on-demand or our sacred right to total sexual freedom ceases to exist. That's our current operating paradigm, without its clothes.

This is why, as an Illinois state senator, Barack Obama opposed the Born-Alive Infants Protection Act, designed to prevent the killing of babies that, despite the abortionist's "best efforts," are born alive—in other words, it was crafted to prevent *precisely the crimes for which Kermit Gosnell was convicted of murder*. But Obama took that extreme position because, once you start allowing for the restriction of abortion in even the slightest way, you are acknowledging the humanity of the unborn (or in this particular case, the *born*) child, and the whole abortion delusion is in danger of unraveling.

MAGIC LINES

In the dream world of "reproductive freedom," women are advised: "Had unprotected sex? Just take the morning-after pill." A few weeks later, "Just take RU486," and a few weeks after that, "Just have a suction abortion. It's not a baby." Yet with each passing week of gestation, the delusion becomes more difficult to sustain. For in just a few more weeks, suddenly anyone killing the same baby risks, like Kermit Gosnell, being branded a despicable child-murderer, prosecuted as a criminal, and sentenced to life without parole. "Any doctor," argued Gosnell's prosecutor, Philly DA Seth Williams, "who cuts into the necks severing the spinal cords of living, breathing babies, who would survive with proper medical attention, is a murderer and a monster."[16]

In a desperate attempt to reconcile these two opposing worlds, we endlessly draw magic lines—arbitrary points before which killing babies is a revered constitutional right, and after which it's a monstrous crime. We create lots of these artificial lines—from "first trimester," "second trimester," and "third trimester," to "heartbeat," "twenty weeks," and "viability."

Of course, overshadowing all these magic lines is an even *more* arbitrary and irrational measure of infant humanity—namely, whether or not the parents want the child! One baby has inestimable value backed by the legal protection of the state solely because the parents want and love it, while another child of identical attributes and age, but whose parents don't want it, is considered worthless medical waste.

Is this not a form of madness?

Is our justification of abortion not akin to the tortured philosophical constructs of Michel Foucault (and many other perverse philosophers), secretly aimed at erasing morality and God's inner laws from people's minds so as to validate their own moral corruption?

In reality—and every sentient adult knows this—life in the womb is a continuum of growth from the moment of fertilization to the moment of birth. There is no "magic line" before which destroying that life is perfectly fine and after which it is a depraved criminal act.

As the Gosnell trial proved, these two warring worlds—the world of love and life versus the world of selfishness and death—inevitably collide somewhere along this continuum. After all, putting aside Gosnell's unsanitary clinic conditions, "racism," and other unseemly atmospherics, the only major difference between his and other abortionists' killings was that his were visible—outside the mother, where others could see it.

Do we really think Gosnell's snipping of infant spinal cords is somehow different or worse than the eighteen thousand other late-term abortions every year in today's America?[17] Is snipping more inhumane than forcibly ripping apart human babies limb from limb, or chemically burning them alive with intrauterine saline and other lethal chemicals, or—as in the recently outlawed intact dilation and extraction (partial-birth abortion) procedure—pulling the living baby feetfirst into the birth canal, except for the head, stabbing the base of the baby's skull with surgical scissors, inserting a tube into the wound, sucking out the baby's brain with a suction machine (causing the skull to collapse), and delivering a now-dead baby?

How can we have the gall to express horror at Gosnell's abortions, but not toward the multitude of other equally abominable but legally sanctioned killings that have scarred and bloodied our nation for more than four decades?

Maybe the Gosnell trial was just a convenient catharsis for "pro-choice" Americans, including the major media, an opportunity to safely take out their pent-up guilt over abortion on one "bad" doctor without endangering all those "good" abortion clinics they dream exist.

Abortion has always been a cosmic collision waiting to happen: in the same society where we are righteously outraged at child murder, we fervently embrace child murder.

"SACRED GROUND"

When the world of reality collides with the dream world of desperately held illusions, extraordinary things happen. In the afterburn of the Gosnell trial and society's rare moral condemnation (the "bad doctor" got three life sentences for multiple first-degree murders of babies), *both good and evil* were mysteriously turbocharged.

The Gosnell verdict was handed down May 13, 2013. Just four weeks later, on June 11, the Texas legislature took up consideration of Senate Bill 5, explicitly drafted to prevent the kind of horrors Gosnell had committed by banning abortions past twenty weeks' gestation, in other words, late-term abortions. Exceptions for the life and physical health of the mother were included, and public support was strong.

However, as we have seen throughout this book, our once-unified nation has become a place of warring opposites. Where light shines, the darkness also rages—and the brighter the light, the angrier and more unhinged the rage grows.

Thus, two weeks later on June 25, then state senator Wendy Davis, a Democrat, engaged in an eleven-hour filibuster (wearing a urinary catheter so she could stay the course)[18] to block passage of the late-term abortion bill before the midnight end of the Texas legislative session.

The big media (who had just finished condemning Gosnell) loved it, with the Associated Press reporting: "Thousands of people watched it live online, with President Barack Obama at one point tweeting,

'Something special is happening in Austin tonight.'"[19] With the help of a raucous mob that would not allow representatives to record their votes by the legal deadline of midnight, Davis succeeded in blocking the bill's passage—for a few weeks, anyway—later parlaying her newfound celebrity into an unsuccessful run for the Texas governorship in 2014.

Remarkably, Davis insisted that late-term abortion is, and I quote, "sacred." In a post-filibuster speech at the National Press Club, she justified her actions to stop the late-term abortion ban by proclaiming, "I'll seek common ground—we all must—but sometimes you have to take a stand on sacred ground."[20] In this, Davis was echoing top congressional Democrat Nancy Pelosi, who earlier had referred to abortion as "sacred ground." While Pelosi called Gosnell's crimes "reprehensible," when a reporter asked her "what's the moral difference" between what Gosnell did to babies born alive and aborting those same infants moments before birth, Pelosi refused to answer, resorting instead to one of her trademark insults to reporters: "I'm not going to have this conversation with you because you obviously have an agenda. You're not interested in having an answer."[21]

To recap: That which just a month earlier had been universally condemned as "monstrous," "sickening," "revolting," and deserving of multiple first-degree murder convictions, had now mysteriously become christened as "sacred ground."

But that was just the beginning. After Davis's filibuster foiled the will of the majority in the Texas legislature, Gov. Rick Perry, vowing his state would not succumb to mob rule, called for a special session the following month to pass the bill into law.

What greeted the new legislative session in July was unprecedented. Proabortion demonstrations can be hostile, but this was downright freakish.

While a pro-life speaker offered her public testimony celebrating life, and others sang "Amazing Grace," supporters of late-term abortion attempted to drown out the pro-lifers' hymn-singing by repeatedly chanting, "Hail Satan!" as multiple videos document.[22]

Then police confiscated bricks, tampons, pads, condoms, urine, and feces that proabortion protestors allegedly intended to throw at pro-life lawmakers before the final vote on the late-term abortion ban. The *Texas Tribune* described the surreal scene at the state capital and what the Texas Department of Public Safety (DPS) was forced to deal with:

> DPS officials have been searching bags before letting people into the gallery, requiring them to throw away paper goods such as magazines, receipts, feminine pads and tampons. One DPS officer said authorities had been instructed by the Senate's sergeant at arms to confiscate anything that could be thrown from the gallery at senators on the floor. She said they had already found objects such as bricks, paint and glitter in bags.
>
> . . . DPS officers have thus far discovered one jar suspected to contain urine, 18 jars suspected to contain feces, and three bottles suspected to contain paint. All of these items—as well as significant quantities of feminine hygiene products, glitter and confetti possessed by individuals—were required to be discarded; otherwise those individuals were denied entry into the gallery.[23]

Is it a coincidence—just weeks after the nation's consciousness was penetrated by the searing realization that the cherished magic line between abortion and murdering babies doesn't actually exist—that those desperately clinging to such delusions would grow even more frenzied as the truth tended to awaken the American mind? So frenzied that, just a few months later, a Wendy Davis supporter would throw a lit Molotov cocktail at a group of Christian pro-life women praying outside Austin's Planned Parenthood?[24]

Make no mistake: the truth about abortion *is* dawning—not just due to the Gosnell trial, of course. But because of the relentless advances in medical science, prenatal care, and imaging technology such as ultrasound, and because of the tireless work of pro-life groups and individuals continually shining a light on the very dark reality of abortion and providing help to desperate women in need of genuine love and support—and because such monumental denial must ultimately, sooner or later, give way to truth.

The shell of denial is cracking. During the 1990s, more Americans considered themselves pro-choice than pro-life by a huge, twenty-point margin, but today those numbers have largely reversed. As of 2013, repeated Gallup polling showed more Americans identifying as pro-life than pro-choice,[25] and in 2014, a nationwide CNN poll showed Americans continuing to trend pro-life, with 58 percent—almost three in five—espousing pro-life views—i.e., that abortion should be legal under "few" or "no" circumstances. Only 40 percent of Americans say abortion should be "always" or "mostly" legal.[26] Likewise, a quarter century ago, in 1991 there were 2,176 surgical abortion clinics in the United States. Today, *fully three-quarters of them are gone,* with only 551 remaining (medication-only facilities are down as well), and the decline has accelerated in recent years.[27]

All of which demonstrates that when long-suppressed truth is effectively brought out into the sunlight—shining and sparkling for all to see—some people are warmed, comforted, renewed, and liberated by it. Others, unfortunately, feel compelled to run away from the light, or worse, attempt to put it out, like the pro-choice woman who lobbed the firebomb from her car at the women praying in Austin.

Such people are lost in a very bad dream. As Operation Rescue president Troy Newman put it, even a peaceful prayer vigil can sometimes enrage abortion advocates because "it reminds them of the horrible day they took the life of their child."[28]

Indeed, let's remember this is a national tragedy: Tens of millions of American women have undergone abortions, many of them severely traumatized, some physically, but millions mentally, emotionally, and spiritually. Some, in great pain and remorse, face up to what they did and seek forgiveness and healing—and find it from a kind and merciful God. Others, for whatever reasons, go into total denial and defend—sometimes maniacally—what they did, because facing it honestly is not yet something they're prepared to do.

WHO WILL RUN THE ASYLUM?

Those in the grip of delusion generally regard those who are not (that is, those who see through the first group's delusion) as themselves delusional. This ongoing battle, with each side regarding the other as dangerous to society, prompts an important concern about America's future under continued progressive-left leadership.

In chapter 1, we saw how the Obama Department of Homeland Security singled out conservatives, pro-lifers, constitutionalists, critics of illegal immigration, and returning war veterans as potentially violent, "right-wing extremists." And peaceful Tea Party folks were accused by left-wing media pundits of acting like "terrorists," "vampires," "zombies," and "cannibals."[29]

Welcome to the history of the Far Left, wherein those who through monumental deceit have conspired to transform Judeo-Christian America, upend her Constitution, and impose an alien new system of governance and morality upon her, have the audacity to accuse the traditionally minded American middle class, which just wants its country back, of being ignorant, deranged, and dangerous.

Psychologists call this "projection," where one person or group literally projects its own wrongs onto another. Thus, for decades, the left—which throughout the 1900s gave the world its bloodiest century in history—has been busy denouncing and "diagnosing" conservatives and Christians. In the Soviet Union, this practice was integral to the ongoing operation of the communist state. Dissidents—the sanest and most courageous people in the country—were confined to psychiatric hospitals for "treatment." If you had a problem with communism, you were mentally ill and diagnosed with made-up conditions like "philosophical intoxication" and "sluggish schizophrenia."[30]

A few of the more well-known "inmates" confined in such mental hospitals included poet Joseph Brodsky and political dissidents Vladimir Bukovsky and Natan Sharansky. As Bukovsky and coauthor Semyon Gluzman later affirmed in *A Manual on Psychiatry for Dissidents*, "the Soviet use of psychiatry as a punitive means is based upon the deliberate interpretation of dissent . . . as a psychiatric problem."[31]

In the United States, the left's political manipulation of psychiatry has been far more subtle—so far. As noted earlier, the homosexual activist movement, an outgrowth of the left, succeeded in the 1970s in pressuring the American Psychiatric Association to remove homosexuality from its official list of disorders, and more recently, to de-pathologize transgender identity disorder. At the same time, we are seeing increasing demonization and, yes, "diagnosing" of conservatives. Is the groundwork being laid for branding American "dissidents"—those dissenting from the immoral and totalitarian drift of today's government and culture—as mentally ill?

Consider: Those who complain their once-great country is being overrun with illegal immigrants are branded "xenophobic," a pathologizing label implying one has a phobia (a mental disorder). Opponents of radically redefining marriage are "homophobic," a made-up pathologizing label. Those objecting to Islamist subversion of the United States are "Islamophobic," another made-up pathologizing label. Same with "biphobia," for people who don't like to be around bisexuals, and "transphobia," for people uncomfortable around transgendered people.

Those questioning "catastrophic man-caused global warming" are "climate-change deniers," an epithet designed to convey not merely pathological denial, but moral equivalence to "Holocaust deniers"—in other words, dangerous derangement. Climate expert Marc Morano, former communications director for the Senate Environment and Public Works Committee, has reported on "a whole slew of new 'research' on conservatives' and global warming skeptics' 'brains.'"

> First off, environment and sociology Prof. Kari Norgaard's new study claims skeptics of man-made global warming fears should be "treated" for their skepticism. . . . Prof. Norgaard's concept of "treating" those who do not follow the current day's political or social orthodoxy is, frighteningly, not new. A quick look at the 20th century totalitarian super-states reveals many similar impulses. It's even more chilling that there is a whole new movement afoot by the promoters of man-made global warming theory to intimidate climate skeptics by using new brain "research."

Other researchers have attempted to tie conservatism (which is identified with the highest number of climate skeptics) to "low brainpower."[32]

Meanwhile, the left-dominated social sciences are also busily accumulating "evidence" that conservatives are the crazy ones, like the study by University College London, which "suggests that conservative brains are structured differently than the brains of other people. . . . Specifically, the research shows that people with conservative tendencies have a larger amygdala and a smaller anterior cingulate than other people. The amygdala—typically thought of as the 'primitive brain'—is responsible for reflexive impulses, like fear."[33]

Or this UC–Berkeley News item claiming:

> Four researchers who culled through 50 years of research literature about the psychology of conservatism report that at the core of political conservatism is the resistance to change and a tolerance for inequality, and that some of the common psychological factors linked to political conservatism include: Fear and aggression; Dogmatism and intolerance of ambiguity; Uncertainty avoidance; Need for cognitive closure; and Terror management.[34]

Ironically, in contrast with such self-serving nonsense (such as conservatives having larger "primitive brain" parts than normal people) is actual objective research suggesting those on the political left are considerably more plagued with mental illness than those on the right.

In an extensive series of surveys involving more than four thousand interviews conducted over the course of four years, Gallup pollsters found that Republicans had "significantly" better mental health than Democrats, with Independents ranking in between the two parties.[35]

"One could be quick to assume," says Gallup's analysis, "that these differences [in mental health] are based on the underlying demographic and socioeconomic patterns related to party identification in America today," noting that "men, those with higher incomes, those with higher education levels, and whites are more likely than others to report excellent mental health. Some of these patterns describe characteristics of Republicans, of course." However, Gallup revealed, "an analysis of the relationship between party identification and self-reported excellent mental health within various categories of age, gender, church attendance, income, education, and other variables shows that the basic pattern persists regardless of these characteristics. In other words, party identification appears to have an independent effect on mental health even when each of these is controlled for."[36]

Likewise, a survey commissioned by the big news-and-entertainment website BuzzFeed found that Democrats suffered mental illness notably more than Republicans in almost every category:

> Does being a Democrat—or a Republican—mean you're more prone to depression, anxiety, or other mental ailments? To find out, BuzzFeed partnered with SurveyMonkey [which provides data collection and analysis for Facebook, Virgin America, Samsung and others] to ask Americans about their political affiliation and whether or not they'd ever been diagnosed with any of 12 mental health conditions and learning disabilities. SurveyMonkey Audience conducted the online survey exclusively for BuzzFeed, gathering a randomly selected, nationally representative sample of 1,117 people.

Key survey results, which showed that Democrats were roughly *twice as likely* to have been diagnosed with a mental disorder as Republicans, included: post-traumatic stress disorder (Democrats 7.95 percent, Republicans 3.97 percent), ADD/ADHD (Democrats 9.13 percent, Republicans 3.97 percent), anxiety (Democrats 20.84 percent, Republicans 10.26 percent), depression (Democrats 34.43 percent, Republicans 23.51 percent).

In fact, in every category polled—dyslexia, ADD/ADHD, Asperger's/autism, depression, anxiety, OCD, bipolar disorder, schizophrenia, PTSD, narcissistic personality disorder, anorexia, and bulimia—Democrats reported higher incidences than Republicans, except for dyslexia.[37]

Nevertheless, the field of psychology is well documented as being dominated by the liberal left,[38] as are America's news and entertainment media, schools and colleges, and even many of her churches. And of course, under Obama, the US government has seen fit to target "dissidents" in a variety of ways, from Homeland Security profiling conservatives as potential "extremists," to the IRS notoriously discriminating against Tea Party groups, to the legal prosecution of Christians for declining to participate in homosexual wedding ceremonies. How big a leap might it be from these forms of persecution to "diagnosing" members of the same groups as "mentally ill," "disordered," or "impaired"? (That would certainly be a handy way to deny firearms ownership to such newly minted "mental-health risks.")

Considering all the past abuses of psychiatry by governments and politically influenced psychiatric establishments, this possibility bears watching, as traditional-minded Americans—the flag-flying, hard-working, Bible-believing folk who built this nation—find themselves increasingly demonized by a lawless government and godless culture, and branded as everything from bigots to "right-wing extremists" to mentally ill.

It's enough to drive you crazy.

Thus, the next chapter will focus on how we can stay sane, healthy, independent, faithful, and endlessly resilient—no matter *what* chaos may be pressing in on us from all sides—and save our country in the process.

11

FREEDOM

Every religious idea, every idea of God, even flirting with the idea of God, is unutterable vileness . . . of the most dangerous kind, contagion of the most abominable kind. Millions of sins, filthy deeds, acts of violence and physical contagions . . . are far less dangerous than the subtle, spiritual idea of God.

—VLADIMIR LENIN, 1913[1]

I n this book, we have surveyed the political and cultural left's hundred-year war on Judeo-Christian America. We've explored not only the outrageous tactics of the lawless Obama presidency, which has plunged America into chaos on virtually every front, but a societal culture that descends lower every year, often in ways so bizarre and degrading that many Americans never imagined such depths existed.

Even more chilling, we've taken a close look at the severe toll this relentless campaign has taken on the American mind and soul.

Our nation is now home to large numbers of people who unashamedly oppose America's core values (polls show millennials now favor socialism over capitalism[2] and are rapidly rejecting Christianity),[3] or are so broken they rely on legal or illegal mind-altering substances, or embrace total sexual anarchy with all its attendant diseases and other grim consequences, or suffer from a multiplicity of addictions and mental disorders. We are likewise faced with tens of millions of rudderless, government-dependent, "low-information" Americans, as well as untold additional millions of aliens, legal and illegal, flooding into our country—the vast majority favoring large, liberal-left government,[4] and many with no love for America and no intent to assimilate or adopt her values.[5]

I say, "even more chilling" because, while a deluded president can be replaced at the next election, one cannot replace a deluded population so easily.

In the face of all these problems, what can we as Americans do, both to redeem our country and to preserve ourselves and our families—body, mind, and spirit?

Unfortunately, when it comes to engaging politics and culture, including even the simplest and most sacred civic act of all, voting, tens of millions of Americans have already checked out.

Sen. Ted Cruz, announcing his 2016 presidential candidacy to a huge crowd at Liberty University, made this shocking statement: "Today roughly half of born-again Christians aren't voting. They're staying home." He added, wistfully, "Imagine, instead, millions of people of faith all across America coming out to the polls and voting our values."[6]

PolitiFact did its own analysis and concluded that about 42 percent of evangelical Christians stay home on Election Day. Since more than 70 percent of Americans self-identify as Christian, and more than 25 percent—one in four—as evangelical (or "born-again"),[7] that means we're talking about *tens of millions of Americans.* These are people who claim to share the Christian values of the nation's founders—values treasured by the vast majority of the brave souls who have fought, bled, and died to preserve America's freedoms—and yet can't find it in themselves to fill out a ballot and vote their values on Election Day.[8]

Why?

Don't say "there's not a dime's worth of difference between the two parties." Today's Far-Left Democratic Party (there are almost no more old-time "moderate Democrats" in Washington in the age of Obama) favors laws and policies that literally promote the killing of viable, late-term, unborn children and the de facto criminalization of Christianity. The Republican Party stands squarely in opposition. Today's Democratic Party is light-years to the left of the party of President John F. Kennedy, who went eyeball-to-eyeball with maniacal Soviet leader Nikita Khrushchev and brought the civilization-threatening Cuban missile crisis to an end. In stark contrast to Obama, Kennedy pledged to give Americans "an across-the-board reduction in personal and corporate income tax rates" to "reduce the burden on private income and the deterrents to private initiative."[9] After Kennedy was assassinated, the massive tax cuts he promised were enacted, resulting in a boom in both the private economy and federal tax revenues for the rest of the decade.

While the party of Obama has little in common with that of JFK, for a better comparison, try exploring the Communist Party USA's website (CPUSA.org), and you'll be stunned at the resemblance between it and today's Democratic Party. You might also take a moment to thoughtfully reflect on the Democrats' candidates who in recent decades were either elected, or nearly elected, as president: Bill Clinton, a serial sexual predator; Al Gore, by many accounts a raving lunatic; John Kerry, who betrayed his fellow Vietnam vets and his country;[10] Barack Obama, a deceitful, America-hating, Far-Left radical; and Hillary Clinton, accurately described by Pulitzer-winning *New York Times* columnist and Presidential Medal of Freedom recipient William Safire as "a congenital liar."[11]

Whatever the Republicans' shortcomings—and they are substantial and sometimes exasperating, on occasion even treacherous—as a whole they are still much closer to the worldview and moral sensibilities of "real America" than today's wantonly left-wing Democratic Party.

In any event, taking the trouble to vote for a president who *isn't* a serial sex predator or Marxist revolutionary seems pretty reasonable for a "born-again Christian," doesn't it?

So, how exactly do tens of millions of American Christians justify being AWOL on Election Day? Their most common rationales: (1) their particular church denomination tells them they are "citizens of heaven" or "not part of this world" and therefore don't need to vote; (2) they're so upset by government corruption they feel contaminated just reading and hearing about it; (3) they believe God will determine who leads America without their help; (4) they believe church and state should be "separate"; (5) they believe their focus should be the gospel, not politics; and finally, underlying all these reasons, (6) they've given up hope of any good ever coming out of Washington, regardless of who is elected.[12] Indeed, many nonvoters are so disillusioned by the lies and hypocrisy dominating politics that they have given up hope and walked away.

Bingo. That's precisely what the Alinsky-left wants, as it serves only to advance and strengthen the anti-Christian transformation of America. There must be another way.

HOPE AND CHANGE

Let's acknowledge a few key realities. First, there is still hope for America.

After all, even if something like half the country has become either indoctrinated, or corrupted, or hopelessly dependent on a nanny state, what about the other half? What about the tens of millions of right-thinking Americans who *haven't* abandoned their nation's founding values—the soldiers and veterans; the hardworking farmers, ranchers, business-owners, and entrepreneurs; the grateful immigrants who came with nothing and achieved the American dream; the inventors and visionaries; and most important, the millions of patriotic citizens who love their country, its history, and its values, as well as the God who blessed them with it? A lot of them are still here!

The American glass is still half-full. However egregiously Obama and the Far Left have transformed America, their efforts have not yet succeeded in transforming all *Americans*.

For every Barack Obama, weaned on bitter resentment toward America's perceived faults and full of radical zeal to impose socialist "change," there's a Ben Carson. Born in poverty, betrayed by a bigamist father (just as Obama was), raised by a mother with a third-grade education, Carson somehow rose above angry victimhood to become a world-famous neurosurgeon, philanthropist, presidential candidate, and Christian role model. And while race-baiting rabble-rousers shamelessly stir up violence and vengeance at every opportunity, we beheld the families of the nine victims murdered in the Charleston, South Carolina, church, who chose to freely and publicly forgive the killer, not wishing to live their lives in hatred and bitterness. This is the real America.

Starkly antithetical to Obama's vision, real America resists utopian change and neutralizes it in uniquely American ways.

For example, after each mass shooting during his presidency—from Sandy Hook to the Aurora movie theater to Emanuel AME Church—Obama has exploited the tragedy in hopes of imposing far-reaching new gun-control measures. In response, freedom-loving Americans' purchases of guns and ammunition have exploded, with firearms manufacturing and sales being among the few business sectors to thrive under Obama.[13] Remember also when Obama tried to ban the sale of high-capacity "assault rifle" magazines (under the apparent belief that a homeowner defending his family against multiple armed invaders couldn't possibly need more than ten rounds total, because he presumably would hit every aggressor with his very first shot, just as in the movies)? In a quintessentially American response, a Texas college student posted online, for free download, instructions on how anyone can *make* his or her own totally functional thirty-round AR-15 magazines at home, using a 3D printer.[14]

Likewise, in response to a breathtakingly biased news media that essentially hoodwinked voters into electing Obama, there's been rapid growth in a more honest, reality-based, pro-American alternative press. Fox News continually crushes its left-leaning cable competitors,[15] talk radio is dominated by conservatives, and a growing number of enormously popular online media organizations (one of the biggest being WND, where I'm honored to serve as managing editor) shine a powerful, cleansing light on the ongoing political and culture wars.

Columnist Don Feder, taking stock of the forces currently

championing traditional American values, concludes that grassroots fervor has "never been stronger":

> Those with a passionate commitment to life, marriage, border security, Second Amendment rights, the free market and fighting jihad are energized and mobilized. The National Rifle Association has 4.5 million members—compared to 300,000 for [the left-wing] People for the American Way. The National Right to Life Committee has more than 3,000 chapters.
>
> Rush Limbaugh has a weekly audience of 13.25 million. Sean Hannity has 12.5 million. There is 7 million each for The Glenn Beck Program and The Mark Levin Show, and 5.25 million for The Savage Nation. The only liberal talk-show in Talkers magazine's list of most-listened-to radio programs is Thom Hartman, with a weekly audience of 2 million.

And "MSNBC," adds Feder, "is moving its studios to a packing crate."[16]

These efforts and many others are part of an ongoing, organic movement to reverse what Marxist theorist Antonio Gramsci called the left's "long march" through America's institutions—only this time around, with the intent of *taking back,* one by one, the foundational building blocks of a renewed Judeo-Christian America.

Regarding my frequent references to "Judeo-Christian values" (*Judeo,* Old Testament, *Christian,* New Testament)—in other words, biblical values—there's a good reason "Judeo-Christian" principles have been singularly successful in the laboratory of world history. They are, quite literally, reflective of God's mind and laws, encouraging the good side of human nature and restraining the bad. In exactly the same way (but in the *opposite direction*), Marxism-socialism and the rest of the cultural left agenda are based on elevating and glorifying everything ignoble about human nature.

Consider: The tenth commandment condemns envy ("Thou shalt not covet"), yet socialism, which, as noted earlier, Churchill identified as "the gospel of envy,"[17] is based on it. Marxism is inherently atheistic because utopian government is a jealous god that countenances worship of no other (violating the first commandment). It intentionally undermines the nuclear family (fifth commandment), has given us by far the greatest mass-murder in world history (sixth commandment), promotes adultery and every form of sexual immorality (seventh commandment), depends on stealing the fruits of others' labor (eighth commandment), and can be implemented only with the aid of massive deception (ninth commandment).

Is it any wonder a society rooted in Judeo-Christian values produces more clear-thinking, moral, competent people than a society based on Marxism, which breeds dependence, envy, blame, theft, sloth, immorality, and violence?

So let's get to it. With the war over America's future raging, what can we do to bring about the best outcome and redeem our great nation?

There are many bold steps—most of them obvious to the non-brainwashed—that need to be taken on a national level, including:

Elect a president who loves America and her Constitution, and who as commander-in-chief will be respected by friends and feared by enemies; stop the progressive abuse and corruption of America's election system; secure the nation's borders and halt rampant illegal immigration; reduce the size of government to affordable, constitutional levels; pass a Human Life Amendment to the Constitution, and another one overruling the Supreme Court's judicial re-definition of marriage; abolish the IRS and replace the current convoluted, punitive tax system with a "flat tax" (uniform rate) or "fair tax" (national sales tax); replace Obamacare with enlightened market-based reforms; abolish the Federal Reserve and reinstitute sound constitutional money, restoring the world's trust in, and reliance upon, the U.S. dollar as global reserve currency; set America's energy sector free to make us energy-independent; keep America's military the strongest, best-trained, and best-equipped in the world; support Israel; abandon political correctness; implement school choice; stop trying to elevate the poor by robbing the rich; embrace Martin Luther King's ideal of a truly color-blind America; stop taxing, regulating, and litigating businesses to death; dare to say no to LGBT social revolutionaries; and end the insane war on Christianity in America.

Of course, while measures like these and others are desperately needed, most are not likely to be implemented anytime soon. Much has to change first.

What, then, can we do right now, on an individual level? Here are a few things to consider:

Besides fulfilling your sacred duty as American citizens to vote for right-thinking public servants who honor God and the Constitution— in other words, people who would implement the types of changes outlined above—consider taking your precious children out of the government indoctrination centers called "public schools" and either homeschooling them or enrolling them in a private school compatible with your values. Remember Lincoln's warning, "The philosophy of the schoolroom in one generation is the philosophy of government in the next"—which is exactly how we got the government we have today!

Become as self-sufficient and independent of government and "the system" as you can. Prepping is good; you're not a nut to "prepare for the worst and live for the best." The world is unstable; so each of us needs to be stable.

Protect your children—and yourself—from today's corrupting, lying, sex-drenched popular culture, which unfortunately is full of people dedicated to tearing down the values you hold dear.

Exercise your Second Amendment right to keep and bear arms, something I emphasize because approximately 300 million privately owned firearms in the hands of free Americans[18] serves as a powerful psychological restraint on out-of-control, power-mad government.

Live a clean life, freely admit when you're wrong, have faith in a great and merciful God, and pray. Paul the Apostle advises that we "pray without ceasing,"[19] and the Old Testament includes a stirring promise from the Almighty: "If my people, which are called by my name, shall humble themselves, and pray, and seek my face, and turn from their wicked ways; then will I hear from heaven, and will forgive their sin, and will heal their land."[20]

You may want to relocate. As we saw in chapter 6, where you live can exert a profound influence on your life. In fact, depending on how bad things get, we could see a trend toward what I call "de facto secession." By *de facto* I mean that actual, legal secession is unlikely simply because the national government won't allow it. We fought a civil war over that issue, and the secessionists lost, costing more than 600,000 lives (and recent research shows the total dead were probably closer to 750,000).[21]

The Internet can play a major role here, facilitating people of like mind finding each other and, if they wish, moving to a common geographic location. During the mid-1800s the Mormons, due to serious persecution, moved en masse to Utah, which became a much friendlier place for them to live.

Today, a state backed by the overwhelming support of a like-minded population can stand up for its Tenth Amendment rights and say no to an overreaching federal government. The feds will probably sue—after all, such insubordination sets a bad example for other states—but so what? Lawsuits can take years, and even if the state loses, it can regroup and find new ways to assert its constitutional autonomy. Ultimately, Washington, preoccupied with genuine problems of its own making (like civil unrest, economic chaos, and terrorism), may just write off the rebel state with all its "wingnuts" and "bitter clingers" and leave it alone. This scenario is, in fact, already playing out in various ways across the country, with dozens of legislative and judicial fights in progress between independent-minded states and the federal government.[22] In the future, the individual states may well hold the key to American freedom.

Another trend to watch for: as the marginalization and legal harassment of Christians becomes even more pronounced in America, we will almost surely see a major rise in civil disobedience. This is true especially since the Supreme Court's five-to-four "gay marriage" ruling, which Texas Attorney General Ken Paxton immediately condemned as "lawless" while advising state workers how to avoid compliance,[23] and which Supreme Court Justice Antonin Scalia described as a "judicial Putsch," calling the liberal-dominated court nothing short of a "threat to American democracy."[24]

On the day of the high court's ruling, the National Organization for Marriage announced its intended non-compliance with the court's "completely illegitimate" decision:

> In his "Letter from a Birmingham Jail," Dr. Martin Luther King discussed the moral importance of disobeying unjust laws, which we submit applies equally to unjust Supreme Court decisions. Dr. King evoked the teaching of St. Thomas Aquinas that an unjust law or decision is one that is "a human law that is not rooted in eternal law or natural law." Today's decision of the Supreme Court lacks both constitutional and moral authority. There is no eternal or natural law that allows for marriage to be redefined. [25]

And evangelical leader Dr. James Dobson voiced his agreement that conscientious Christians have been thrust into an era of inevitable civil disobedience, adding that he "will not . . . bend to any rule purporting to force us to bless immoral sexual partnerships [or] treat them as marriages."[26]

Months earlier, Dobson had similarly announced he would not contribute to Obamacare's controversial abortion insurance surcharge: "To pay one cent for the killing of babies is egregious to me, and I will do all I can to correct a government that lies to me about its intentions and then tries to coerce my acquiescence with extortion. It would be a violation of my most deeply held convictions to disobey what I consider to be the principles in Scripture. The Creator will not hold us guiltless if we turn a deaf ear to the cries of His innocent babies. So come and get me if you must, Mr. President. I will not bow before your wicked regulation."[27]

If the beloved, aging Dr. Dobson and other thought leaders are moving in the direction of civil disobedience, rest assured others will follow, just as dozens of bakers, photographers, florists, bed-and-breakfast owners, and other Christian businesspeople, for refusing on religious grounds to personally celebrate and participate in homosexual weddings, have already sacrificed much. As Ronald Reagan frequently said, freedom isn't free.

In every era, unconstitutional laws that violate core liberties and freedom of conscience, or result in harm to innocents, have a way of inspiring what Mahatma Gandhi called "non-violent non-coopera- tion."[28] During the 1960s civil rights movement, peaceful civil disobe- dience awakened the conscience of millions and transformed America's attitudes and laws regarding segregation in a single generation.

Let us pause now and consider something even more fundamental than all the preceding. Before we can help our country, or even our com- munities or families, we need to take personal stock of ourselves. Too many of us, as this book has documented, are simply overwhelmed by the stress and chaos of living in today's world. So let's briefly explore, as Kipling put it at the outset of his classic poem "If," how you can "keep your head when all about you are losing theirs and blaming it on you."[29]

When it comes to overcoming stress and staying healthy, physically, mentally, and spiritually, there are, of course, many worthy actions to consider. But there are three absolutely paramount factors we ignore at our peril: diet, exercise, and personal time for spiritual growth. Let's take a fresh look at each.

THE KEY TO EATING RIGHT

"Health is 90 percent diet related," says Lee Heib, MD, past president of the Association of American Physicians and Surgeons and an ortho- pedic surgeon who served at Camp Lejeune, North Carolina. And "the first step in eating correctly," the good doctor advises, "is to absolutely forget any government recommendation you have ever heard about what to eat."[30]

Heib is *not* talking about Michelle Obama's infamous school- lunch recommendations that have ignited near-universal rebellion among high-schoolers,[31] but rather the federal government's official Dietary Guidelines Advisory Committee. To cite just one example, the committee recently "decided to drop its caution about eating choles-terol-laden food, a move that could undo almost 40 years of government warnings about its consumption," according to the *Washington Post.*[32]

That's right. After scaring Americans to death about eating eggs for four decades, the government experts have suddenly realized, the *Post* reports, that "eating foods high in cholesterol may *not* significantly affect the level of cholesterol in the blood or increase the risk of heart disease."

At the same time, dozens of congressmen jumped all over the feds' diet-recommending panel for allegedly being motivated not by science, but "environmental" politics, in determining what Americans should eat!

Speaking for seventy-one members of Congress, Rep. Tim Huelskamp, R-KS, said, "We are disappointed with reports from observers that the approach of the 2015 [Dietary Guidelines Advisory Committee] suggests studies were either selected or excluded to sup-port pre-determined conclusions. . . . [The] recommendation on lean red meat directly contradicts years of peer-reviewed scientific research on the benefits of lean red meat as a high quality source of protein in a healthy diet."

It seems the government panel called for Americans to eat less meat, "in part, because of meat production's impact on the environment," reported *Roll Call,* prompting six dozen congressmen to condemn this "latest attempt by the administration to use federal agencies to push the president's political agenda."[33]

Fortunately, there is plenty of enlightened, state-of-the-art research *not* influenced by politics or ideology, and the resulting dietary wisdom can be boiled down to some key points: Eat a variety of fresh, natural foods, especially vegetables and fruits and particularly lots of enzyme-rich raw foods. Nuts are good. Fish (try for wild-caught) and chicken (antibiotic-free) are fine; so is red meat in moderation (grass-fed/no hormones is best); same with dairy (milk, especially in cultured form, like yogurt or kefir, and butter—not margarine). In general, buy natural/ organic whenever possible.

"Eggs are a nearly perfect human food," says Heib, but "try to get omega-3 eggs or eggs from free-range chickens." What about oils? Stick with butter, olive oil, coconut, palm, and fish oils (naturally occurring omega-3 oils), she advises. And "avoid all soda pop."

There's much more, of course, and this rapid-fire summary just skims the surface of an enormously important subject. "Past generations suffered from scarcity of food," observes Heib, "but the food they did eat was real and compatible with the human body's genetic blueprint."

Noting the large role diet plays in "the diseases of modern civilization—diabetes, stroke, heart disease, and cancer," Heib says the problem "is not just overeating. It is eating substances that look like food, but in reality are like Frankenstein—artificial, manmade, and unholy creations that even bacteria will avoid." To reach and maintain optimal health, she concludes, "we need to consciously reestablish the eating patterns of our ancestors."[34]

It would benefit readers greatly to do a little research of their own. Heib's book, *Surviving the Medical Meltdown: Your Guide to Living Through the Disaster of Obamacare,* has a comprehensive chapter on diet. I also suggest Sally Fallon's classic work, *Nourishing Traditions: The Cookbook that Challenges Politically Correct Nutrition and the Diet Dictocrats* and Jordan Rubin's *The Maker's Diet.* Also, check out the "Dietary Guidelines" page at the Westin A. Price Foundation website (WestonAPrice.org).[35]

"THE RESTORATIVE POWER OF EXERCISE"

Exercise not only helps keep our hearts (and the rest of us) healthy, it confers untold benefits, tangible and intangible. And as the world-famous Mayo Clinic puts it, "Exercise in almost any form can act as a stress reliever":

> Physical activity helps bump up the production of your brain's feel-good neurotransmitters, called endorphins. Although this function is often referred to as a runner's high, a rousing game of tennis or a nature hike also can contribute to this same feeling.

It's meditation in motion. After a fast-paced game of racquetball or several laps in the pool, you'll often find that you've forgotten the day's irritations and concentrated only on your body's movements.

As you begin to regularly shed your daily tensions through movement and physical activity, you may find that this focus on a single task, and the resulting energy and optimism, can help you remain calm and clear in everything you do.

It improves your mood. Regular exercise can increase self-confidence, it can relax you, and it can lower the symptoms associated with mild depression and anxiety. Exercise can also improve your sleep, which is often disrupted by stress, depression and anxiety.[36]

There's more. According to the experts at *Harvard Men's Health Watch*, "Aerobic exercise is the key for your head, just as it is for your heart. It has a unique capacity to exhilarate and relax, to provide stimulation and calm, to counter depression and dissipate stress." Harvard's medical team adds:

> Endurance athletes commonly experience the restorative power of exercise, and this has been verified in clinical trials that have used exercise to treat anxiety and depression. How can exercise contend with problems as difficult as anxiety and depression? There are several explanations, some chemical, others behavioral. The mental benefits of aerobic exercise have a neurochemical basis. Exercise reduces levels of the body's stress hormones, such as adrenaline and cortisol. It also stimulates the production of endorphins, the body's natural painkillers and mood elevators.[37]

Personally, I walk. Not in a sweaty workout center, breathing stale air with hip-hop blaring in my ears, but a good, long, brisk walk out in nature, several times a week, rain or shine, just looking at what's there—observing, not necessarily thinking about anything in particular, just staying in neutral. That's when many interesting and valuable ideas and insights occur. The mind sorts itself out; stresses dissipate; heart, lungs, muscles, and other things get exercised; and a general feeling of energy and well-being emerges. It's a tremendously good and necessary habit on many levels.

I'm no exercise expert, but our friend Chuck Norris is, and I'm glad to say the six-time world karate champion and reputed "world's toughest man" is offering much the same advice I am:

> Though the current national exercise base line is 150 minutes a week of moderate physical activity, many experts are suggesting that much more is needed to achieve optimal benefits. According to two studies recently published in JAMA Internal Medicine involving more than a half-million people, those who exercised 450 minutes a week (which comes out to about an hour each day) were 39 percent less likely to die prematurely. Achieving this level of activity does not require a gym membership or a personal trainer. You can get the benefit with a mix of vigorous to moderate actions, including taking a brisk walk. My strong recommendation is that you direct it toward nature.
>
> I know I have been hitting this "call to the wild" pretty hard recently, but with reason. In multiple studies of exercise behavior, it has been found that one of the most reliable indicators of whether people will continue to exercise is that they find exercise satisfying. Outdoor exercise has been shown to contribute to increased energy and revitalization—along with decreased anger, depression and tension—when compared with indoor exercise, and participants enjoy their workouts more and are likelier to stay with them. Researchers believe that our state of mindfulness during exercise, which they define simply as awareness of what is happening in the moment, affects the exercise. It can alter our sense of satisfaction. People seem to find more pleasure in movement when it occurs outdoors.[38]

Enough said. As Nike says, "Just do it."

DAY OF REST

From the Hebrew *Shabbath*—literally "day of rest"—the idea of taking one day in seven to rest from work and turn one's attention to higher things goes back thousands of years—to Moses and the Ten Commandments, the fourth being to "Remember the sabbath day, to keep it holy."

Whether our initial impetus for this observance is religious or merely practical (that is, you're tired and need to rest and unwind after working all week), there is a great deal of good in this practice, not all of it obvious. I'll let Dennis Prager, the insightful columnist/radio talker, and a religious Jew, explain why cultivating this simple habit "may well be the best single thing you can do—that you are probably not doing now—to improve the quality of your life, your family's life and, ultimately, the life of our society."

To begin with, notes Prager, "Many people—even among those who revere the Ten Commandments—do not think that the fourth commandment, the Sabbath Day, is particularly important, let alone binding. Once you understand it, however, you will recognize how both life-changing and world-changing it is."

For one thing, he explains, "No matter how materially poor we may be, at least on the Sabbath Day, we are not just material beings. We are elevated. Recall that the commandment tells us to keep the day holy, not merely not to work." Therefore, regardless of our circumstances, "we must remind ourselves at least one day a week that we are sacred beings; we have a soul to feed, not just a body." Furthermore, says Prager:

> In the biblical view, unless necessary for survival, people who choose to work seven days a week are essentially slaves—slaves to work or perhaps to money, but slaves nonetheless. The millionaire who works seven days a week is simply a rich slave.
>
> The Sabbath almost singlehandedly creates and strengthens family ties and friendships. When a person takes off from work one day every week, that day almost inevitably becomes a day spent with other people—namely, family and/or friends. It has similar positive effects on marriages."

Here's another amazing benefit: "Just as faith in God brings people to the Sabbath," notes Prager, "observing the Sabbath brings people to faith in God. In our secularized modern societies, very few activities bring people to a relationship with God as effectively as devoting a day each week to the spiritual, not just the material."

That, he concludes, is "why the Sabbath is one of the Ten Commandments," adding that "those who have it in their lives are often happier, with richer family lives, more serenity, a community of friends, and, yes, are even healthier."[39]

While I personally observe the Sabbath, I admit I don't do so in a rigid and ceremonial way. I just appreciate the day off, read the Bible and perhaps other religious books, catch up on rest, maybe watch a good movie or visit with family and friends, take a long walk—and don't work. Jesus, a Torah-observant Jew, nevertheless repeatedly ran afoul of the inflexibly legalistic religious authorities of his day. He rebuked them for absurdly complaining when he healed people on the Sabbath and when his disciples walked through a cornfield on the Sabbath, picking ears of corn to eat. Pointing out that King David had done much the same thing, Jesus told the Pharisees to get their priorities straight, declaring, "The sabbath was made for man, and not man for the sabbath."[40]

WHAT ABOUT MEDITATION?

Today it seems virtually every stress expert, doctor, hospital, and health organization advocates meditation for its proven benefits, like reduced stress, increased focus, and lowered blood pressure.[41]

Yet, admits ABC News anchor Dan Harris in his No. 1 *New York Times* best seller, *10% Happier: How I Tamed the Voice in My Head, Reduced Stress Without Losing My Edge, and Found Self-Help That Actually Works,* "Meditation suffers from a towering PR problem, largely because its most prominent proponents talk as if they have a perpetual pan flute accompaniment." Despite its association with Eastern religious traditions, he explains, an impressive body of recent neuroscience research "has led to the flowering of an elite subculture of executives, athletes, and Marines who are using meditation to improve their focus, curb their addiction to technology, and stop being yanked around by their emotions."[42]

This is all true enough. With current estimates ranging from 10 to 20 million Americans practicing meditation,[43] there are now scores of peer-reviewed medical studies documenting its beneficial effects on health.[44] The National Institutes of Health recommends it for everything from lowering blood pressure and easing symptoms of anxiety, depression, and insomnia to specifically helping with disease conditions from irritable bowel syndrome to ulcerative colitis,[45] and the American Heart Association praises its proven ability to reduce incidence of heart attacks and high blood pressure.[46]

There are, however, different forms of meditation, and though they may look much the same from the outside, it is what goes on inside the mind that matters. Some of the Eastern religious varieties, particularly mantra meditations, where one repeats a certain word or sound over and over again internally, can be very hypnotic. Focusing on the breath, a common Buddhist practice but widely used in the West, is better.

However, the technique I recommend, used by hundreds of thousands of Americans, including many in the US military, provides not only relief from stress and all the related health benefits, but is Judeo-Christian in origin. It's called "Be Still and Know," named for the Psalm, "Be still, and know that I am God." A simple exercise in which you objectively and non-judgmentally observe your own thoughts and feelings while anchoring your attention in the present moment, it was introduced decades ago by the patriarch of Western stress experts, British-born Roy Masters.[47]

The exercise is so effective, says Masters, because "it enables you to become objective, a little bit separate and disentangled from all your troublesome thoughts, emotions, heartaches, fears and traumatic memories—and that, all by itself, is extremely helpful, and actually healing."

Remarkably, "Be Still and Know" has been endorsed by both the Army's chief of chaplains, Maj. Gen. Douglas L. Carver (ret.), a Southern Baptist chaplain who calls it "a great resource for our Soldiers," and its top psychiatrist, Col. John Bradley, MD (former chief of psychiatry at Walter Reed), who says he even "rendered a positive opinion to the Surgeon General."[48] I've interviewed combat vets, generals, chaplains, and doctors who recommend this particular practice, and all agree it's a valuable tool for everyone, in or out of the military. It is available at FHU.com.

By the way, this practice has also proven helpful in overcoming one of the biggest stumbling blocks we human beings encounter in this life—anger, our own and others'.

And that leads us to the final, and probably most important, item on my list.

LEARN TO RISE ABOVE ANGER

For if ye forgive men their trespasses, your heavenly Father will also forgive you: But if ye forgive not men their trespasses, neither will your Father forgive your trespasses. —MATTHEW 6:14–15

Being angry is dangerous. There's really no need to itemize everything wrong with being mad, resentful, hostile, judgmental, impatient, irritated, fuming, and brooding. It's no coincidence that the word *mad* can mean both "angry" and "insane"—since becoming very angry can amount to a sort of temporary insanity, wherein we think, speak, and act very differently than when we're calm and centered. And as any good psychiatrist will tell you, anger plays a major role in clinical depression[49] and other mental illnesses.[50]

Our anger hurts our children, poisons our relationships, breaks up our families, and undermines our businesses. It also wrecks our health. A recent study shows anger can flat-out *cause* a heart attack. As Emmy-winning medical journalist Dr. Maria Simbra explains, this latest research "shows intense feelings of anger can trigger a heart attack, even up to two hours later. This is most likely related to the surge of stress hormones, the rise in pulse and blood pressure, and constriction of the heart's blood vessels."[51]

Anger can also destroy entire societies. Although the left reflexively brands all criticism of its agenda as "hate" ("hate speech," "racism," "war on women," "Islamophobia," "homophobia," "transphobia," "xeno-phobia," "intolerance," "bigotry"), in reality, hate is at the heart of the radical left, with many activists openly admitting they're fueled by rage. For example, LGBT thought leaders Marshall Kirk and Hunter Madsen, authors of the famous gay-rights strategy book *After the Ball,* reveal—at the very end of their treatise—where the motivation and energy for their cause originates:

> It's practically a Western tradition to close one's call to arms with the sugary invocation of love as the best way to move mountains. Well, love is an excellent end in itself, but it isn't half so compelling as a means. Over history, love has severed no colonies from their mother countries, nor overthrown any czars, nor obliterated any Nazis, nor produced any civil rights movements. You may discount what the pious tell you, because it is actually *rage,* not love, that lay behind all those progressive events.

Today's America, Kirk and Madsen counsel activists, "is the time and place for rage—ice-cold, controlled, directed rage."[52]

Another way anger could result in a tremendous loss of freedom would be if some who claim to stand for God, country, and the Constitution became so enraged at the Left's provocations and outrages that they resorted to violence in some deluded attempt to "strike a blow for liberty," all the while reassuring themselves they were channeling America's founding generation—you know, refreshing "the tree of liberty," as Jefferson said, with "the blood of patriots and tyrants."

Such deplorable actions would not only fail to achieve anything good, but innocent people would suffer, and the result would undoubtedly be a level of government repression unprecedented in modern times. "Right-wing extremism" would, perversely enough, then appear to validate all the delusions and self-projections of hatred and violence of which the Far Left is guilty, but continually ascribes to normal Americans.

At the outset of our journey together, I quoted Rush Limbaugh's on-air observation that Barack Obama, in hot pursuit of his stated goal of "fundamentally transforming the United States of America,"[53] seemed intent on driving normal folks over the edge.

"I think he *wants* people to snap," said Limbaugh. "I think Obama is challenging everybody's sanity. . . . Obama is literally pushing people to snap, attacking the very sanity of the country." He added, "Everything that people hold dear is under assault, *deliberately making people upset! This is not what presidents do.*"[54]

Yet as we have seen, this is no ordinary president, and these are no ordinary times. It's an era of lawless government and godless culture, and millions are indeed "snapping."

"Snapping" implies a sudden and dramatic break with reality, but also a preceding period of time during which pressure builds toward that breaking point. The left's ascension to political and cultural power in America has occurred over several decades, yet it is only in the last few years that we have witnessed the rapid-fire break with reality: the wholesale abandonment of millennia-old values like reverence for God and the Bible, marriage, morality, fidelity, gender, the rule of law, personal responsibility, defense of the innocent, and the sacredness of human life.

Sadly, we're also seeing the widespread plunge of human souls into bondage that inevitably results when we fall away from the protection of God's law.

Yet, at its core, that's exactly what the left's assault on traditional Judeo-Christian America is all about—a rebellion against God and His laws. That's why it manifests, first and foremost, as an attack on Americans of faith and the common-sense values they cherish—or as Limbaugh put it, on "the very sanity of the country."

Many of the leftist assaults on normality described throughout this book—from the Obama administration singling out mainstream conservatives as potential "right-wing extremists," to the legal targeting of Christian businesses for declining to participate in same-sex weddings or provide abortifacients to their employees, to incidents like the pro-choice woman throwing a Molotov cocktail at people praying out-side a Texas abortion clinic—amount to a campaign of anti-Christian vilification and intimidation in a once-Christian nation. No, it isn't the terrible, murderous persecution occurring daily in various parts of the Islamic world and in communist nations like North Korea. But the abuse is nevertheless intended to crush the faith, courage, and convictions of Americans holding to traditional biblical values, since such people are incompatible with—indeed, are the primary roadblock to—realization of the left's utopian dreams.

With this Christian persecution theme in mind, let me end this chapter with a true story that dramatically captures the "missing ingre-dient" we all need if we are to withstand the present onslaught and, in the end, allow goodness to prevail in America.

"NOT THE SLIGHTEST BITTERNESS"

> *But I say unto you, Love your enemies, bless them that curse you, do good to them that hate you, and pray for them which despitefully use you, and persecute you; That ye may be the children of your Father which is in heaven.* —MATTHEW 5:44-45

Meet Richard Wurmbrand. In case you don't know his story, he is the heroic Romanian evangelical pastor who spent fourteen years in a Romanian prison, three of them in solitary confinement, suffering starvation and torture for the crime of boldly preaching the Christian gospel in what was then a brutally repressive communist nation. When, two years after his final release from captivity, Wurmbrand testified before the US Senate's Internal Security Subcommittee, he stripped to the waist to reveal eighteen deep wounds covering his torso, the result of years of unspeakable abuse.[55]

And yet, as Wurmbrand explained in his classic book, *Tortured for Christ,* he and his fellow Christian prisoners well understood that the communists, especially those who imprisoned and abused them, were themselves prisoners.

With striking compassion for his jailers and torturers, Wurmbrand writes:

> The enormous amount of drunkenness in communist countries exposes the longing for a more meaningful life, which communism cannot give. The average Russian is a deep, big-hearted, generous person. Communism is shallow and superficial. He seeks the deep life and, finding it nowhere else, he seeks it in alcohol. He expresses in alcoholism his horror about the brutal and deceitful life he must live. For a few moments alcohol sets him free, as truth would set him free forever if he could know it.[56]

So genuine was Wurmbrand's concern for the souls of his tormentors that, over the years of his incarceration, he converted many of them to the Christian faith, some of whom actually ended up in prison with him—and were glad for it!

Contemplate, if you can, Wurmbrand's last act before leaving Romania after years of living thirty feet underground in a communist prison—no sunshine or fresh air, always hungry, treated brutally and sadistically day after day, year after year.

"In December 1965," writes Wurmbrand, "my family and I were allowed to leave Romania":

> My last deed before leaving was to go to the grave of the colonel who had given the order for my arrest and who had ordered my years of torture. I placed a flower on his grave. By doing this I dedicated myself to bringing the joys of Christ that I have to the communists who are so empty spiritually.
>
> I hate the communist system but I love the men. I hate the sin but I love the sinner. I love the communists with all of my heart. Communists can kill Christians but they cannot kill their love toward even those who killed them. I have not the slightest bitterness or resentment against the communists or my torturers.[57]

How is such an attitude possible? Explains Wurmbrand, "I have seen Christians in communist prisons with fifty pounds of chains on their feet, tortured with red-hot iron pokers, in whose throats spoonfuls of salt had been forced, being kept afterward without water, starving, whipped, suffering from cold—and praying with fervor for the communists. This is humanly inexplicable! It is the love of Christ, which was poured out in our hearts."[58]

Finally, in words reminiscent of some of the early Christian martyrs of the first century, Richard Wurmbrand shares with the reader the presence of God he experienced in his prison cell:

> God is "the Truth." The Bible is the "truth about the Truth." Theology is the "truth about the truth about the Truth." Christian people live in these many truths about the Truth, and, because of them, have not "the Truth."
>
> Hungry, beaten, and drugged, we had forgotten theology and the Bible. We had forgotten the "truths about the Truth," therefore we lived in "the Truth." It is written, "The Son of man is coming at an hour when you do not expect Him" (Matthew 24:44). We could not think anymore. In our darkest hours of torture, the Son of Man came to us, making the prison walls shine like diamonds and filling the cells with light. Somewhere, far away, were the torturers below us in the sphere of the body. But the spirit rejoiced in the Lord. We would not have given up this joy for that of kingly palaces.[59]

Just as it is difficult to comprehend the dark depths to which humans can descend, it may seem equally hard to grasp the heights of God's blessings and light some people are graced to discover when they need it most, welling up from a hidden spring. It's a well from which we all need to drink.

In our final chapter, we'll explore this mystery a little more deeply. Fasten your seat belt, because we're going on a wild ride.

12

MESSIAHS FALSE AND TRUE

Decades ago, as a young person, I liked to visit the National Air and Space Museum in Washington, DC, where one exhibit featured a nine-minute film that played continuously in a loop. I would stand there, in awe, watching it over and over again.

It was called *Powers of Ten: A Film Dealing with the Relative Size of Things in the Universe—and the Effect of Adding Another Zero.* (You can watch it on YouTube.)[1]

Narrated by MIT physics professor Philip Morrison, the short movie takes viewers on a spellbinding high-speed voyage into outer space, zooming away from Earth another order of magnitude (ten times farther) every ten seconds, thus traversing through our solar system and vastly beyond, eventually past the Milky Way galaxy unto the outer reaches of the known universe—ending up *100 million light-years from home.* Upon returning to Earth, the cosmic roller coaster slows down and pauses temporarily at its initial starting point at the planet's surface, but now continues on "in the other direction"—that is, *inward.* Microscopically traveling by a new order of magnitude (ten times smaller) every ten seconds, the same rate as the previous journey, this time the fantastic voyage targets something "far off," deep inside a man's hand. We survey skin cells and other structures, then chromosomes and DNA, and as the magnification increases exponentially, molecules and atoms come into view, until finally we arrive at our destination: a single shimmering proton within the nucleus of a carbon atom.

Not only does "Powers of Ten" (as well as a later remake called

"Cosmic Voyage")[2] provide a glimpse of the astonishing complexity and magnificence of creation and the relative size of all things known; it also, intriguingly, shows man to be more or less smack in the middle of two universes, one infinitely larger than us and the other infinitesimally smaller.

Think of it: Zoom out to, say, one light-year of distance from Earth (10^{16} meters), and our sun is seen as a tiny speck in space. But zoom inward, toward the center of a carbon atom, and you've traveled the same number of orders of magnitude, sixteen (10^{-16} meters, or 0.000001 angstroms), and the atomic nucleus is likewise seen as a tiny speck in space.

With this mind-blowing relativity in mind, man is obviously not "small," as we're often reminded, except when compared to the distances, speeds, and heavenly bodies inhabiting outer space. But relative to the equally mind-bogglingly small constellations of inner space—well, let's just say, you and I are to the tiny particles in the nucleus of an atom as the Milky Way galaxy is to us.

Thus perched between these "parallel universes," we human beings exist on this remarkably beautiful blue, green, and brown spinning sphere called Earth. And as such, we are faced with a great enigma: why a Creator who can conceive universes large and small, equally incomprehensible in both their largeness and their smallness (not to mention their complexity and wonder), would place, right in the middle of it all, human beings, full of all our vexing and even malignant flaws.

For what purpose?

That's a mystery. It is *the* mystery.

In our life on this earth, our first and most tangible reality is the wondrous natural world surrounding us and providing for all our material needs. We are likewise blessed with marvelous faculties—two little spherical cameras called eyes with which to see, ears to hear, plus all our other senses and abilities, all topped off with an astonishing supercomputer: our brain. All this that we may perceive, navigate, and live out our lives successfully within this natural world, like the rest of the animal kingdom.

Alas, we're not just animals, ordained to locate food, stay warm in winter, procreate, and steer clear of predators. For, coexisting with this natural world is a mysterious moral dimension in which we humans are also immersed. Animals don't share this moral realm, nor do plants, rocks, mountains, oceans, stars, or galaxies, all of which act in accord with their given nature, all without honor or dishonor, reward or punishment. Kittens aren't good, and man-eating sharks aren't evil. Man alone dwells in this peculiar moral realm wherein good and evil not only manifest, but seem to be focused on recruiting us! As such, we inevitably are drawn into becoming conduits of good, or of evil—or more often, of both good and evil, as both realms strive relentlessly to claim our minds, hearts, loyalties, and ultimately our souls.

This moral (or spiritual) dimension courses through our very being. It is what imbues us with a capacity for consciousness, reverence, and ultimate meaning, for realizing there is an infinitely great Creator and that every blade of grass and every heartbeat in our chest is a miracle. However, this moral sphere is also the matrix from which most of our problems emerge, overshadowing and often utterly overwhelming everything else in our lives.

For despite all that is amazing about human beings—the civilizations we've built, literature and art we've created, diseases we've conquered, dizzying scientific and technological wonders we've achieved, and most important, our genuine capacity for nobility, generosity, courage, and self-sacrifice—we are greatly troubled creatures. The human race is a giant mess and, from everything we know, always has been. Along with our conscience (a little speck of God's mind that He graciously enfolds within each one of us) and the many virtues with which we are blessed, we're also mightily beset by pride, envy, anger, selfishness, blindness, greed, and lust, and have a prodigious capacity for denial and delusion. We seem effortlessly able to follow destructive proclivities of every imaginable and unimaginable sort, almost as though we had a genetic predisposition toward them. Some of us become full-fledged monsters.

As a result, our world encompasses entire nations that resemble huge mind-control cults where the most deranged and predatory people are those in positions of authority. Each culture, religion, and political ideology has a set of core beliefs about which adherents are absolutely certain, yet which are utterly at odds with the core beliefs of all other cultures, religions, and political ideologies. Worse yet, in the case of major expansionist utopian systems like communism and Islam, millions are programmed not only to embrace terribly dehumanizing beliefs and practices, but to believe they are required to force everyone else on earth to adopt their beliefs—or else be subjugated or slaughtered.

This "moral dimension" in which we exist has one unique and defining feature: *choice.* Animals have no choice. They have one nature, one type of internal programming, and they live according to it. In contrast, human beings have the freedom to hearken to either of two spiritual dimensions, good and evil—diametrically opposite sources of direction, each offering to guide us along our path through this life.

The classic question, "Why does evil exist?" actually has a fairly self-evident answer: "Good" can't exist without "evil," just as "hot" is meaningless without "cold"; "courage" can't exist without "cowardice," and "above" means nothing if there is no "below." This is not semantics: Without evil, good literally could not manifest, and the entire universe would then amount to just so much elegant, fiery, but ultimately meaningless cosmic clockwork.

Still, why would anyone be attracted to evil, especially considering that each of us possesses an inborn knowing of right from wrong ("conscience" literally means "with knowing")?

THE SIN VIRUS

Evil, being the master of disguise it is, doesn't assume the form depicted by artists—a snarling red supervillain with horns and forked tail—since few would be attracted to such a hideous monster. Rather, it takes a much more subtle approach.

When we first enter this world, we're beautiful and innocent, a source of joy, delight, and wonder. But before long—as though a mysterious, ancient curse resides within each of us, a latent virus awaiting activation—something happens that disturbs our blissful existence and redirects the course of our lives.

It can take many forms. Perhaps someone—a parent, sibling, friend, or teacher—does something cruel or otherwise violating to us. The experience shocks and confuses us, and in our resulting emotional turmoil, something starts to change inside us.

More such experiences occur, giving rise to yet more anger and confusion. Soon we are thinking, feeling, and acting differently than we did before, our carefree happiness mysteriously replaced by anxiety, insecurity, fear, resentment . . . and strange ideas.

In fact, we start to act a little bit like the people who were cruel to us (or who teased, bullied, lied to, cheated, mocked, were impatient with, ignored, betrayed, or molested us). Their adverse influence on us might be obvious (as when a Palestinian child indoctrinated to hate Jews and love death decides to become a suicide bomber) or it might be more subtle (as when a child bullied by an older child takes it out on someone weaker). One way or another, we all tend to do to others what was done to us—just the opposite of the Golden Rule.

As all this unfolds—as we are progressively torn away from our original inner, wordless, faith bond with our Creator, and instead increasingly are transformed in the image of other lost souls—a whole other mind-set is growing within us, with its own thoughts, emotions, anxieties, obsessions, and cravings, in competition with our real self. All too often, this false self, which the Bible calls the "sin" nature, comes to dominate and ultimately destroy our lives—and others'.

Indeed, this syndrome spreads throughout the human race like a pandemic, the sin "virus" mutating endlessly into all manner of anger, pride, jealousy, rebellion, insecurity, suggestibility, confusion, and delusion—and beyond that point into full-blown corruption, violence, madness, criminality, and war.

Take a good panoramic look at life on Earth today, and that's pretty much what we're witnessing, isn't it?

FALSE MESSIAHS

Clearly there's something in our makeup, some mysterious inheritance from ancient times, that beckons us to so easily cross the line of conscience and reason—to violate God's laws, to become spiritual outlaws. In Christian shorthand, we're all "born in sin."

It's one of the great mysteries of life that some people—usually after great suffering and soul-searching—manage to mature into responsible, conscientious, moral adults, while others unfortunately become ever more entangled in dark thoughts and feelings, leading to self-destructive or predatory behaviors.

But here's the rub. Even in those who eventually leave behind their former sinful behavior, the nature that gave rise to it seems to linger somewhere deep within us like a latent virus. Moreover, even if we *are* somehow graced to become totally free of our troublesome nature, we still cannot undo the wrongs we committed in the past. In a cosmic legal sense, we're still guilty. We're like offenders who have broken the law and violated and damaged other people, and though we may now sincerely regret what we did, we're still guilty of having done it! How can our guilt then be taken away? Can the past magically be wiped out? Can we ever finally live in peace and happiness? This is where the idea of a messiah comes in.

Unfortunately, because repenting and facing our own corrupt, sinful nature can be painful and requires humility and raw honesty, many people are more inclined to skip the introspection part and just appoint an earthly savior to rescue them from their misery. The most notorious example of a false messiah in modern times was Adolf Hitler, although both Joseph Stalin and Mao Zedong were responsible for far more deaths. All of these mass-murdering psychopaths demanded obedience and worship in return for a glorious kingdom on earth, but of course it didn't work out. It never does—but we keep trying.

As former New Left leader David Horowitz explains, progressive true-believers "regard the past, which is real, with contempt, and are focused exclusively on a future which is imaginary." He explains the strange thinking inherent in this political ideology:

Think of progressives as a species of religious fundamentalists planning a redemption. Like fundamentalists, they look at the world as fallen—a place corrupted by racism, sexism and class division. But the truly religious understand that we are the *source* of corruption and that redemption is only possible through the work of a Divinity. In contrast, progressives see *themselves* as the redeemers, which is why they are so dangerous, because they regard those who oppose them as the eternally damned. Progressives are on a mission to create the kingdom of heaven on earth by redistributing income and using the state to enforce politically correct attitudes and practices in everyone's life.[3]

Of course, the communist/socialist dream has never delivered on its utopian promises, with 100 to 200 million dead bodies resulting from it in the last century. How strange, then, that the stench emanating from those mountains of rotting corpses is somehow overcome by the sweet aroma of an impossible dream, the delusion that we can reform and redeem mankind through the "enlightened" coercion of an all-powerful government. Socialism, the strange religion of the left, still energizes and excites true believers—including Barack Obama.

Indeed, in America, many people saw Obama as nothing less than a messiah and invested all their hopes and dreams for the future in him, with 69 million voters casting their ballots for him in 2008.

"We thought that he was going to be—I shouldn't say this at Christmastime—but the next messiah," veteran broadcast journalist Barbara Walters told Piers Morgan on CNN.[4] *Newsweek* editor Evan Thomas told MSNBC, "I mean, in a way, Obama's standing above the country, above—above the world, he's sort of God."[5] And upon Obama's 2012 reelection, *Newsweek* celebrated the occasion with the front-cover headline "THE SECOND COMING."[6]

A messiah, at least in the Christian sense, is not only supposed to lead people out of bondage and oppression, but to take away their guilt, sins, and ultimate condemnation. Obama was, in effect, anointed by the majority of American voters to absolve their guilt over our great national sin of slavery (and later, racial segregation). But instead of cleansing us of our national guilt, Obama and his administration, especially his attorney general, Eric Holder, cynically *magnified and enlarged* that guilt, using it as a mighty weapon to upset and divide Americans over race, all for the unholy purpose of amassing ever more power.

Most Americans—some sooner, some later—have ultimately realized that not only is Obama not a messiah, but he's almost certainly the most dishonest and perversely *anti-Christian* president in US history. His radical-left administration has caused tremendous harm not just to the nation's constitutional system of government, its economy, security, and culture—but to its national soul. That's because, to "fundamentally transform" a uniquely great and Christian nation like America into just one more pitiful, secular, redistributionist welfare state presided over by an all-powerful nanny government, the American people must be seduced into becoming less Christian and less moral than they once were, less rugged and resilient, less rational and competent, less principled and courageous—in short, they must become lesser people than they once were. This, alas, is the true legacy of the Obama presidency: the degradation and demoralization of America.

The desire for a messiah—a God-anointed person who will lead us into lasting peace and happiness—is embedded deep in the human soul. The messiah is central not just to Christianity and to Judaism, but also to Islam, which has its own exotic version of a last-days deliverer.

In fact, polls reveal that a large percentage of Muslims currently living in the Middle East believe they will see, in their lifetime, the coming of their messiah—whom they call the Mahdi.[7] But believe it or not, Islam anticipates that the Mahdi will return with a sidekick—Jesus, whom Muslims call "Isa." The Muslim Jesus is expected to tell the entire world that He is *not* the Son of God, was *not* crucified, and was *not* resurrected from the dead. Rather, according to Muslim teachings, Jesus' message upon His return will be that He does indeed exist, but that He is—surprise!—a Muslim, and that all the world must convert to Islam.

The fact that human beings have proven again and again to disastrously appoint false "messiahs" to absolve their sins and lead them to peace and freedom highlights the millennia-old question of whether the true messiah is a political (group) savior, or a spiritual (individual) one.

Twenty centuries ago, when Jesus of Nazareth walked the earth, the Jewish people, citing the biblical prophets, were awaiting a great leader descended from King David who would rescue and lead them into a time of lasting peace on earth. However, Jesus, though urged to lead a rebellion against the Roman oppressors, responded that He had come to lead a different sort of revolution—an inner one, within each person.

TRUE MESSIAH

If we're completely honest, at some point during our lives we come to realize we are broken in such a deep way that we cannot fix ourselves. Our problem with sin, with deep roots going back to our childhood and beyond, seems to cling to us all of our lives. Even in the best of us, the traumas of life have become so much a part of us, the perverse cravings of our hearts so strong, and the hold sin has on us so powerful, that even with our best efforts we remain a shadow of the person we'd like to be. We never seem to be totally healed—not through living a clean, law-abiding, moral life, not with the help of modern medicine and antidepressants, not with church attendance and sermons and hymns and good deeds, not even by diligently trying to obey all of God's commandments.

We need something we cannot give ourselves.

We need true healing; we need forgiveness; we need a new identity; we need new life.

This mystery of otherworldly redemption is alluded to throughout the Old Testament, the prophet Isaiah writing: "Come now, and let us reason together, saith the LORD: though your sins be as scarlet, they shall be as white as snow; though they be red like crimson, they shall be as wool."[8]

All of which brings us to the coming of the Messiah—the real one.

What more compassionate and needed gift could God possibly give His struggling, wayward children than a perfect, in-the-flesh example of how to live, a great lover of our souls who would suffer greatly for our redemption and dramatically demonstrate real love, and one who would actually do battle with the dark spiritual forces that oppress the human race?

Why, indeed, would a Creator so great as to imagine into existence such an astonishingly magnificent universe *not* provide for us the example, the teacher, and the savior we so desperately need?

The simplicity and sincerity of Christ's essential message is conveyed by one of my very favorite scriptures, courtesy of John the apostle: "Here is the message we heard from him [Jesus] and pass on to you: that God is light, and in him there is no darkness at all. If we claim to be sharing in his life while we walk in the dark, our words and our lives are a lie; but if we walk in the light as he himself is in the light, then we share together a common life, and we are being cleansed from every sin by the blood of Jesus his Son" (1 John 1:5–7 NEB).

John mentions here no complicated dogma, no required religious observances, rituals, pilgrimages, or special diet. Just a sincere appreciation of God's forgiveness and this glistening instruction: If we "walk in the light, as he himself is in the light"—that is, if we calmly and humbly welcome God's light of understanding to shine in our minds and souls, by which light we will observe our sinful nature—He will grace us with repentance. And "then," assures John, "we share together a common life, and we are being cleansed from every sin by the blood of Jesus his Son."

Again, living "in the light"—not losing ourselves in worry over the past, or anxiety and fear over the future, but staying faithful in the present moment, in the presence of God—involves facing our own vexing imperfections and faults, without condemning ourselves, or covering up the sin, or struggling with it to fix it, but just patiently waiting on God for help. When we do that, we are, in that very moment, being transformed, redeemed, graced to "share together a common life" with God.

These are, of course, simply my reflections on an enormously profound subject. But I believe such deep matters are meant to be pondered by each of us in our hearts, without worry, without pressure, without fear of hellfire hanging over us. If we don't understand something, it's okay. If we experience doubt or confusion, it's okay—just honestly admit it. God sees all, and will help.

Our lives are an adventure playing out in two different worlds simultaneously: We're meant not only to live our lives on this earth the best we can manage, but also to embrace an inner journey that is ultimately far more important. Sadly, some of us lead unexamined lives, but as Socrates said at his trial, "The unexamined life is not worth living." Still others simply don't want to face reality no matter what, stubbornly preferring to inhabit their own alternate universe, their mad dreamworld, in which they inevitably hurt many people, and themselves.

That seems to be the great divide in humanity. It's not a racial, ethnic, cultural, class, or generational one, nor is it even a philosophical, ideological, or religious divide per se. Rather, it is simply that there are people who are willing to honestly face their sinful nature no matter how uncomfortable or humbling, and to truly repent in the light of God and thereby find reconciliation with Him. And then there are people who are not. There are those who, even in the worst of circumstances, find this blessed place, and others who, though benefitting from the best of circumstances, reject it. Our deep-down love of truth—or lack of it—forms the invisible nucleus around which orbit all our beliefs and attitudes. What kind of person we become in this life emanates naturally from our willingness or unwillingness to face the sometimes painful mystery of ourselves with honesty and integrity.

Earlier we considered why God would position the human race betwixt alternate universes—magnificent cosmic clockwork large and small—and immerse us likewise in two opposing spiritual dimensions of good and evil, virtue and wickedness, sanity and madness.

Why are we here? What is God intent on creating in this special realm—the realm of man—that He couldn't bring into being any other way, or anywhere else in the universe, even 100 million light-years out?

Love, sacrifice, courage, character—in a word, goodness. Manifesting real love and goodness in this world has more to do with patient suffering, endurance, forgiveness, and self-sacrifice than anything else, but how does God create that kind of person with purely natural processes? Can He create love the way He creates stars, with giant explosions of dense clouds of hydrogen gas? Or the way He causes an acorn to follow an invisible blueprint and grow into a towering oak?

God is seeking people who will truly love Him and love one another—and even, as Jesus taught and exemplified, love and pray for their *enemies*. That means He's looking for something that simply cannot be brought into being any other way than as an end result of the troubled lives we lead in this difficult world and the hard-won lessons of humility and faith we ultimately embrace. And to help us, to guide us—indeed to make it possible—He sends His Son, the true Messiah, our best friend, to lift the curse and destroy the virus through some wondrous magic from beyond the ends of the universe.

So, the solution to our mystery of why God put such imperfect beings in the midst of colliding galaxies and subatomic constellations may simply be that, in the Creator's mind, all that dazzling stuff just serves as the ornate setting, and we—we're the crown jewel of His creation. Not that we're anything praiseworthy, mind you. Not at all. It's just that God wanted children—and all the stars, planets, oceans, rocks, trees, and birds just wouldn't do.

God does not create loving and obedient children the same way He creates the rest of the universe. But in leaving a race of prodigal sons and daughters here, untethered in a moral wilderness with the freedom to follow their own folly for a season and thereby learn precious lessons, God knew many would eventually come to their senses and come back home to Him. May it be so with you.

NOTES

INTRODUCTION

1. Rebecca Riffkin, "Government, Economy, Immigration Are Top U.S. Problems," Gallup Politics, August 13, 2014, http://www.gallup.com/poll/174809/government-economy-immigration-top-problems.aspx?utm_source=alert&utm_medium=email&utm_campaign=syndication&utm_content=morelink&utm_term=Politics.

2. See EnemiesList.info: The complete, annotated Nixon's Enemies List, http://www.enemieslist.info/; and "The Nixon Administration and Watergate: Nixon Campaign 'Dirty Tricks,'" History Commons, http://www.historycommons.org/timeline.jsp?timeline=nixon_and_watergate_tmln&nixon_and_watergate_tmln_watergate_campaign_conspiracy=nixon_and_watergate_tmln_nixon_campaign__dirty_tricks_.

3. Jimmy Carter, "Carter's 'Crisis of Confidence' Speech," *American Experience*, http://www.pbs.org/wgbh/americanexperience/features/general-article/carter-crisis-speech/.

4. See sundance, "Fabian = Progressive: Crisis Is Fundamental to 'Fundamental Transformation,'" *The Last Refuge* (blog), December 31, 2012, http://theconservativetreehouse.com/2012/12/31/fabian-progressive-crisis-is-fundamental-to-fundamental-transformation/.

5. Ian R. H. Rockett et al., "Leading Causes of Unintentional and Intentional Injury Mortality: United States, 2000–2009," *American Journal of Public Health* 102, no. 11 (November 2012): e84–e92 http://ajph.aphapublications.org/doi/abs/10.2105/AJPH.2012.300960.

6. Megan McCloskey, "More soldier suicides than combat deaths in 2012," *Stars and Stripes*, December 20, 2012, http://www.stripes.com/news/more-soldier-suicides-than-combat-deaths-in-2012-1.201440.

7. Alan Schwarz and Sarah Cohen, "A.D.H.D. Seen in 11% of U.S. Children as Diagnoses Rise," *New York Times*, March 31, 2013, http://www.nytimes.com/2013/04/01/health/more-diagnoses-of-hyperactivity-causing-concern.html?_r=2&.

8. Carl Campanile, "1 in 5 city preteens have mental woes," *New York Post*, March 25, 2013, http://nypost.com/2013/03/25/1-in-5-city-preteens-have-mental-woes/.

9. Lauren Paxman, "One in 12 teenagers self-harm (but most grow out of it by their twenties)," *Daily Mail*, November 17, 2011, http://www.dailymail.co.uk/health/article-2062629/One-12-teenagers-self-harm-grow-twenties.html.

10. "Self-Inflicted Injury Prevention, Children Ages 10 to 19 Years," New York State Department of Health, https://www.health.ny.gov/prevention/injury_prevention/children/fact_sheets/10-19_years/self-inflcited_injury_prevention_10-19_years.htm.

11. Lauren Weber and Sue Shellenbarger, "Office Stress: His vs. Hers," *Wall Street Journal*, March 5, 2013, http://online.wsj.com/news/articles/SB10001424127887324678604578340332290414820.

12. Elwood Watson, "Millennial Stress College Years and Beyond," *Diverse: Issues in Higher Education*, March 6, 2013, http://diverseeducation.com/article/51755/.

13. Hayley Dixon, "Stress makes you susceptible to illness," *Telegraph*, March 15, 2013, http://www.telegraph.co.uk/health/healthnews/9932987/Stress-makes-you-susceptible-to-illness.html.

14. Archana S. Nagaraja, Guillermo N. Armaiz-Pena, Susan K. Lutgendorf, Anil K. Sood, "Why stress is BAD for cancer patients," The Journal of Clinical Investigation, February 1, 2013, www.jci.org/articles/view/67887?key=741bcde7c39c877f58de.

15. "Heart Disease Facts," Centers for Disease Control and Prevention, http://www.cdc.gov/heartdisease/facts.htm.

16. Anna Hodgekiss, "Being stressed is as damaging for your heart as smoking five cigarettes a day," *Daily Mail*, December 18, 2012, http://www.dailymail.co.uk/health/article-2250106/Stress-bad-heart-smoking-cigarettes-day.html.

17. "School and Mass Shootings," SSRIstories.com, http://ssristories.org/category/violence/school-or-other-mass-shooting/.

18. "Antidepressant Use in Persons Aged 12 and Over: United States, 2005–2008," NCHS Data Brief Number 76, Centers for Disease Control and Prevention, October 2011, http://www.cdc.gov/nchs/data/databriefs/db76.htm.

19. Alan Schwarz and Sarah Cohen, "A.D.H.D. Seen in 11% of U.S. Children as Diagnoses Rise," *New York Times*, March 31, 2013, http://www.nytimes.com/2013/04/01/health/more-diagnoses-of-hyperactivity-causing-concern.html?_r=2&.

20. "Alcoholism and Alcohol Abuse," *New York Times* Health Guide, November 21, 2013, http://www.nytimes.com/health/guides/disease/alcoholism/risk-factors.html.

21. Substance Abuse and Mental Health Services Administration, Results from the 2013 National Survey on Drug Use and Health: Summary of National Findings, NSDUH Series H-48, HHS Publication No. (SMA) 14-4863. Rockville, MD: Substance Abuse and Mental Health Services Administration, 2014, http://www.samhsa.gov/data/sites/default/files/NSDUHresultsPDFWHTML2013/Web/NSDUHresults2013.pdf.

22. Covenant Eyes, "Pornography Statistics: Annual Report 2014," http://www.covenanteyes.com/pornstats/.

23. Bahar Gholipour, "Hidden STD Epidemic: Maps Show Infection Rates in 50 States," LiveScience.com, October 6, 2014, http://www.livescience.com/48100-sexually-transmitted-infections-50-states-map.html.

24. "Prevalence of Childhood and Adult Obesity in the United States, 2011–2012," *Journal of the American Medical Association*, February 26, 2014, http://jama.jamanetwork.com/article.aspx?articleid=1832542.

25. Kate Kelland, "Nearly 40 percent of Europeans suffer mental illness," Reuters, September 4, 2011, http://www.reuters.com/article/2011/09/04/us-europe-mental-illness-idUSTRE7832JJ20110904.

26. *Merriam-Webster Dictionary*, s.v. "revolutionary," http://www.merriam-webster.com/dictionary/revolutionary, accessed May 20, 2015.

27. Rush Limbaugh, "A Newly Minted NRA Member'" (transcript), the official website of *The Rush Limbaugh Show*, January 16, 2013, http://www.rushlimbaugh.com/daily/2013/01/16/a_newly_minted_nra_member.

28. Rush Limbaugh, "Revenge on the Bitter Clingers" (transcript), the official website of *The Rush Limbaugh Show*, January 16, 2013, http://www.rushlimbaugh.com/daily/2013/01/16/revenge_on_the_bitter_clingers.

29. Chris Stirewalt, "Amid more bad news, Obama returns to base baiting," FoxNews.com, July 1, 2014, http://www.foxnews.com/politics/2014/07/01/amid-more-bad-news-obama-returns-to-base-baiting/.

30. David Limbaugh, "Let's Recognize Who the Real Haters Are," *Townhall.com*, April 3, 2015, http://townhall.com/columnists/davidlimbaugh/2015/04/03/lets-recognize-who-the-real-haters-are-n1980212.

CHAPTER 1: BIZARRO AMERICA

1. "Bizarro," Fact Index, accessed May 20, 2015, http://www.fact-index.com/b/bi/bizarro.html.

2. "Twitter Users Wish Death on Sarah Palin," YouTube video, 4:00, posted by shinhwa, January 11, 2011, https://www.youtube.com/watch?v=3s4YfBKs39Y.

3. Ryan Kellett, "Read the Palin e-mails," *Washington Post*, June 9, 2011, http://www.washingtonpost.com/blogs/the-fix/post/help-analyze-the-palin-emails/2011/06/08/AGZAaHNH_blog.html; Derek Willis, "Help Us Review the Sarah Palin E-Mail Records," *The Caucus* (NYT blog), June 9, 2011, http://thecaucus.blogs.nytimes.com/2011/06/09/help-us-investigate-the-sarah-palin-e-mail-records/.

4. Howard Kurtz, "Martin Bashir quits at MSNBC over Palin slur," Fox News, December 5, 2013, http://www.foxnews.com/politics/2013/12/05/martin-bashir-quits-at-msnbc-over-palin-slur/.

5. David Kupelian, *How Evil Works* (New York: Threshold Editions, 2010), 238–9.

6. Robin of Berkeley, "Why the Left Hates Sarah Palin," *American Thinker*, January 19, 2011, http://conservatives4palin.com/2011/01/robin-of-berkeley-why-the-left-hates-sarah-palin.html.

7. Lori Preuitt and Shawn Brouwer, "Salinas Teacher Calls This Drawing 'Offensive,'" NBC Bay Area, May 11, 2010, http://www.nbcbayarea.com/news/politics/Salinas-Teacher-Calls-Flag-Drawing-Offensive-93423139.html.

8. Wilson Ring, "Lisa Miller Must Give Child To Ex-Partner, Judge Rules," *Huffington Post*, March 18, 2010, http://www.huffingtonpost.com/2009/12/29/lisa-miller-must-give-chi_n_406699.html.

9. "Rightwing Extremism: Current Economic and Political Climate Fueling Resurgence in Radicalization and Recruitment," U.S. Department of Homeland Security, April 7, 2009, http://fas.org/irp/eprint/rightwing.pdf.

10. Ibid. See in particular, pp. 2–6. See also *Huffington Post*/AP, "Homeland Security Report Warns Of Rising Right-Wing Extremism," *HuffPost* Politics, May 15, 2009, http://www.huffingtonpost.com/2009/04/14/homeland-security-report_n_186834.html.

11. Col. Oliver North, "I Am an Extremist," Fox News, May 16, 2009, http://www.foxnews.com/on-air/war-stories/2009/04/16/i-am-extremist.

12. Maureen Dowd, "Washington Chain Saw Massacre," *New York Times*, August 2, 2011, http://www.nytimes.com/2011/08/03/opinion/washington-chain-saw-massacre.html?_r=2&ref=columnists&gwh=95B4FC7D20BFF72DF5A98CDE8EF5ADBC&gwt=pay&assetType=opinion.

13. Alex Fitzsimmons, "MSNBC 'Morning Joe' Panelists (Yet Again) Call Tea Partiers 'Economic Terrorists,'" MRC NewsBusters, July 29, 2011, http://newsbusters.org/blogs/alex-fitzsimmons/2011/07/29/msnbc-morning-joe-panelists-yet-again-call-tea-partiers-economic-t.

14. Noel Sheppard, "Charles Krauthammer Scolds Margaret Carlson for Saying Tea Party 'Strapped Explosives to the Capitol,'" NewsBusters, July 29, 2011, http://newsbusters.org/blogs/noel-sheppard/2011/07/29/krauthammer-scolds-lib-columnist-claiming-tea-party-has-strapped-expl.

15. Scott Whitlock, "Chris Matthews Smears the 'Scary' GOP as the 'Wahhabis of American Government,'" NewsBusters.org, July 5, 2011, http://newsbusters.org/blogs/scott-whitlock/2011/07/05/chris-matthews-smears-scary-gop-wahhabis-american-government.

16. Frances Martel, "Bernie Goldberg and Bill O'Reilly Make Fun of Liberals Labeling Tea Partiers 'Terrorists,'" Mediaite, August 1, 2011, http://www.mediaite.com/tv/bernie-goldberg-and-bill-oreilly-make-fun-of-liberals-labeling-tea-partiers-terrorists/.

17. "Norman Rockwell Receives Presidential Medal of Freedom," Norman Rockwell Museum website, accessed May 20, 2015, http://www.nrm.org/MT/text/MedalFreedom.html.

18. Blake Gopnik, "National Portrait Gallery bows to censors, withdraws Wojnarowicz video on gay love," *Washington Post*, November 30, 2010, http://www.washingtonpost.com/wp-dyn/content/article/2010/11/30/AR2010113006911.html.

19. Ibid.

20. Dinesh D'Souza, "Exceptionally good or exceptionally evil? Two competing and utterly opposite visions for America battle for ascendency," Whistleblower magazine, published by WND.com, July 2014 issue, "The Real America," http://superstore.wnd.com/SUBSCRIPTIONS/2010-2008/Whistleblower-Single-Issue-July-2014.

21. Jon Swaine, "White House admits it did return Winston Churchill bust to Britain," *Telegraph*, July 29, 2012, http://www.telegraph.co.uk/news/worldnews/barackobama/9436526/White-House-admits-it-did-return-Winston-Churchill-bust-to-Britain.html.

22. Marc A. Thiessen, "Obama's offensive against Netanyahu backfires," *Washington Post*, February 2, 2015, http://www.washingtonpost.com/opinions/marc-thiessen-obamas-offensive-against-netanyahu-backfires/2015/02/02/5f800ab2-aae1-11e4-ad71-7b9eba0f87d6_story.html.

23. Stephen Dinan, "DHS released another 30,000 criminal aliens onto streets," *Washington Times*, March 18, 2015, http://www.washingtontimes.com/news/2015/mar/18/dhs-released-another-30000-criminal-aliens-streets/#ixzz3UlphxIiD.

24. Michelle Spitzer, "NASA Chief Bolden's Muslim Remark to Al-Jazeera Causes Stir," Space.com, July 7, 2010, http://www.space.com/8725-nasa-chief-bolden-muslim-remark-al-jazeera-stir.html.

25. "New Inquisition: Punish climate-change 'deniers,'" WND, March 21, 2015, http://www.wnd.com/2015/03/new-inquisition-punish-climate-change-deniers/.

26. Michael Bastasch, "Al Gore: Spend $90 Trillion to Ban Cars from Every Major City in the World," *Daily Caller*, January 23, 2015, http://dailycaller.com/2015/01/23/al-gore-spend-90-trillion-to-ban-cars-from-every-major-city-in-the-world/.

27. "Global gross domestic product (GDP) at current prices from 2004 to 2014," Statista, http://www.statista.com/statistics/268750/global-gross-domestic-product-gdp/.

28. David Rosenberg, "A Boys' Camp to Redefine Gender," *Slate*, July 15, 2013, http://www.slate.com/blogs/behold/2013/07/15/_you_are_you_looks_at_a_gender_nonconforming_camp_for_boys_photos.html.

29. Cheryl K. Chumley, "Satanic 'black mass' in Oklahoma draws hundreds of protesters," *Washington Times*, September 22, 2014, http://www.washingtontimes.com/news/2014/sep/22/satanic-black-mass-oklahoma-draws-hundreds-protest/.

30. Hawes Spencer, "Child Handcuffed and School Policies Questioned," WVTF, December 9, 2014, http://wvtf.org/post/child-handcuffed-and-school-policies-questioned.

31. Daniel Bukszpan, "Fifty Shades of Grey: How Wal-Mart, Target and Vermont Teddy Bear are cashing in," *Fortune*, February 14, 2015, http://fortune.com/2015/02/14/fifty-shades-of-grey-how-wal-mart-target-and-vermont-teddy-bear-are-cashing-in/.

32. Philip Hickey, "Homosexuality: The Mental Illness That Went Away," Behaviorism and Mental Health, Oct. 8, 2011, http://www.behaviorismandmentalhealth.com/2011/10/08/homosexuality-the-mental-illness-that-went-away/.

CHAPTER 2: THE BLUR

1. Kyle Drennen, "Newsweek's Evan Thomas: Obama Is 'Sort of God,'" *NewsBusters*, June 5, 2009, http://newsbusters.org/blogs/kyle-drennen/2009/06/05/newsweek-s-evan-thomas-obama-sort-god.

2. Barack Obama, The Audacity of Hope: Thoughts on Reclaiming the American Dream (New York: Vintage, 2008), 16.

3. FactCheck.org, "Obama's Legislative Record," September 25, 2008, http://www.factcheck.org/2008/09/obamas-legislative-record/.

4. Jon Meacham, "We Are All Socialists Now," *Newsweek*, February 6, 2009, http://www.newsweek.com/we-are-all-socialists-now-82577.

5. Breitbart News, "Horowitz at Heritage Foundation: 'The Communist Party Is the Democratic Party,'" Breitbart, November 12, 2013, http://www.breitbart.com/big-journalism/2013/11/12/horowitz-blasts-left-heritage/.

6. Patrick Buchanan, The Death of the West: How Dying Populations and Immigrant Invasions Imperil Our Country and Civilization (New York: St. Martin's Griffin, 2002), 73–74.

7. Ibid., 75.

8. Ibid.

9. Ibid., 76.

10. Ibid., 77.

11. "Kupelian on Hannity: Obama staging 'socialist coup,'" WND, April 6, 2010, http://www.wnd.com/2010/04/137513/.

12. The Communist Party USA, "What is Marxism? How can I learn more?," FAQ, accessed May 21, 2015, http://www.cpusa.org/faq/.

13. Williams S. Lind, "Who Stole Our Culture?," WND.com, May 24, 2007, http://www.wnd.com/2007/05/41737/.

14. Buchanan, The Death of the West, 78.

15. Ibid., 79.

16. Ibid., 83.

17. Ibid., 85.

18. *glbtq*, s.v. "Marcuse, Herbert," http://www.glbtq.com/social-sciences/marcuse_h.html, accessed May 21, 2015.

19. Buchanan, The Death of the West, 87.

20. Mikhail Heller, Cogs in the Wheel (New York: Knopf, 1988), pp. 168–79.

21. Phyllis Schlafly, *Who Killed the American Family?* (Washington, DC: WND Books, 2014), 5.

22. Ibid., 7.

23. Ibid., 8.

24. Ibid., 32.

25. Dennis Cauchon, "Marriage gap could sway elections," *USA Today*, September 27, 2006, http://usatoday30.usatoday.com/news/washington/2006-09-26-marriage-gap_x.htm.

26. John Zogby, "Demographics and the Election of 2012: The 'Marriage Gap,'" *Forbes*, July 12, 2012, http://www.forbes.com/sites/johnzogby/2012/07/12/zogby-demographics-and-the-election-of-2012-the-marriage-gap/.

27. Schlafly, Who Killed the American Family?, xiii.

28. See "Obama: 'Fundamentally Transforming the United States of America' Long Version, YouTube video, 1:37, submitted by jbranstetter04, https://www.youtube.com/watch?v=KrefKCaV8m4.

29. Jacob Laksin, "National Council of Churches: Worldviews, Activities, and Agendas," DiscoverTheNetworks.org, 2005, http://www.discoverthenetworks.org/Articles/nccexpandedagenasactivities.html.

30. Ryan Mauro, "Homeland Security's Mohammed Elibiary: Caliphate Inevitable," Clarion Project, June 25, 2014, http://www.clarionproject.org/analysis/homeland-securitys-mohammed-elibiary-caliphate-inevitable.

31. Lisa Gardiner, "American Muslim leader urges faithful to spread Islam's message," *San Ramon Valley Herald,* July 4, 1998, cached at http://www.danielpipes.org/rr/394.pdf.

32. The Investigative Project on Terrorism, *Omar Ahmad and the Palestine Committee: An IPT Investigative Report,* n.d., http://www.investigativeproject.org/documents/misc/635.pdf, 4 (see note 39); see also "The Philadelphia Meeting," *Anti-*CAIR *Report,* Anti-CAIR News & Analysis, October 6, 2008, http://www.anti-cair-net.org/FBItiesCAIRHamas.

33. Lou Gelfland, "Reader says use of 'fundamentalist' hurting Muslims," *Minneapolis Star Tribune,* April 4, 1993, 31A, cached at http://www.anti-cair-net.org/HooperStarTrib.

34. Sun Tzu's Art of War, http://suntzusaid.com/book/3/.

CHAPTER 3: DISINFORMATION AGE

1. President Ronald Reagan, congratulatory retirement letter to Vahey S. Kupelian, March 30, 1988.

2. Peter Schweizer, *Reagan's War: The Epic Story of His Forty-Year Struggle and Final Triumph over Communism* (New York: Doubleday, 2002), 8.

3. Paul Kengor, "Dreams from Frank Marshall Davis," *American Spectator,* October 2012, http://spectator.org/articles/34799/dreams-frank-marshall-davis.

4. Jamie Glazov, "Young Obama's Dreams of a Communist Revolution in America," *FrontPage Mag,* August 8, 2012, http://www.frontpagemag.com/2012/jamie-glazov/young-obama%E2%80%99s-dreams-of-a-communist-revolution-in-america/.

5. Christopher Andersen, *Barack and Michelle: Portrait of an American Marriage* (New York: HarperCollins, 2009), 165–66, 169–70.

6. "Anita Dunn Favorite Philosopher Mao Tse-Tung," OrthodoxNet.com, October 16, 2009, http://www.orthodoxytoday.org/blog/2009/10/anita-dunn-favorite-philosopher-mao-tse-tung/.

7. Aaron Klein, "Czar's 'communist manifesto' scrubbed from Net," WND, August 30, 2009, http://www.wnd.com/2009/08/108445/.

8. Ion Mihai Pacepa and Ronald J. Rychlak, *Disinformation: Former Spy Chief Reveals Secret Strategies for Undermining Freedom, Attacking Religion, and Promoting Terrorism* (Washington, DC: WND Books, 2014), 96.

9. Ibid, 298–99.

10. Ibid., 299.

11. David Mccormack and Annabel Grossman, "They're among the brightest young minds in the country . . . and they think America is a bigger threat to world peace than ISIS," *Daily Mail,* October 9, 2014, http://www.dailymail.co.uk/news/article-2786764/Harvard-students-think-America-bigger-threat-world-peace-ISIS.html.

12. "Ward Churchill: 'U.S. by Its Own Rules Is Subject to Being Bombed,'" *Fox News Insider,* September 9, 2014, http://insider.foxnews.com/2014/09/09/ward-churchill-%E2%80%98us-its-own-rules-subject-being-bombed%E2%80%99.

13. Pacepa and Rychlak, *Disinformation,* 96–97.

14. Ion Mihai Pacepa, "The KGB's Man," *Wall Street Journal,* September 22, 2003, http://online.wsj.com/articles/SB106419296113226300.

15. Pacepa and Rychlak, *Disinformation,* vii–viii.

16. Ibid., 15.

17. Ibid., 2.

18. Michael Fumento, "The Great Black Church-Burning Hoax," *Wall Street Journal*, 1998, http://fumento.com/racism/column8.html. See also http://fumento.com/arson/.
19. Pacepa and Rychlak, *Disinformation*, 4.
20. Ibid., 2–3.
21. Ibid., 3.
22. Ibid.
23. *Wikipedia* defines "elite media" as "newspapers, radio stations, TV channels, and other media that influence the political agenda of other mass media." *Wikipedia*, s.v. "elite media," http://en.wikipedia.org/wiki/Elite_media, accessed May 21, 2015.
24. Askold Krushelnycky, "Ukrainians want pro-Stalin writer stripped of Pulitzer," *Guardian*, May 3, 2003, http://www.theguardian.com/world/2003/may/04/russia.usa.
25. Jacques Steinberg, "Times Should Lose Pulitzer from 30's, Consultant Says," *New York Times*, October 23, 2003, http://www.nytimes.com/2003/10/23/us/times-should-lose-pulitzer-from-30-s-consultant-says.html.
26. Askold Krushelnycky, "Ukrainians want pro-Stalin writer stripped of Pulitzer," *Guardian*, May 3, 2003, http://www.theguardian.com/world/2003/may/04/russia.usa.
27. David Kupelian, The Marketing of Evil: How Radicals, Elitists, and Pseudo-Experts Sell Us Corruption Disguised as Freedom (Washington, DC: WND Books, 2005), 190–92.

CHAPTER 4: CHAOS THEORY

1. Al Weaver, "Cheney: President Obama Wants 'to Take America Down,'" *Daily Caller*, April 7, 2015, http://dailycaller.com/2015/04/07/cheney-president-obama-wants-to-take-america-down-video/.
2. Ali Meyer, "Record 20% of Households on Food Stamps in 2013," CNSNews.com, January 21, 2014, http://cnsnews.com/news/article/ali-meyer/record-20-households-food-stamps-2013.
3. See "Obama: 'If you like your health care plan, you'll be able to keep your health care plan,'" Politifact.com, http://www.politifact.com/obama-like-health-care-keep/.
4. Sally Nelson, "Report: 83 percent of doctors have considered quitting over Obamacare," *Daily Caller*, July 9, 2012, http://dailycaller.com/2012/07/09/report-83-of-doctors-have-considered-quitting-over-obamacare/.
5. Vince Coglianese, "Obama tells Latinos to 'punish our enemies,' the GOP," *Daily Caller*, October 25, 2010, http://dailycaller.com/2010/10/25/obama-tells-latinos-to-punish-our-enemies-the-gop/.
6. "Krauthammer: 'Obama Clearly a Narcissist,' 'Lives in a Cocoon Surrounded by Sycophants,'" Fox News, September 16, 2014, http://nation.foxnews.com/2014/09/16/krauthammer-obama-clearly-narcissist-lives-cocoon-surrounded-sycophants.
7. Jerome R. Corsi, "Congressmen: Obama using 'Cloward-Piven maneuver,'" WND, June 11, 2014, http://www.wnd.com/2014/06/congressmen-obama-using-cloward-piven-maneuver/.
8. Frances Fox Piven and Richard Cloward, "The Weight of the Poor: A Strategy to End Poverty," *The Nation*, May 2, 1966, http://www.thenation.com/article/weight-poor-strategy-end-poverty#.
9. Richard Poe, "The Cloward-Piven Strategy," DiscoverTheNetworks.org, 2005, http://www.discoverthenetworks.org/Articles/theclowardpivenstrategypoe.html.
10. Ibid.
11. Sol Stern, "ACORN's Nutty Regime for Cities," *City Journal*, Spring 2003, http://www.city-journal.org/html/13_2_acorns_nutty_regime.html.
12. Eleanor Goldberg, "80% of Central American Women, Girls Are Raped Crossing Into the U.S.," *Huffington Post*, September 12, 2014, http://www.huffingtonpost.com/2014/09/12/central-america-migrants-rape_n_5806972.html.

13. Tony Lee, "L.A. Times Concedes 'Serious Diseases' Come from Mexico, Central America," Breitbart, February 18, 2015, http://www.breitbart.com/big-journalism/2015/02/18/l-a-times-concedes-serious-diseases-come-from-mexico-central-america/.

14. Elizabeth Lee Vliet, "Deadly Diseases Crossing Border with Illegals," WND, June 17, 2014, http://www.wnd.com/2014/06/deadly-diseases-crossing-border-with-illegals/.

15. Jennifer Harper, "No laughing matter: Perry's Texas jails 203,000 'criminal aliens' for 640K crimes," *Washington Times*, July 22, 2014, http://www.washingtontimes.com/news/2014/jul/22/rick-perry-county-jails-texas-have-taken-203000-cr/.

16. John Boehner's "22 Times President Obama Said He Couldn't Ignore or Create His Own Immigration Law" at http://www.speaker.gov/general/22-times-president-obama-said-he-couldn-t-ignore-or-create-his-own-immigration-law.

17. Leo Hohmann, "U.S. cities 'secretly selected' for importing Muslims," WND, April 8, 2015, http://www.wnd.com/2015/04/u-s-cities-secretly-selected-for-muslim-immigration/.

18. Jessica Vaughan, "ICE Document Details 36,000 Criminal Alien Releases in 2013," Center for Immigration Studies, May 2014, http://cis.org/ICE-Document-Details-36000-Criminal-Aliens-Release-in-2013.

19. Gerald F. Seib, "In Crisis, Opportunity for Obama," Wall Street Journal, November 21, 2008, http://www.wsj.com/articles/SB122721278056345271.

20. Lyle H. Rossiter, Jr., *The Liberal Mind: The Psychological Causes of Political Madness* (St. Charles, IL: Free World Books, 2006), 332.

21. Ibid., 333.

22. William Sargant, Battle for the Mind: A Physiology of Conversion and Brainwashing—How Evangelists, Psychiatrists, Politicians, and Medicine Men Can Change Your Beliefs and Behavior (Cambridge, MA: Major Books, 1997), 151.

23. Ibid., 154–55.

24. "Lifton's Brainwashing Processes," ChangingMinds.org, accessed May 21, 2015, http://changingminds.org/techniques/conversion/lifton_brainwashing.htm.

25. Julia Layton, "How Brainwashing Works," HowStuffWorks.com, accessed May 21, 2015, http://science.howstuffworks.com/life/inside-the-mind/human-brain/brainwashing1.htm.

26. Dinesh D'Souza, "Obama and Post-Racist America," TownHall.com, January 28, 2009, http://townhall.com/columnists/dineshdsouza/2009/01/28/obama_and_post-racist_america/page/full.

27. Beth Fouhy, "Obama Addresses Question of Experience," *Washington Post*, April 21, 2007, http://www.washingtonpost.com/wp-dyn/content/article/2007/04/21/AR2007042100650.html.

28. Mark Sherman, "Supreme Court declares nationwide right to same-sex marriage," Associated Press, June 26, 2015, http://hosted.ap.org/dynamic/stories/U/US_SUPREME_COURT_GAY_MARRIAGE?SITE=AP&SECTION=HOME&TEMPLATE=DEFAULT&CTIME=2015-06-26-10-02-52.

29. David Nakamura, "Obama on same-sex marriage ruling: 'We have made our union a little more perfect,'" *Washington Post*, June 26, 2015, http://www.washingtonpost.com/blogs/post-politics/wp/2015/06/26/obama-on-same-sex-marriage-ruling-we-have-made-our-union-a-little-more-perfect/.

30. Saul Alinsky, *Rules for Radicals: A Pragmatic Primer for Realistic Radicals* (New York: Vintage, 1971), xix.

31. Ibid., xxi–xxii.

32. Ibid., 128.

33. Ibid., 129.

34. Ibid., 129–30.
35. Ibid., 136.
36. Ibid.
37. Ibid., 137.

CHAPTER 5: MAGIC WORDS

1. National Annenberg Election Survey, "Most Indians Say Name of Washington 'Redskins' Is Acceptable While 9 Percent Call It Offensive," the Annenberg Public Policy Center, September 24, 2004, http://www.annenbergpublicpolicycenter.org/most-indians-say-name-of-washington-redskins-is-acceptable-while-9-percent-call-it-offensive/.

2. Jessica Chasmar, "White House calls illegal immigrants 'Americans-in-waiting,'" *Washington Times*, February 25, 2015, http://www.washingtontimes.com/news/2015/feb/25/white-house-calls-illegal-immigrants-americans-in-/.

3. Ingrid Newkirk, cofounder of People for the Ethical Treatment of Animals (PETA) famously told Vogue magazine in 1989, "A rat is a pig is a dog is a boy. They are all mammals."

4. Doctors on Fetal Pain, "Fetal Pain: The Evidence," March 14, 2011, http://www.doctorsonfetalpain.com/.

5. Jay Sekulow, "UN's twisted logic: Free speech equals 'torture,'" Fox News, May 16, 2014, http://www.foxnews.com/opinion/2014/05/16/un-twisted-logic-free-speech-equals-torture/.

6. Center for Reproductive Rights, Argument to the United Nations Committee Against Torture, April 11, 2014, http://tbinternet.ohchr.org/Treaties/CAT/Shared%20Documents/VAT/INT_CAT_NGO_VAT_17038_E.pdf.

7. Jerry Adler et al., "Taking Offense: Is this the new enlightenment on campus or the new McCarthyism?," *Newsweek*, December 24, 1990, cached at the website of Bob Just, at http://bobjust.com/cgi-bin/imcart/read_v2.cgi?article_id=1&sub=3.

8. Ibid.

9. Ibid.

10. Ibid.

11. William Lind, "The Origins of Political Correctness," Accuracy in Academia, February 5, 2000, http://www.academia.org/the-origins-of-political-correctness/.

12. Ibid.

13. Mao Zedong, "Where Do Correct Ideas Come From?," People's Publishing House, Beijing, May 1963, 1.

14. Mao Zedong, "Combat Liberalism," September 7, 1937, in *Selected Works*, vol. 2 (Peking, China: Foreign Language Press, 1937), 33.

15. Mao Zedong, "Methods of Work of Party Committees," March 13, 1949, in Selected Works, vol. 4 (Peking, China: Foreign Language Press, 1945), 378–79.

16. Mao Zedong, "On Khrushchev's Phony Communism and Its Historical Lessons for the World," July 14, 1964, 72–74.

17. Wen Hua, "A Tribute to He Zizhen, Abandoned Wife of Mao Zedong," *Epoch Times*, September 12, 2006, http://www.theepochtimes.com/news/6-9-12/45882.html.

18. Li Zhisui, *The Private Life of Chairman Mao* (New York: Random House, 1995).

19. Winston Churchill quotes on socialism, website of the National Churchill Museum, accessed June 9, 2015, https://www.nationalchurchillmuseum.org/socialism-quotes.html.

20. M. Scott Peck, *People of the Lie: The Hope for Healing Human Evil* (New York: Touchstone, 1983), 78.

CHAPTER 6: URBAN WARFARE

1. Kurt Badenhausen, "Detroit Tops 2013 List of America's Most Miserable Cities," *Forbes*, February 21, 2013, http://www.forbes.com/sites/kurtbadenhausen/2013/02/21/detroit-tops-2013-list-of-americas-most-miserable-cities/.

2. Alana Semuels, "Thousands go without water as Detroit cuts service for nonpayment," *Los Angeles Times*, June 28, 2014, http://www.latimes.com/nation/la-na-detroit-water-20140629-story.html#page=1.

3. Kurt Badenhausen, "America's Most Miserable Cities 2013," February 21, 2013, *Forbes*, http://www.forbes.com/pictures/mli45lmhg/1-detroit-mich/.

4. Mark Newman, "Maps of the 2012 U.S. presidential election results," Department of Physics and Center for the Study of Complex Systems, November 8, 2012, http://www-personal.umich.edu/~mejn/election/2012/.

5. Josh Kron, "Red State, Blue City: How the Urban-Rural Divide Is Splitting America," *Atlantic*, November 30, 2012, http://www.theatlantic.com/politics/archive/2012/11/red-state-blue-city-how-the-urban-rural-divide-is-splitting-america/265686/.

6. Ibid.

7. "Election 2012—Oregon, Map of Presidential Results," *New York Times*, http://elections.nytimes.com/2012/results/states/oregon.

8. Kron, "Red State, Blue City."

9. Drew DeSilver, "How the most ideologically polarized Americans live different lives," Pew Research, June 13, 2014, http://www.pewresearch.org/fact-tank/2014/06/13/big-houses-art-museums-and-in-laws-how-the-most-ideologically-polarized-americans-live-different-lives/.

10. Laura Meckler and Dante Chinni, "City vs. Country: How Where We Live Deepens the Nation's Political Divide," *Wall Street Journal*, March 21, 2014, http://online.wsj.com/articles/SB10001424052702303636404579395532755485004.

11. Darren Schreiber et al., "Red Brain, Blue Brain: Evaluative Processes Differ in Democrats and Republicans," PLOS One, February 13, 2013, http://journals.plos.org/plosone/article?id=10.1371/journal.pone.0052970.

12. James G. Gimpel, "Migration, Immigration and the Politics of Places," Center for Immigration Studies, October 1999, http://cis.org/InternalMigration-GeographicMobility.

13. James G. Gimpel, "Immigration's Impact on Republican Political Prospects, 1980 to 2012," Center for Immigration Studies, April 2014, http://cis.org/immigration-impacts-on-republican-prospects-1980-2012.

14. Eileen Patten and Mark Hugo Lopez, "Are unauthorized immigrants overwhelmingly Democrats?," Pew Research, July 22, 2013, http://www.pewresearch.org/fact-tank/2013/07/22/are-unauthorized-immigrants-overwhelmingly-democrats/.

15. Steve Salvi, "Sanctuary Cities: What are they?," The Original list of Sanctuary Cities, USA, Ohio Jobs & Justice PAC, http://www.ojjpac.org/sanctuary.asp, accessed May 22, 2015.

16. Jerome Corsi, "Congressmen: Obama using 'Cloward-Piven maneuver': 'Attempt to flood the border with illegals' part of infamous socialist strategy," WND, June 11, 2014, http://www.wnd.com/2014/06/congressmen-obama-using-cloward-piven-maneuver/.

17. Breitbart TV, "Gohmert: Obama Is Flooding Texas with Immigrants to 'Turn It Blue,'" Breitbart, July 7, 2014, http://www.breitbart.com/Breitbart-TV/2014/07/07/Gohmert-Obama-Flooding-Texas-With-Immigrants-To-Turn-it-Blue.

18. Philip Bump, "What the 2012 election could have looked like with 100 percent turnout," *Washington Post*, March 19, 2015, http://www.washingtonpost.com/blogs/the-fix/wp/2015/03/19/what-the-2012-election-could-have-looked-like-with-100-percent-turnout/.

19. Michelle Malkin, "That Rioting in Baltimore? It's All Our Fault," *National Review*, April 29, 2015, http://www.nationalreview.com/article/417638/rioting-baltimore-its-all-our-fault-michelle-malkin.

20. Kevin D. Williamson, "Riot-Plagued Baltimore Is a Catastrophe Entirely of the Democratic Party's Own Making," *National Review*, April 28, 2015, http://www.nationalreview.com/article/417601/riot-plagued-baltimore-catastrophe-entirely-democratic-partys-own-making-kevin-d.

21. Daniel Greenfield, "The American City Is Dying," *FrontPage Mag*, January 30, 2013, http://www.frontpagemag.com/2013/dgreenfield/the-american-city-is-dying/.

22. Angelo M. Codevilla, "America's Ruling Class—and the Perils of Revolution," *American Spectator*, July–August 2010, http://spectator.org/articles/39326/americas-ruling-class-and-perils-revolution.

CHAPTER 7: THE REAL ZOMBIE APOCALYPSE

1. "Medical Marijuana," accessed May 22, 2015, http://medicalmarijuana.com/treatments-with-medical-marijuana-cannabis.

2. Nick Taborek, Callie Bost, and Nikolaj Gammeltoft, "Pot Shares Rally 21% to 1,700% as Speculators See Green," Bloomberg News, January 9, 2014, http://www.bloomberg.com/news/2014-01-09/pot-shares-rally-21-to-1-700-as-speculators-see-green.html.

3. Aldo Svaldi, "High Times launches private equity fund for marijuana investment," *Denver Post*, January 4, 2014, http://www.denverpost.com/business/ci_24844193/high-times-launches-fund-cannabis-investment.

4. Bruce Kennedy, "Ad agencies prepare for the legal marijuana market," CBS News, January 6, 2014, http://www.cbsnews.com/news/ad-agencies-prepare-for-the-legal-marijuana-market/.

5. Shannon Bond, "Bob Marley: Marlboro Man of marijuana," *Financial Times*, November 18, 2014, http://www.ft.com/intl/cms/s/2/01da3e7e-6e81-11e4-a65a-00144feabdc0.html#axzz3JXZVK3ut.

6. Joanne Ostrow, "Pot plays big on TV in 'Glee,' 'Parenthood' and 'Mad Men,'" *Denver Post*, December 23, 2013, http://www.sltrib.com/sltrib/entertainment2/57270472-223/pot-colorado-marijuana-post.html.csp.

7. Aly Weisman, "11 Celebrities Who Are Outspoken about Their Love of Weed," *Business Insider*, April 20, 2013, http://www.businessinsider.com/celebrities-who-smoke-weed-2013-4?op=1.

8. CNN Political Unit, "CNN Poll: Support for legal marijuana soaring," *Political Ticker* (blog), January 6, 2014, http://politicalticker.blogs.cnn.com/2014/01/06/cnn-poll-support-for-legal-marijuana-soaring/.

9. David Remnick, "Going the Distance: On and off the road with Barack Obama," *New Yorker*, January 27, 2014, http://www.newyorker.com/magazine/2014/01/27/going-the-distance-2?currentPage=all.

10. Madeline H. Meier et al., "Persistent cannabis users show neuropsychological decline from childhood to midlife," *PNAS* 109, no. 40, http://www.pnas.org/content/109/40/E2657.abstract.

11. Gillian Mohney, "Colorado Teen Addiction Centers Gear Up for Legal Pot," ABC News, January 3, 2014, http://abcnews.go.com/blogs/health/2014/01/03/colo-teen-addiction-centers-gear-up-for-legal-pot/.

12. "Strong cannabis causes one in four cases of psychosis," *Daily Mail*, February 15, 2015, http://www.dailymail.co.uk/news/article-2955020/Strong-cannabis-causes-one-four-cases-psychosis-Users-three-times-likely-episode-never-tried-it.html.

13. Substance Abuse and Mental Health Services Administration, Results from the 2013 National Survey on Drug Use and Health: Summary of National Findings, NSDUH Series H-48, HHS Publication No. (SMA) 14-4863. Rockville, MD: Substance Abuse and Mental Health Services Administration, 2014, http://www.samhsa.gov/data/sites/default/files/NSDUHresultsPDFWHTML2013/Web/NSDUHresults2013.pdf.

14. Ibid.

15. "In an average year 30 million Americans drive drunk - 10 million drive impaired by illicit drugs," Substance Abuse and Mental Health Services Administration, December 9, 2010, http://www.samhsa.gov/newsroom/press-announcements/201012091230.

16. Substance Abuse and Mental Health Services Administration, Results from the 2013 National Survey on Drug Use and Health: Summary of National Findings, NSDUH Series H-48, HHS Publication No. (SMA) 14-4863. Rockville, MD: Substance Abuse and Mental Health Services Administration, 2014, http://www.samhsa.gov/data/sites/default/files/NSDUHresultsPDFWHTML2013/Web/NSDUHresults2013.pdf.

17. Centers for Disease Control and Prevention, "CDC Grand Rounds: Prescription Drug Overdoses—a U.S. Epidemic," *Morbidity and Mortality Weekly Report*, January 13, 2012, http://www.cdc.gov/mmwr/preview/mmwrhtml/mm6101a3.htm.

18. "Opiate Pain Relievers for Chronic Pain," WebMD, http://www.webmd.com/pain-management/opioid-analgesics-for-chronic-pain.

19. Allison McCabe, "America's Number One Prescription Sleep Aid Could Trigger 'Zombies,' Murder and Other Disturbing Behavior," *The Fix*, as reprinted on AlterNet, January 15, 2014, http://www.alternet.org/drugs/americas-number-one-prescription-sleep-aid-could-trigger-zombies-murder-and-other-disturbing?ak_proof=1&akid=.1121926.wDJK8-.&rd=1&src=newsletter948677&t=11.

20. U.S. Food and Drug Administration, Ambien approved labeling April 23, 2008.

21. Sabrina Tavernise, "Drug Agency Recommends Lower Doses of Sleep Aids for Women," *New York Times*, January 10, 2013, http://www.nytimes.com/2013/01/11/health/fda-requires-cuts-to-dosages-of-ambien-and-other-sleep-drugs.html?_r=2&.

22. Thomas Insel, "Director's Blog: Antidepressants: A complicated picture," National Institute of Mental Health, December 6, 2011, http://www.nimh.nih.gov/about/director/2011/antidepressants-a-complicated-picture.shtml.

23. U.S. Food and Drug Administration, "Antidepressant Use in Children, Adolescents, and Adults," May 2, 2007, online at http://www.fda.gov/Drugs/DrugSafety/InformationbyDrugClass/UCM096273.

24. SSRI Stories: Antidepressant Nightmares, "Our Stories," accessed May 22, 2015, http://www.ssristories.org/.

25. Angela K. Brown, "Antidepressant used by Yates questioned," Associated Press, July 9, 2006, http://www.washingtonpost.com/wp-dyn/content/article/2006/07/09/AR2006070900582_pf.html.

26. "Antidepressant Nightmares," SSRI Stories, http://ssristories.org/.

27. Kara M. Conners, "Antidepressants: Can They Turn Kids into Killers? New Cases, Evidence to Test 'Prozac Defense,'" Press & Sun-Bulletin, February 20, 2005.

28. Centers for Disease Control and Prevention, "Attention-Deficit/ Hyperactivity Disorder (ADHD): Data & Statistics," accessed May 22, 2015, http://www.cdc.gov/ncbddd/adhd/data.html.

29. U.S. Drug Enforcement Administration, "Methylphenidate (Ritalin)," Drug Fact Sheets, accessed May 22, 2015, http://www.dea.gov/druginfo/concern_meth.shtml.

30. New Hampshire Department of Health and Human Services, "Controlled Substances: Federal Controlled Substance Schedule," accessed May 22, 2015, http://www.dhhs.nh.gov/dcbcs/bdas/controlledsubstances.htm.

31. Robert Whitaker, *"New York Times*: When Stimulants Are Bad," Mad in America, June 11, 2012, https://www.madinamerica.com/2012/06/the-ny-times-when-stimulants-are-bad/.

32. Centers for Disease Control and Prevention, "2011–2012 National Survey of Children's Health," State and Local Area Integrated Telephone Survey, http://www.cdc.gov/nchs/slaits/nsch.htm.

33. Garth Kant, "Radical increase in kids prescribed Ritalin," WND, April 1, 2013, http://www.wnd.com/2013/04/radical-increase-in-kids-prescribed-ritalin/.

34. Robert S. Mendelsohn, M.D., *The People's Doctor*, No. 4, Vol. 12: 1988.

35. National Institute of Mental Health, "What is Depression?," accessed May 22, 2015, http://www.nimh.nih.gov/health/publications/depression/index.shtml.

36. The remaining quotes in this section are from Gary Greenberg, "The Psychiatric Drug Crisis," *New Yorker*, September 3, 2013, http://www.newyorker.com/tech/elements/the-psychiatric-drug-crisis.

37. Ibid.38.

38. Virginia Hughes, "How Scientists Are Learning to Shape Our Memory," *Popular Science*, November 25, 2013, http://www.popsci.com/article/science/how-scientists-are-learning-shape-our-memory.

39. Katie Rucke, "Are Psychedelic Drugs the New Marijuana?," Mint Press News, September 4, 2013, http://www.mintpressnews.com/are-psychedelics-the-new-marijuana/168289/.

CHAPTER 8: ADDICT NATION

1. "Addiction Medicine: Closing the Gap between Science and Practice," The National Center on Addiction and Substance Abuse at Columbia University, June 2012, http://www.casacolumbia.org/addiction-research/reports/addiction-medicine.

2. Graeme Paton, "Infants 'unable to use toy building blocks' due to iPad addiction," *Telegraph*, April 15, 2014, http://www.telegraph.co.uk/education/educationnews/10767878/Infants-unable-to-use-toy-building-blocks-due-to-iPad-addiction.html.

3. Nancy M. Petry1 and Charles P. O'Brien, "Internet gaming disorder and the DSM-5," May 13, 2013, http://onlinelibrary.wiley.com/doi/10.1111/add.12162/full.

4. Karl Turner, "17-year-old accused of killing mother over Halo 3 video game may get verdict soon," Cleveland.com, December 16, 2008, http://blog.cleveland.com/metro/2008/12/trial_of_boy_accused_of_killin.html.

5. Romeo Vitelli, "Are Video Games Addictive?," *Psychology Today*, August 19, 2013, http://www.psychologytoday.com/blog/media-spotlight/201308/are-video-games-addictive.

6. Jordan Steffen, "12-year-old allegedly tries to poison mom for taking away iPhone," *Denver Post*, March 20, 2015, http://www.denverpost.com/news/ci_27753705/12-year-old-allegedly-tries-poison-mom-taking.

7. Tom Phillips, "Chinese teen chops hand off to 'cure' internet addiction," *Telegraph*, February 3, 2015, http://www.telegraph.co.uk/news/worldnews/asia/china/11386325/Chinese-teen-chops-hand-off-to-cure-internet-addiction.html.

8. Phill Dunn, "Online gambling spurs addiction fears," *USA Today*, March 16, 2014, http://www.usatoday.com/story/news/nation/2014/03/16/online-gambling-addiction/6476761/.

9. "Report: Nearly a Quarter of All Teens Go Online 'Almost Constantly," Philadelphia CBS Local, April 14, 2015, http://philadelphia.cbslocal.com/2015/04/14/report-nearly-a-quarter-of-all-teens-go-online-almost-constantly/.

10. "Pornography Statistics: Annual Report 2014," Covenant Eyes, http://www.covenanteyes.com/pornstats/.

11. ProvenMen.org, "Pornography Addiction Survey (conducted by the Barna Group), Proven Men, accessed May 22, 2015, http://www.provenmen.org/2014pornsurvey/pornography-use-and-addiction/.

12. "Internet pornography by the numbers; a significant threat to society," Webroot, accessed May 22, 2015, http://www.webroot.com/us/en/home/resources/tips/digital-family-life/internet-pornography-by-the-numbers.

13. Carolyn Kellogg, "'Fifty Shades of Grey' trilogy tops 100 million in worldwide sales," *Los Angeles Times*, February 26, 2014, http://articles.latimes.com/2014/feb/26/entertainment/la-et-jc-fifty-shades-of-grey-tops-100-million-in-worldwide-sales-20140226.

14. Cynthia L. Ogden et al., "Prevalence of Childhood and Adult Obesity in the United States, 2011–2012," *Journal of the American Medical Association*, February 26, 2014, http://jama.jamanetwork.com/article.aspx?articleid=1832542.

15. Ashley N. Gearhardt et al., "Can Food Be Addictive? Public Health and Policy Implications," February 14, 2011, http://www.ncbi.nlm.nih.gov/pmc/articles/PMC3171738/.

16. Ibid.

17. Tara Parker-Pope, "How the Food Makers Captured Our Brains," *New York Times*, June 22, 2009, http://www.nytimes.com/2009/06/23/health/23well.html?_r=2&.

18. George Dvorsky, "Is it true that Oreos are more addictive to lab rats than cocaine?," *io9* (blog), October 16, 2013, http://io9.com/is-it-true-that-oreos-are-more-addictive-to-lab-rats-th-1446363299.

19. Lauren Paxman, "One in 12 teenagers self-harm (but most grow out of it by their twenties)," *Daily Mail*, November 17, 2011, http://www.dailymail.co.uk/health/article-2062629/One-12-teenagers-self-harm-grow-twenties.html.

20. Harvard Health, "Understanding Addiction: How Addiction Hijacks the Brain," HelpGuide.org, accessed May 22, 2015, http://www.helpguide.org/harvard/how-addiction-hijacks-the-brain.htm.

21. Jeremy Laurance, "Addicted! Scientists show how internet dependency alters the human brain," *Independent*, January 12, 2012, http://www.independent.co.uk/news/science/addicted-scientists-show-how-internet-dependency-alters-the-human-brain-6288344.html.

22. "Internet addiction affects the brain 'like a drink or drug problem,'" *Telegraph*, December 1, 2012, http://www.telegraph.co.uk/technology/internet/9009125/Internet-addiction-affects-the-brain-like-a-drink-or-drug-problem.html?mobile=basic.

23. See "My Strange Addiction (2010–)," IMDb, http://www.imdb.com/title/tt1809014/.

24. David Hinckley, "'My Strange Addiction' has a gallery of weird cravings: eating tires, cat fur, VapoRub," *New York Daily News*, March 6, 2013, http://www.nydailynews.com/entertainment/tv-movies/strange-addiction-delivers-big-grosses-article-1.1279987.

25. *Wikipedia*, s.v. "My Strange Addiction," http://en.wikipedia.org/wiki/My_Strange_Addiction, accessed May 22, 2015.

26. Ben Tufft, "Heroin to be prescribed to Canadian addicts by doctors," *Independent*, November 23, 2014, http://www.independent.co.uk/news/science/heroin-to-be-prescribed-to-canadian-addicts-by-doctors-9878322.html.

27. Carl Erik Fisher, "Psychiatrists Embrace Deep-Brain Stimulation," *Scientific American*, December 19, 2013, http://www.scientificamerican.com/article/psychiatrists-embrace-deep-brain-stimulation/.

28. *Frontline*, "What is addiction, and how can we treat it?," PBS, http://www.pbs.org/wgbh/pages/frontline/shows/drugs/buyers/treatment.html.

29. Harvard Health, "Understanding Addiction."

30. CasaColumbia, *Addiction Medicine: Closing the Gap between Science and Practice,* The National Center on Addiction and Substance Abuse at Columbia University, June 2012, http://www.casacolumbia.org/addiction-research/reports/addiction-medicine.

31. Dr. Keith Ablow, "Obesity is not a disease—and neither is alcoholism," FoxNews.com, June 20, 2013, http://www.foxnews.com/health/2013/06/20/dr-keith-ablow-obesity-is-not-disease-and-neither-is-alcoholism/.

32. Ibid.

33. Ibid.

34. Stephen Diamond, "Avoidance, Sobriety and Reality: The Psychology of Addiction," *Evil Deeds (Psychology Today* blog), February 28, 2010, http://www.psychologytoday.com/blog/evil-deeds/201002/avoidance-sobriety-and-reality-the-psychology-addiction.

35. Candy Finnigan and Sean Finnigan, When Enough is Enough: A Comprehensive Guide to Successful Intervention (New York: Avery, 2008), 3–4.

36. "Problem Gambling," Comprehensive Mental Health Services website, accessed May 22, 2015, http://www.thecmhs.com/Gambling_Addictions.html.

37. Susan Donaldson James, "Auto-Erotic Asphyxia's Deadly Thrill," ABC News, June 5, 2009, http://abcnews.go.com/Health/story?id=7764618.

38. Finnigan and Finnigan, *When Enough Is Enough*, 4.

39. WHO, *Global Status Report on Alcohol and Health* (World Health Organization, 2011), www.who.int/substance_abuse/publications/global_alcohol_report/msbgsruprofiles.pdf, p. 27.

40. Pauline Jelinek, "Military culture of drinking and drug abuse called crisis in report," *Seattle Times*, September 17, 2012, http://www.seattletimes.com/nation-world/military-culture-of-drinking-and-drug-abuse-called-crisis-in-report/.

41. Sarah Portlock, "Contracting GDP Is Rare Outside of Recessions," *Real Time Economics*, May 29, 2014, http://blogs.wsj.com/economics/2014/05/29/contracting-gdp-is-rare-outside-of-recessions/.

42. Terence P. Jeffrey, "92,594,000: Americans Not in Labor Force Hits All-Time Record," CNSNews.com, May 2, 2014, http://www.cnsnews.com/news/article/terence-p-jeffrey/92594000-americans-not-labor-force-hits-all-time-record-participation.

43. Pete Baklinski, "Lesbian teacher: How I convince kids to accept gay 'marriage', starting at 4-years-old," LifeSite News, April 20, 2015, https://www.lifesitenews.com/news/lesbian-teacher-how-i-convince-kids-to-accept-gay-marriage-starting-at-4-ye.

CHAPTER 9: GENDER MADNESS

1. Melissa Thompson, "My anorexia battle: I survived on an apple and laxatives then my baby saved my life," *Daily Mirror*, June 5, 2013, http://www.mirror.co.uk/news/real-life-stories/anorexia-battle-survived-apple-laxatives-1932129.

2. Ruth Styles, "Having a baby cured my anorexia," June 5, 2013, http://www.dailymail.co.uk/femail/article-2336424/Mother-reveals-having-child-helped-beat-anorexia.html.

3. "Anorexia Nervosa," the National Eating Disorders Association, http://www.nationaleatingdisorders.org/anorexia-nervosa, accessed May 23, 2015.

4. "The Transgender Tipping Point," *Time*, May 29, 2014, http://time.com/135480/transgender-tipping-point/.

5. Sophia Gubb, "What It Feels Like to Be Transgender (and Why Trans Genders Are Valid)," Sophia Gubb's Blog, August 23, 2013, http://www.sophiagubb.com/what-does-it-feel-like-to-be-transgender/.

6. "Transgender and wanting to avoid mirrors?," Yahoo! Answers, accessed May 23, 2015, https://answers.yahoo.com/question/index?qid=20130620175733AAsv6l0.

7. Voices.Yahoo.com, http://voices.yahoo.com/transsexuals-please-explain-why-sex-surgery-necessary-2224286.html.

8. Jessica Roy, "'I Am a Woman' and 14 More Moving Statements from Bruce Jenner's 20/20 Interview," *TV Guide*, April 25, 2015, http://www.tvguide.com/news/quotes-bruce-jenner-2020-interview/.

9. Buzz Bissinger, "Introducing Caitlyn Jenner," *Vanity Fair*, July 2015, http://www.vanityfair.com/hollywood/2015/06/caitlyn-jenner-bruce-cover-annie-leibovitz.

10. "What is OCD?," International OCD Foundation, http://www.ocfoundation.org/whatisocd.aspx, accessed May 23, 2015.

11. "Statistics," National Institute of Mental Health, http://www.nimh.nih.gov/health/publications/the-numbers-count-mental-disorders-in-america/index.shtml, accessed May 23, 2015.

12. Rachel Pomerance, "One in 50 American kids has autism: What the latest figures tell us," *U.S. News and World Report*, March 29, 2013, http://www.nydailynews.com/life-style/health/50-american-kids-autism-latest-figures-article-1.1302872.

13. Luke Malone, "Transgender Suicide Attempt Rates Are Staggering," Vocativ, March 5, 2015, http://www.vocativ.com/culture/lgbt/transgender-suicide/.

14. Robin S. Rosenberg, "Abnormal Is the New Normal," *Slate*, April 12, 2013, http://www.slate.com/articles/health_and_science/medical_examiner/2013/04/diagnostic_and_statistical_manual_fifth_edition_why_will_half_the_u_s_population.html.

15. Traci G. Lee, "Being transgender no longer a 'mental disorder': APA," NBC News, December 7, 2012, http://www.nbcnews.com/id/50075205/t/being-transgender-no-longer-mental-disorder-apa/#.VIEVHWcRc3l.

16. Lin Frasera et al., "Recommendations for Revision of the DSM Diagnoses of Gender Identity Disorders from the World Professional Association for Transgender Health," *International Journal of Transgenderism* 12, no. 2 (2010): 80–85, http://www.tandfonline.com/doi/abs/10.1080/15532739.2010.509202#.VIEiMmcRc9l.

17. Ibid.

18. Louise K. Newman, "Sex, Gender and Culture: Issues in the Definition, Assessment and Treatment of Gender Identity Disorder," *Clinical Child Psychology and Psychiatry*, July 2002, http://ccp.sagepub.com/content/7/3/352.

19. Clara Moskowitz, "Transgender Americans face high suicide risk," NBC News, November 19, 2010, http://www.nbcnews.com/id/40279043/ns/health-health_care/#.VIEkiWcRc3l.

20. Stella Morabito, "Trouble in Transtopia: Murmurs of Sex Change Regret," *Federalist*, November 11, 2014, http://thefederalist.com/2014/11/11/trouble-in-transtopia-murmurs-of-sex-change-regret/.

21. Michael W. Chapman, "Johns Hopkins Psychiatrist: Transgender Is 'Mental Disorder;' Sex Change 'Biologically Impossible,'" CNSNews.com, August 20, 2014, http://cnsnews.com/news/article/michael-w-chapman/johns-hopkins-psychiatrist-transgender-mental-disorder-sex-change.

22. Paul McHugh, "Transgender Surgery Isn't the Solution," *Wall Street Journal*, June 12, 2014, http://www.wsj.com/articles/paul-mchugh-transgender-surgery-isnt-the-solution-1402615120.

23. Mary J. Moss, "Camp Aranu'tiq: A Safe Haven for Transgender Kids," *Huffington Post*, August 11, 2014, http://www.huffingtonpost.com/mary-j-moss/camp-aranutiqa-safe-haven_b_5665060.html.

24. Matthey Cullinan Hoffman, "Former president of APA says organization controlled by 'gay rights' movement," LifeSite News, June 4, 2012, https://www.lifesitenews.com/news/

former-president-of-apa-says-organization-controlled-by-gay-rights-movement?utm_
source=LifeSiteNews.com+Daily+Newsletter&utm_campaign=710f05a9f1-LifeSiteNews_com_
US_Headlines_06_04_2012&utm_medium=email.

25. Jenny Kutner, "Genetic sexual attraction is normal, and very real," *Salon*, February 17, 2015, http://
www.salon.com/2015/02/17/genetic_sexual_attraction_is_normal_and_very_real_a_woman_
describes_the_reality_of_parent_child_incest/.

26. Cheryl Wetzstein, "APA to correct manual: Pedophilia is not a 'sexual orientation,'" *Washington
Times*, October 31, 2013, http://www.washingtontimes.com/news/2013/oct/31/apa-correct-manual-
clarification-pedophilia-not-se/.

27. Salynn Boyles, "Do Sexually Abused Kids Become Abusers?," WebMD Health News, February 6,
2003, http://www.webmd.com/mental-health/news/20030206/do-sexually-abused-kids-become-
abusers.

28. Bruno Waterfield, "Belgian killed by euthanasia after a botched sex change operation," *Telegraph*,
October 1, 2013, http://www.telegraph.co.uk/news/worldnews/europe/belgium/10346616/Belgian-
killed-by-euthanasia-after-a-botched-sex-change-operation.html.

29. S. Lloyd and D. Operario, "HIV risk among men who have sex with men who have experienced
childhood sexual abuse: systematic review and meta-analysis," *Aids Education and Prevention* 24,
no. 3 (June 24, 2012): 228-41, http://www.ncbi.nlm.nih.gov/pubmed/22676462.

30. M. S. Friedman et al., "A meta-analysis of disparities in childhood sexual abuse, parental physical
abuse, and peer victimization among sexual minority and sexual nonminority individuals,"
American Journal of Public Health 101, no. 8 (August 2011): 1481–94, http://www.ncbi.nlm.nih.
gov/pubmed/21680921.

31. K. A. McLaughlin et al., "Disproportionate exposure to early-life adversity and sexual orientation
disparities in psychiatric morbidity," *Childhood Abuse & Neglect* 36, no. 9 (September 2012): 645–55,
http://www.ncbi.nlm.nih.gov/pubmed/22964371.

32. D. J. Brennan et al., "History of childhood sexual abuse and HIV risk behaviors in homosexual
and bisexual men," *American Journal of Public Health* 97, no. 6 (June 2007): 1107–12, http://www.
ncbi.nlm.nih.gov/pubmed/17463386.

33. S. B. Austin et al., "Disparities in child abuse victimization in lesbian, bisexual, and heterosexual
women in the Nurses' Health Study II," *Journal of Women's Health* 17, no. 4 (May 2008): 597–606,
http://www.ncbi.nlm.nih.gov/pubmed/18447763.

34. Andrea L. Roberts, M. Maria Glymour, and Karestan C. Koenen, "Does Maltreatment in
Childhood Affect Sexual Orientation in Adulthood?," *Archives of Sexual Behavior* 42, no. 2
(September 14, 2012): 161–71, http://www.ncbi.nlm.nih.gov/pmc/articles/PMC3535560/.

35. Ibid.

36. Drew Altman, "Behind the Increase in HIV Infections among Gay and Bisexual Men," *Wall Street
Journal*, September 25, 2014, http://blogs.wsj.com/washwire/2014/09/25/behind-the-increase-in-
hiv-infections-among-gay-and-bisexual-men/.

37. Sarah Boesveld, "Becoming disabled by choice, not chance: 'Transabled' people feel like impostors
in their fully working bodies," The National Post, June 3, 2015, http://news.nationalpost.com/
news/canada/becoming-disabled-by-choice-not-chance-transabled-people-feel-like-impostors-in-
their-fully-working-bodies.

38. Shannon Larratt, "One Hand Jason: BIID Interview in BME/News, " February 19, 2008, http://
news.bme.com/2008/02/19/one-hand-jason-biid-interview-in-bmenews-publishers-ring/.

39. Ann Oldenburg, "Benham brothers: 'If faith cost us TV show, so be it,'" *USA Today*, May 8, 2014,
http://www.usatoday.com/story/life/tv/2014/05/07/hgtv-nixes-benham-brothers-series-anti-gay-
extremist-abortion/8810393/.

40. Clare O'Connor, "Chick-fil-A CEO Cathy: Gay Marriage Still Wrong, but I'll Shut Up about It and Sell Chicken," *Forbes*, March 19, 2014, http://www.forbes.com/sites/clareoconnor/2014/03/19/chick-fil-a-ceo-cathy-gay-marriage-still-wrong-but-ill-shut-up-about-it-and-sell-chicken/.

41. Mary Katharine Ham, "FRC shooter: I targeted them because SPLC list said they were 'anti-gay,'" *Hot Air*, April 24, 2013, http://hotair.com/archives/2013/04/24/frc-shooter-i-targeted-them-because-splc-list-said-they-were-anti-gay/.

42. Case citations courtesy of Peter LaBarbera, Americans for Truth about Homosexuality, http://americansfortruth.com/.

43. "Fleur Cakes, Oregon Bakery, Turns Away Lesbian Couple Seeking Wedding Cake," *HuffPost* Gay Voice, May 15, 2013, http://www.huffingtonpost.com/2013/05/15/fleur-cakes-gay-wedding-oregon_n_3279833.html.

44. *Seattle Times* staff, "Bar owner fined for banning transgender patrons," *Seattle Times*, August 31, 2013, http://seattletimes.com/html/localnews/2021731073_transgenderpenaltyxml.html.

45. Katy Steinmetz, "The Transgender Tipping Point," *Time*, May 29, 2014, http://time.com/135480/transgender-tipping-point/.

46. Jennifer Bendery, "Joe Biden: Transgender Discrimination Is 'The Civil Rights Issue of Our Time,'" *Huffington Post*, October 30, 2012, http://www.huffingtonpost.com/2012/10/30/joe-biden-transgender-rights_n_2047275.html.

47. Eleanor Harding, "Parents anger after children as young as THREE told to sign contract promising not to use 'transphobic language' at nursery," *Daily Mail*, April 24, 2015, http://www.dailymail.co.uk/news/article-3054592/Parents-anger-children-young-THREE-told-sign-contract-promising-not-use-transphobic-language-nursery.html.

48. Chapman, "Johns Hopkins Psychiatrist: Transgender Is 'Mental Disorder.'"

CHAPTER 10: WAKING UP

1. Dinesh D'Souza, "How Obama Thinks," *Forbes*, September 9, 2010, http://www.forbes.com/forbes/2010/0927/politics-socialism-capitalism-private-enterprises-obama-business-problem.html.

2. Dinesh D'Souza, *The Roots of Obama's Rage* (Washington, DC: Regnery, 2010), 198.

3. Jon Henley, "Calls for legal child sex rebound on luminaries of May 68," *Guardian* (UK), February 23, 2001, http://www.theguardian.com/world/2001/feb/24/jonhenley.

4. Dinesh D'Souza, "Exceptionally good or exceptionally evil?," *Whistleblower* magazine, July 2014, http://www.wnd.com/2014/08/america-exceptionally-good-or-exceptionally-evil/.

5. Adam Edelman and Corky Siemaszko, "Georgia boys face murder charges after cold-blooded killing of infant being strolled by mother," *New York Daily News*, March 22, 2013, http://www.nydailynews.com/news/crime/cops-hunt-young-boys-baby-mom-shooting-article-1.1296312.

6. "Black Teens Murder White Baby for the Fun of It In Georgia," LiveLeak, accessed June 9, 2015, http://www.liveleak.com/view?i=e21_1377810920.

7. National Criminal Justice Reference Service, quoting P. T. D'Orban, "Women Who Kill Their Children," *British Journal of Psychiatry* 134 (1979): 560–71, https://www.ncjrs.gov/App/publications/Abstract.aspx?id=75522.

8. R. Seth Williams, *Report of the Grand Jury: In the Court of Common Pleas: First Judicial District of Pennsylvania Criminal Trial Division* (Misc. No. 0009901-2008), January 14, 2011, www.phila.gov/districtattorney/pdfs/grandjurywomensmedical.pdf, 1.

9. Elizabeth Harrington, "Gosnell Trial Witness: Baby Abortion Survivor Was 'Swimming' in Toilet 'Trying to Get Out'," CNS News, April 18, 2013, http://cnsnews.com/news/article/gosnell-trial-witness-baby-abortion-survivor-was-swimming-toilet-trying-get-out.

10. Kirsten Powers, "Philadelphia abortion clinic horror," USA Today, April 11, 2013, http://www.usatoday.com/story/opinion/2013/04/10/philadelphia-abortion-clinic-horror-column/2072577/.

11. Conor Friedersdorf, "Why Dr. Kermit Gosnell's Trial Should Be a Front-Page Story," Atlantic, April 12, 2013, http://www.theatlantic.com/national/archive/2013/04/why-dr-kermit-gosnells-trial-should-be-a-front-page-story/274944/.

12. David C. Reardon, "The After Effects of Abortion," AbortionFacts.com, accessed June 9, 2015, http://www.abortionfacts.com/reardon/the-after-effects-of-abortion.

13. Randy Hall, "Abortion Causing 'Black Genocide,' Activists Say," Crosswalk.com, February 7, 2005, http://www.crosswalk.com/1311395/.

14. Mark Crutcher, Lime 5: Exploited by Choice (Denton, TX: Life Dynamics, 1996), 100–2.

15. Powers, "Philadelphia abortion clinic horror."

16. Associated Press and FoxNews.com, "Philadelphia DA calls abortion doctor Kermit Gosnell a 'monster' after he's sentenced to life in prison without parole," Fox News, May 15, 2013, http://www.foxnews.com/us/2013/05/15/gosnell-gets-life-in-prison-no-parole/.

17. Steven Ertelt, "18,000 Viable Unborn Babies Die Every Year in Painful Late Abortions in the United States," LifeNews.com, June 11, 2015, http://www.lifenews.com/2015/06/11/18000-viable-unborn-babies-die-every-year-in-painful-late-abortions-in-the-united-states/.

18. Cheryl Chumley, "Texas Sen. Wendy Davis dons urinary catheter for 11-hour abortion filibuster," Washington Times, June 28, 2013, http://www.washingtontimes.com/news/2013/jun/28/texas-sen-wendy-davis-dons-urinary-catheter-11-hou/.

19. Associated Press, "Texas Candidate Says She Ended Pregnancies," New York Times, September 5, 2014, http://www.nytimes.com/2014/09/06/us/texas-candidate-says-she-ended-pregnancies.html?_r=0.

20. Ed Morrissey, "Wendy Davis: Late term abortion rights 'sacred ground,'" Hot Air, August 5, 2013, http://hotair.com/archives/2013/08/05/wendy-davis-late-term-abortion-rights-sacred-ground/.

21. John McCormack, "Pelosi Can't Explain Difference Between Gosnell Slayings and Late-Term Abortions," Weekly Standard, June 13, 2013, http://www.weeklystandard.com/blogs/pelosi-late-term-abortions-sacred_735188.html.

22. Drew Zahn, "'Creepier' pro-abortion 'Satan' video emerges," WND, July 5, 2013, http://wp.wnd.com/2013/07/creepier-pro-abortion-satan-video-emerges/.

23. Morgan Smith, Becca Aaronson, and Shefali Luthra, "Abortion Bill Finally Passes Texas Legislature," Texas Tribune, July 13, 2013, http://www.texastribune.org/2013/07/13/texas-abortion-regulations-debate-nears-climax/.

24. Casey Claiborne, "APD: 'Molotov Cocktail' thrown at pro-life group," myFOXaustin, March 24, 2015, http://www.myfoxaustin.com/story/28605285/apd-molotov-cocktail-thrown-at-pro-life-group.

25. Jeffrey H. Anderson, "Gallup: More Americans Are Pro-Life than Pro-Choice," Weekly Standard, July 2, 2013, http://www.weeklystandard.com/blogs/gallup-more-americans-are-pro-life-pro-choice_738558.html.

26. Guy Benson, "CNN Poll: 58 Percent of Americans Oppose Abortion in All or Most Cases," Townhall.com, March 10, 2014, http://townhall.com/tipsheet/guybenson/2014/03/10/cnn-poll-58-percent-of-americans-oppose-abortion-in-all-or-most-circumstances-n1806283.

27. "75% of Abortion Clinics Closed: Jan. 2015 vs. 1991," *Culture News*, January 3, 2015, http://culturecampaign.blogspot.com/2015/01/75-of-abortion-clinics-closed-jan-2015.html.

28. Bob Unruh, "Wendy Davis supporter hurls bomb at pro-lifers," WND.com, March 26, 2015, http://www.wnd.com/2015/03/wendy-davis-supporter-hurls-bomb-at-pro-lifers/.

29. See chapter 1, notes 9–10, 12–15.

30. Young Su Park et al., "Psychiatry in Former Socialist Countries: Implications for North Korean Psychiatry," *Psychiatry Investigation*, October 2014, http://www.ncbi.nlm.nih.gov/pmc/articles/PMC4225199/.

31. Sidney Bloch and Peter Reddaway, *Russia's Political Hospitals: The Abuse of Psychiatry in the Soviet Union* (n.p.: Victor Gollancz, 1977), 425.

32. Marc Morano, "If Only We All Had (Liberal) Brains, We'd All Believe in Man-Made Global Warming," CNSNews.com, March 30, 2012, http://cnsnews.com/blog/marc-morano/if-only-we-all-had-liberal-brains-wed-all-believe-man-made-global-warming.

33. Christopher R. Walker, "Study: Conservatives have larger 'fear center,'" *Salon*, December 29, 2010, http://www.salon.com/2010/12/29/conservative_brains/.

34. Kathleen Maclay, "Researchers help define what makes a political conservative," *UCBerkeleyNews*, July 22, 2003, http://www.berkeley.edu/news/media/releases/2003/07/22_politics.shtml.

35. Frank Newport, "Republicans Report Much Better Mental Health Than Others," Gallup, November 30, 2007, http://www.gallup.com/poll/102943/republicans-report-much-better-mental-health-than-others.aspx.

36. Ibid.

37. Anna North, "What Your Politics Say about Your Mental Health," Buzz Feed, May 17, 2013, http://www.buzzfeed.com/annanorth/what-your-politics-say-about-your-mental-health.

38. Lee Jussim, "Liberal Bias in Social Psychology: Personal Experience I," *Psychology Today*, September 13, 2013, https://www.psychologytoday.com/blog/rabble-rouser/201309/liberal-bias-in-social-psychology-personal-experience-i.

CHAPTER 11: FREEDOM

1. V. I. Lenin in a Nov. 13, 1913, letter to colleague Maxim Gorky, from V.I. Lenin, *Complete Collected Works*, 45 vols. (Moscow, USSR: Progress Publishers, 1978), 35:122.

2. Pew, "America's Changing Religious Landscape," Pew Research Center, Religion & Public Life, May 12, 2015, http://www.pewforum.org/2015/05/12/americas-changing-religious-landscape/.

3. Sarah Pulliam Bailey, "Christianity faces sharp decline as Americans are becoming even less affiliated with religion," *Washington Post*, May 12, 2015, http://www.washingtonpost.com/news/acts-of-faith/wp/2015/05/12/christianity-faces-sharp-decline-as-americans-are-becoming-even-less-affiliated-with-religion/.

4. *How Mass (Legal) Immigration Dooms a Conservative Republican Party* (Washington, DC: Eagle Forum, 2014), http://www.eagleforum.org/wp-content/uploads/2014/06/2014_ImmigrationBook-6-12-14.pdf.

5. Leo Hohmann, "Hundreds of Muslim refugees headed to Idaho," WND, April 30, 2015, http://www.wnd.com/2015/04/hundreds-of-muslim-refugees-headed-to-idaho/.

6. Transcript: Ted Cruz's speech at Liberty University, *Washington Post*, March 23, 2015, http://www.washingtonpost.com/politics/transcript-ted-cruzs-speech-at-liberty-university/2015/03/23/41c4011a-d168-11e4-a62f-ee745911a4ff_story.html.

7. Pew, "America's Changing Religious Landscape."

8. W. Gardner Selby, "Ted Cruz says today, roughly half of born-again Christians aren't voting," March 30, 2015, http://www.politifact.com/texas/statements/2015/mar/30/ted-cruz/ted-cruz-says-today-roughly-half-born-again-christ/.

9. Peter Ferrara, "Obama Democrats Versus Kennedy Democrats," *Forbes*, March 10, 2014, http://www.forbes.com/sites/peterferrara/2014/03/10/obama-democrats-versus-kennedy-democrats/.

10. John E. O'Neill and Jerome Corsi, *Unfit for Command: Swift Boat Veterans Speak Out Against John Kerry* (Washington, DC: Regnery, 2004).

11. William Safire, "Blizzard of Lies," *New York Times*, January 8, 1996, http://www.nytimes.com/1996/01/08/opinion/essay-blizzard-of-lies.html.

12. Shane Idleman, "Top 5 Reasons Why Young Christians, Some Pastors Don't Vote and Avoid Politics," *Christian Post*, November 3, 2014, http://www.christianpost.com/news/top-5-reasons-why-young-christians-some-pastors-dont-vote-and-avoid-politics-129037/.

13. Philip Bump, "Barack Obama has likely given a $9 billion boost to the gun industry (at least)," *Washington Post*, March 11, 2015, http://www.washingtonpost.com/blogs/the-fix/wp/2015/03/11/barack-obama-may-have-been-at-least-a-9-billion-boon-to-the-gun-industry-so-far/.

14. Andy Greenberg, "Gunsmiths 3D-Print High Capacity Ammo Clips to Thwart Proposed Gun Laws," *Forbes*, January 14, 2013, http://www.forbes.com/sites/andygreenberg/2013/01/14/gunsmiths-3d-print-high-capacity-ammo-clips-to-thwart-proposed-gun-laws/.

15. Dominic Patten, "MSNBC Ratings Crater to All-Time Lows, Fox News Tops Q1 Results, CNN Up, *Deadline* Hollywood, March 31, 2015, http://deadline.com/2015/03/msnbc-ratings-all-time-low-fox-news-wins-cnn-1201402274/.

16. Don Feder, "Seven Reasons to Hope for America," GrassTopsUSA, May 25, 2015, http://www.grasstopsusa.com/df052515.html.

17. Winston Churchill quotes on socialism, website of the National Churchill Museum, accessed June 9, 2015, https://www.nationalchurchillmuseum.org/socialism-quotes.html.

18. Drew DeSilver, "A minority of Americans own guns, but just how many is unclear," Pew Research, June 4, 2013, http://www.pewresearch.org/fact-tank/2013/06/04/a-minority-of-americans-own-guns-but-just-how-many-is-unclear/.

19. 1 Thessalonians 5:16–18.

20. 2 Chronicles 7:14.

21. Guy Gugliotta, "New Estimate Raises Civil War Death Toll," *New York Times*, April 2, 2012, http://www.nytimes.com/2012/04/03/science/civil-war-toll-up-by-20-percent-in-new-estimate.html?_r=0.

22. Tenther Action Center, Tenth Amendment Center, http://tracking.tenthamendmentcenter.com/.

23. Betsy Blaney, "Texas Officials Say They Can Deny Marriage Licences," Associated Press, June 28, 2015, http://www.usnews.com/news/politics/articles/2015/06/28/paxton-state-workers-can-deny-licenses-to-same-sex-couples.

24. U.S. Supreme Court Justice Antonin Scalia's dissenting opinion in the Obergefell v. Hodges (same-sex marriage) case, decided June 26, 2015, http://www.supremecourt.gov/opinions/14pdf/14-556_3204.pdf.

25. National Organization for Marriage (NOM) statement following US Supreme Court decision on marriage, June 26, 2015, http://www.nomblog.com/40488/.

26. James Dobson, "I fear judgment befalling America," WND, June 26, 2015, http://www.wnd.com/2015/06/i-fear-judgment-befalling-america/.

27. Garth Kant, "Dobson tears into Obama: 'Come and get me,'" WND, May 1, 2014, http://www.wnd.com/2014/05/dobson-obama-is-abortion-president/.

28. "Nonviolent Non-Cooperation," MKGandhi.org, accessed June 9, 2015, http://www.mkgandhi. org/biography/nnviolnt.htm.

29. Rudyard Kipling, "If," from *Rewards and Fairies* (Garden City: Doubleday, Page & Co., 1910).

30. Lee Heib, Surviving the Medical Meltdown: Your Guide to Living Through the Disaster of Obamacare (Washington, DC: WND Books, 2015), 79.

31. Elizabeth Harrington, "1M kids stop school lunch due to Michelle Obama's standards," *Washington Times*, March 6, 2014, http://www.washingtontimes.com/news/2014/mar/6/1m-kids-stop-school-lunch-due-michelle-obamas-stan/?page=all.

32. Peter Whoriskey, "The U.S. government is poised to withdraw longstanding warnings about cholesterol," *Washington Post*, February 10, 2015, http://www.washingtonpost.com/blogs/wonkblog/wp/2015/02/10/feds-poised-to-withdraw-longstanding-warnings-about-dietary-cholesterol/.

33. David Eldridge, "Conservatives Find Political Red Meat in USDA Diet Guidelines," *Roll Call*, April 9, 2015, http://www3.blogs.rollcall.com/218/usda-meat-guidelines-conseervatives/?dcz.

34. Heib, Surviving the Medical Meltdown, 98.

35. Jill Nienhiser, "Dietary Guidelines," Westin A. Price Foundation, http://www.westonaprice.org/health-topics/abcs-of-nutrition/dietary-guidelines/.

36. Mayo Clinic Staff, "Exercise and stress: Get moving to manage stress," May Clinic website, accessed June 9, 2015, http://www.mayoclinic.org/healthy-lifestyle/stress-management/in-depth/exercise-and-stress/art-20044469.

37. "Benefits of exercise—reduces stress, anxiety, and helps fight depression, from Harvard Men's Health Watch," Harvard Health Publications website, accessed June 9, 2015, http://www.health.harvard.edu/press_releases/benefits-of-exercisereduces-stress-anxiety-and-helps-fight-depression.

38. Chuck Norris, "Chuck Norris kicks open 'call of the wild'," WND, May 22, 2015, http://www.wnd.com/2015/05/chuck-norris-kicks-open-call-of-the-wild/.

39. Dennis Prager, "The greatest days of your life," WND, December 29, 2014, http://www.wnd.com/2014/12/the-greatest-days-of-your-life/.

40. Mark 2:27.

41. Sumathi Reddy, "Doctor's Orders: 20 Minutes of Meditation Twice a Day," *Wall Street Journal*, April 15, 2013, http://www.wsj.com/articles/SB10001424127887324345804578424863782143682.

42. Dan Harris, *10% Happier: How I Tamed the Voice in My Head, Reduced Stress Without Losing My Edge, and Found Self-Help That Actually Works—A True Story* (New York: It Books, 2014), xiv–xv.

43. John Hancmay, "A Few of the Paths to a Calmer Life," *New York Times*, May 9, 2012, http://www.nytimes.com/2012/05/10/business/retirementspecial/a-few-of-the-paths-to-a-calmer-life.html?_r=0.

44. J. David Creswell et al., "Brief mindfulness meditation training alters psychological and neuroendocrine responses to social evaluative stress," *Psychoneuroendocrinology* 44 (June 2014): 1–12, http://www.psyneuen-journal.com/article/S0306-4530%2814%2900058-4/abstract.

45. "Meditation: What You Need to Know," website of the National Institutes of Health, National Center for Complementary and Integrative Health, accessed June 9, 2015, https://nccih.nih.gov/health/meditation/overview.htm.

46. "Meditation and Heart Health," American Heart Association's website, accessed June 9, 2015, http://www.heart.org/HEARTORG/Conditions/More/MyHeartandStrokeNews/Meditation-and-Heart-Disease-Stroke_UCM_452930_Article.jsp.

47. See his Foundation of Human Understanding website at https://www.fhu.com/.

48. David Kupelian, "Military praises 'fantastic' new stress therapy," WND, July 19, 2011, http://www.wnd.com/2011/07/319737/.

49. Lewis L. Judd et al., "Overt Irritability/Anger in Unipolar Major Depressive Episodes," *JAMA Psychiatry* 70, no. 11 (November 2013): 1171–80, http://archpsyc.jamanetwork.com/article. aspx?articleid=1737169.

50. "Mental Illness and Anger," HealthyPlace, accessed June 9, 2015, http://www.healthyplace.com/ other-info/mental-health-newsletter/mental-illness-and-anger/.

51. Maria Simbra, "Australian Study Shows Anger Increases Risk of Heart Attack," CBS Pittsburgh, February 24, 2015, http://pittsburgh.cbslocal.com/2015/02/24/australian-study-shows-anger-increases-risk-of-heart-attack/.

52. Marshall Kirk and Hunter Madsen, *After the Ball: How America Will Conquer Its Fear and Hatred of Gays in the '90s* (New York: Penguin, 1990), 382.

53. See "Obama: 'Fundamentally Transforming the United States of America,' Long Version," YouTube video, 1:37, submitted by jbranstetter04, October 30, 2008, https://www.youtube.com/ watch?v=KrefKCaV8m4.

54. See Rush Limbaugh, "A Newly Minted NRA Member" (transcript); and "Revenge on the Bitter Clingers" (transcript), on the official website of *The Rush Limbaugh Show*, January 16, 2013, http://www.rushlimbaugh.com/daily/2013/01/16/a_newly_minted_nra_member and http://www. rushlimbaugh.com/daily/2013/01/16/revenge_on_the_bitter_clingers.

55. "Richard Wurmbrand" (obituary), *Telegraph* (UK), February 23, 2001, http://www.telegraph. co.uk/news/obituaries/1323729/Richard-Wurmbrand.html.

56. Richard Wurmbrand, *Tortured for Christ* (Bartlesville, OK: Voice of the Martyrs, 1967), 113.

57-. Ibid., 59.

58. Ibid., 63.

59. Ibid., 81.

CHAPTER 12: MESSIAHS FALSE AND TRUE

1. Charles and Ray Eames, "Powers of Ten (1977), YouTube video, 9:00, posted by Earnes Office, August 26, 2010, https://www.youtube.com/watch?v=0fKBhvDjuy0.

2. Cosmic Voyage, Inc., "Cosmic Voyage," National Air and Space Museum, narrated by Morgan Freeman, tps://www.youtube.com/watch?v=FVFvH8Sfj98.

3. David Horowitz, "The Threat We Face," *FrontPage Mag*, October 10, 2013, http://www. frontpagemag.com/2013/david-horowitz/the-threat-we-face-2/.

4. "Barbara Walters: We Thought Obama Was Going to Be 'The Next Messiah,'" *Washington Free Beacon*, December 18, 2013, http://freebeacon.com/culture/barbara-walters-we-thought-obama-was-going-to-be-the-next-messiah/.

5. Kyle Drennen, "Newsweek's Evan Thomas: Obama Is 'Sort of God,'" *NewsBusters*, June 5, 2009, http://newsbusters.org/blogs/kyle-drennen/2009/06/05/newsweek-s-evan-thomas-obama-sort-god.

6. Brent Baker, "Newsweek Makes It Official: Obama's Inauguration Is 'The Second Coming,'" *NewsBusters*, January 18, 2013, http://newsbusters.org/blogs/brent-baker/2013/01/18/newsweek-makes-it-official-obama-s-inauguration-second-coming.

7. "The World's Muslims: Unity and Diversity," Pew Research Center, August 9, 2012, http://www. pewforum.org/2012/08/09/the-worlds-muslims-unity-and-diversity-3-articles-of-faith/.

8. Isaiah 1:18.

INDEX

A

Abbas, Mahmoud, 56
Ablow, Keith, 143–44
abortion, 14, 18, 19, 23, 35, 62–64, 89, 94,
    119–20, 179–89, 204
Abzug, Bella, 36
ACLU (American Civil Liberties Union), 27, 169
Adams, John, 83
addiction. *See ch. 8, "Addict Nation"* (135–51).
    For drug addiction see also ch. 7, "The
    Real Zombie Apocalypse" (117–34).
    food, 4, 138–39, 145, 146
    effects on the brain, 140, 42
    how American culture encourages, 147–51
    Internet-related, 136, 140
    number of Americans touched by, 147
    two competing paradigms for understand-
        ing and treating, 142–45
Addiction Medicine: Closing the Gap between Sci-
    ence and Practice, 142
ADHD (attention deficit/hyperactivity disorder),
    3, 4, 127–28, 156, 160, 193
Adorno, Theodor, 34
After the Ball (Kirk and Madsen), 214
Ahmad, Omar, 40–41
AIDS, 118, 177
alcohol, 4, 10, 20, 117, 119, 120, 122–23, 125,
    135, 138, 139, 140, 142, 143, 145,
    147–148, 149, 162, 217
Alcoholics Anonymous, 141
alcoholism, 134, 142, 143, 147–48, 162, 217
Alinsky, Saul, 5–6, 27, 31, 49, 79–81, 82–83, 94
Aloha Bed & Breakfast (HI), 169
al-Qaeda, 40, 56
Ambien, 124–25, 126
American Civil Liberties Union (ACLU), 27, 169
American exceptionalism, Obama's hostility
    toward, 87
American Medical Association, 143, 144

American Psychiatric Association, 129–30, 143,
    157–58, 160, 161, 191
American Psychological Association, 137, 160
Americans for Truth, 168
amnesty, 65, 70
amphetamines, 127
Andropov, Yuri, 55, 56–57
Aniston, Jennifer, 118
anorexia nervosa, 153, 193
anti-Americanism, 54, 56
antianxiety drugs (Valium, Xanax), 124, 125, 131
anti-bullying, 93
antidepressants, 4, 125–26, 130–32, 227
anti-Semitism, 41, 55, 56, 146
anti-Zionism, 56
anxiety, 3, 69, 73, 74, 78, 79, 145, 150, 157, 172,
    193, 208, 212, 223, 228
anxiety disorder, number of American adults hav-
    ing an, 155
Arafat, Yasser, 55–56
Armenian Genocide, 23, 45
arson, 58–59, 113
atheism, 24
Atlantic, 105, 107, 108, 180–81
attention deficit/hyperactivity disorder (ADHD),
    3, 4, 127–28, 156, 160, 193
Audacity of Hope, The (Obama), 25
Aurora movie theater shooting, 199
Ayd, Frank, 131–32
Ayers, William, 10, 31, 49

B

Babel, 103, 114
Baker, Shukri Abu, 40
Baldwin, Roger, 27
Baril, Alexandre, 165
Bashir, Martin, 12
Battle for the Mind: A Physiology of Conversion and
    Brainwashing (Sargent), 73–74

G

Gallup poll, 119, 189, 192–93
gambling, 136, 139 , 140, 145, 146
Gandhi, Mahatma, 205
gender. *See in general ch. 9, "Gender Madness"*
    (153–73)
gender dysphoria (gender identity disorder),
    153–54, 157–58
generalized anxiety disorder, 156, 157
genetics, blaming of addiction on, 142–43
genetic sexual attraction (incest), 161
Giffords, Gabrielle, 12
girls
    addicted to "cutting," 3, 139, 148
    exposed to porn before age eighteen, num-
        ber of, 137
    number engaging in repeated self-harm,
        3, 139
    percent being diagnosed with ADHD, 128
    percent who have viewed online child porn,
        homosexual sex, group sex,
        bestiality, bondage, 137
    percent who suffer from anorexia nervosa,
        153
    result of abuse by men, 165
GlaxoSmithKline, 127, 131
*glbtq: an encyclopedia of gay, lesbian, bisexual, trans-
    gender, and queer culture*, 34
Glee (TV show), 118
Glenn Beck (show), 200
global warming, 20, 191
Gluzman, Semyon, 190
Gohmert, Louis, 111
Goldberg, Bernie, 16
Goldberg, Whoopi, 118
Gopnik, Blake, 17
Gore, Al, 21, 197
Gosnell, Kermit, 179–88
governors, imprisoned Illinois, 104
Graf, William, 128
Gramsci, Antonio, 29–30, 32, 43, 62, 200
Great American Panel, 30
Greenberg, Gary, 130–32
Greenfield, Daniel, 114
GTMO, 66

H

Hall, G. Stanley, 27
hallucinogens, 4, 121, 124, 125

Hamas, 40, 41, 45
Hannity, Sean, 30–31, 200
Harris, Dan, 211
Harris, Eric, 126
Harvard Health, 142
Harvard Medical School, 75, 140, 164
Harvard Men's Health Watch, 208
hashish, 121
Hathaway, Taryn, 13
health care system, 66, 72
heart disease, 3, 206, 207
Heib, Lee, 205, 206–7
Heller, Mikhail, 35
heroin, 4, 121, 123, 140, 141, 143, 145
Hilton, Perez, 168
Hinckley, John, 126–27
Hiss, Alger, 53
Hitler, Adolf, 28, 98, 224
Holder, Eric, 77, 226
Hollywood, 46, 47, 118
Holocaust, 23, 59, 191
"homicidal ideation" (in antidepressant users),
    126
homicides by illegal aliens, 19, 70
"homophobic," 33, 191
Homeschooling, 201
homosexuality, 13, 79, 93, 96, 160, 161, 163,
    164, 165, 167, 169, 170, 171, 177,
    191
    clinical evidence that childhood abuse plays
        a huge role in later, 163–64
Hooper, Ibrahim, 41
Horowitz, David, 26, 224–25
How Evil Works (Kupelian), 12
Huelskamp, Tim, 206
Huguenin, Jon and Elaine, 168
hydrocodone (brand names Norco, Vicodin) and
        hydromorphone (Dilaudid, Exalgo),
        123

I

illegal drugs, number of Americans using, 121
illegal immigration, 1, 14, 15, 19–20, 65, 69–70,
        89, 110, 190, 191, 201
Illinois governors who went to prison, 104
illnesses, the invention of, 141–47
immigrants, favoring of big government and
        liberal values by, 110
incest, 161
income tax, 77, 197